The Battle Within

CHRISTINA TWOMEY is Professor of History at Monash University, Melbourne. She is the author of three books, *A History of Australia* (co-authored with Mark Peel, 2nd Edition, 2017), *Australia's Forgotten Prisoners: Civilians Interned by the Japanese in World War Two* (2007) and *Deserted and Destitute: Motherhood, Wife Desertion and Colonial Welfare* (2002). Christina has also published widely on the cultural history of war, with a focus on issues of imprisonment, captivity, witnessing, the photography of atrocity, gender and memory.

The Battle Within

POWs in Postwar Australia

CHRISTINA TWOMEY

NEWSOUTH

A NewSouth book

Published by
NewSouth Publishing
University of New South Wales Press Ltd
University of New South Wales
Sydney NSW 2052
AUSTRALIA
newsouthpublishing.com

© Christina Twomey 2018

10 9 8 7 6 5 4 3 2 1

This book is copyright. Apart from any fair dealing for the purpose of private study, research, criticism or review, as permitted under the Copyright Act, no part of this book may be reproduced by any process without written permission. Inquiries should be addressed to the publisher.

National Library of Australia
Cataloguing-in-Publication entry
Creator: Twomey, Christina, author.
Title: The battle within : POWs in postwar Australia / Christina Twomey.
ISBN: 9781742235684 (paperback)
        9781742244099 (ebook)
        9781742248493 (ePDF)
Notes: Includes bibliographical references and index.
Subjects: World War, 1939–1945—Prisoners and prisons, Japanese.
           World War, 1939–1945—Personal narratives, Australian.
           Australia—History.

Design Josephine Pajor-Markus
Cover design Lisa White
Front cover image Australian POWs arrive in Sydney, 27 January 1944. Fairfax Syndication
Back cover image Burma–Thailand Railway, c. 1943. Prisoners of war (POWs) carrying sleepers in Burma, about 40 kilometres south of Thanbyuzayat (probably Beke Taung). Australian War Memorial C41423.

All reasonable efforts were taken to obtain permission to use copyright material reproduced in this book, but in some cases copyright could not be traced. The author welcomes information in this regard.

For
Norman James Sherrington (1919–2009)
and
Alma Jessie Keir, née Sherrington (1922–2008),

who first told me about the war

Contents

Prologue		ix
Introduction		1

Part I Official attitudes to POWs
1	A matter of dishonour?	15
2	A bit queer	33
3	Three bob a day	54
4	The Prisoners of War Trust Fund	75

Part II The POW story
5	Rebuilding a life	103
6	POW marriages	132

Part III Coming to terms with Asia
7	Reconciliation with Japan	157
8	Rewards and regional relationships	187

Part IV The battle resolved
9	Prisoners in the time of trauma	213
	Epilogue	241
	Coda	248

Acknowledgments	249
Notes	253
Bibliography	279
Index	294

Prologue

Before dawn on 25 April 2012 I walked along the remains of the Thai–Burma Railway. Its iron tracks had been ripped up long ago. The original wooden sleepers, their surface at once cracked and polished by monsoonal rains, were partly obscured by small grey stones. The railway cutting is deep and narrow, with rock face looming on each side. Asian *romusha* (forced labourers) and Allied prisoners of war (POWs) chiselled out this railway pass in the early 1940s to facilitate Japan's Thai–Burma Railway project. Seventy years later the beauty of this man-made valley, with its floor of pale stones and crown of green foliage, flames from bamboo lanterns illuminating its orange walls, belied the human cost of its creation. On the morning of my visit, no one spoke as they picked their way along the pathway of sleepers towards the black stone memorial. The crunch of gravel beneath our feet was reminiscent of a purposeful march.

The remote location of Hellfire Pass, in the western Thai province of Kanchanaburi, near the border with Burma, is several hours' journey by bus from Bangkok. Yet at least 1000 other people were there that morning, many of them Australians. All of those present had descended the wide wooden steps to the railway cutting from the Hellfire Pass Memorial Museum, an institution built and funded by Australia's federal government. They gathered at this dawn service to hear the Anzac Day address and to pay their respects to the people who had suffered and died on the railway.

Anzac Day is a solemn occasion and reverence was the dominant mood. The New Zealand Ambassador delivered the address and referred to those gathered before him as being there to 'bear witness'. Two former POWs laid an official wreath. Later that morning they travelled back from Hellfire Pass to the Kanchanaburi War Cemetery to attend the 11 a.m. wreath-laying ceremony. The Australian Ambassador acknowledged the presence of the elderly men, which brought forth warm applause. One of them delivered the ex-POW address, in which he stated that he and his comrades had attempted to slow Japan's advance south towards Australia and that, once they had been captured, mateship had been the key to their survival. The other read the 'Ode of Remembrance' and then introduced the two minutes' silence. Still connected to the microphone, he leaned to one side and said to the Master of Ceremonies, 'How are we doing?' followed by, 'Are you doing the timing?' People in the crowd, who heard the asides broadcast to the entire gathering, suppressed giggles. At the conclusion of the dawn service back up in the hills there had been a ripple of applause, at which one seasoned observer had cautioned, 'No!' A woman sitting behind me whispered to her friend, 'This is our national day. Why can't we sing our national anthem?'

The Anzac Day services in Thailand epitomise the place that POWs of Japan hold in Australian memories and stories about the Second World War. Prisoners have come to embody the damage and trauma of war. Australians pay deference to the accounts of individual survivors, visit the scenes of their incarceration in the Asia-Pacific region and 'bear witness' to their suffering. POWs are an acceptable face of Anzac, with its blend of patriotism and theatre; hence, members of the audience want to clap, sing 'Advance Australia Fair' and laugh at the slip-ups. The federal government has shown commitment to honouring

POWs, through the millions of dollars invested in the Hellfire Pass Memorial Museum, opened in 1998; by sending Governor-General Quentin Bryce to deliver the Anzac Day address there in 2011; and by giving each surviving POW a $25 000 compensation payment in 2001.

※

I had been to Kanchanaburi once before, as a twelve-year-old girl, in 1980. There were no tourists walking along Hellfire Pass in those days; it was ninety kilometres further up the mountain from the main town and the jungle had reclaimed that section of the railway known to local people as Konyu Cutting. The only way through the pass would have been with a sickle. Tourist activity in the province of Kanchanaburi centred on the town itself, where a steel bridge across the river gained fame after the release of the 1957 Academy Award–winning film *The Bridge on the River Kwai*. Based on a Pierre Boulle novel, the film fictionalised events surrounding the construction of a wooden trestle bridge, which in reality bore little resemblance to the wartime steel structure in Kanchanaburi.[1] Indeed, during the Second World War, the river flowing under the steel bridge was known as the Mae Khlong. Capitalising on the region's connection with the film, locals renamed this section of the river as the Kwae Yai, thus blurring the lines between fiction and history. Replicas of the bridge were available on fridge magnets, key rings and T-shirts. There were some train engines and carriages, rusting and out of place, near to the marketplace. This was during the period when the Australian government refused to sanction any official memorial activity in relation to POWs other than honouring the bodies of those who died with individual memorial plaques at the Commonwealth War Graves Commission cemeteries in town and at nearby Chungkai.

Apart from the graves, in 1980 the main references to POWs were to be found at the JEATH War Museum. Thai monks had established this slightly gruesome collection of material in the grounds of a temple. A well-meaning and small-scale affair of *atap* huts filled with a few relics, newspaper clippings and photographs that were rotting away due to the humidity, the museum sought to pay tribute to the nations involved in the construction of the railway: Japan, England, Australia, Thailand and Holland (JEATH). The images of beheadings and emaciated men in loin cloths were terrifying to a child who had never seen anything like it.

In 1980 it was unusual for an Australian family to take a holiday in Kanchanaburi. My own had only done so because we were living in the region as part of the Royal Australian Air Force commitment at Butterworth in Malaysia. In that expatriate community, consciousness of the Second World War was ever present, and not just because the men were serving military personnel. There were crumbling ruins referred to as the 'Japanese forts'. Rumours circulated that some of the single women in their forties and fifties who worked as amahs for Australian families had been ill-used by the Japanese during the occupation and had remained unmarried as a result. Perhaps such stories were apocryphal; even so, they were certainly evidence that the war remained part of the emotional and physical landscape well into the 1970s.

A trip to Thailand was sometimes on the travel itinerary for air force families in the 1970s, but journeys to Singapore were more popular. Butterworth and Penang, the adjacent island on which many of us lived, were then rather more down at heel than the rapidly modernising Singapore. Bright lights, theme parks, and shopping strips full of the latest electronic equipment held great appeal for Australians far from home. There were also

Prologue

Second World War attractions for those who liked to mix tourism and history. The Surrender Chambers at Fort Siloso included the chance to see waxwork exhibits depicting the British and Japanese surrenders. On the day of my family's visit, as we stood pondering the wax figure of Lord Louis Mountbatten, an attendant walked past and said, 'Him dead, boom'. My mother, perplexed, carefully explained that, *no*, he had not been killed in the war. That attendant's comment now allows me to date our excursion to August 1979, when Mountbatten, who indeed had survived the Second World War, had that very day been assassinated by the Irish Republican Army while boating off the Irish coast. Such news, riveting for my parents, was relatively inconsequential for a child, but on that trip I still managed to register that Changi, the jail on Singapore, had been home to men, women and children. There was always a consciousness among the Australian expatriate community in Malaysia that people with whom we identified – British women and children – had spent the war years under Japanese control.

When my family returned to Australia in the early 1980s the revival of interest in POWs was underway. There was plenty of historical drama on the television to fuel curiosity about the experiences of prisoners and civilian internees in the Asia-Pacific in the Second World War. *A Town like Alice* (1981) was one of the first Australian miniseries, based on Nevil Shute's 1950 novel and starring Bryan Brown as former POW Joe Harman. There were three series of *Tenko* (1981–84), a British Broadcasting Corporation and Australian Broadcasting Commission (ABC[2]) co-production, which focused on British, Dutch and Australian women interned by the Japanese. These programs were compelling for my mother and me, as they were, it transpired, for many feminists interested in stories of sisterhood. But for us, it was like our own experience in the region turned upside down.

The early 1980s was also a period when Australian students were being encouraged to study Asian languages as part of that generation's efforts to reorient the nation towards Asia. At high school I learned Bahasa Indonesia, which did not feel completely foreign after a few years spent listening to television ads in Malay. '*Minum Milo anda jadi sehat dan kuat*', we used to sing in the playground ('Drink Milo and you will be healthy and strong'). My great-uncle Norman, a Queensland Second World War veteran who had served in what he always called 'the islands', was delighted. I suddenly understood the words that spliced his vocabulary: *telinga* (ear), *anak-anak* (children), *gula* (sugar), *susu* (milk), *terima kasih* (thank you).

The thirty years that elapsed between my original visit to Kanchanaburi in 1980 and my return journey in 2012 witnessed remarkable change in the memorialisation of POWs who worked on the Thai–Burma Railway. The decaying JEATH Museum, never a model of curatorial practice and by my second visit even worse for wear, had been upstaged. There was now a large and impressive private museum in the town, the Thailand–Burma Railway Centre, and the Australian government's multimillion-dollar facility at Hellfire Pass. The 1980s and 1990s were pivotal decades in the rediscovery and recovery of POW history in Australia itself, with a slew of radio and television documentaries, scholarly books and exhibitions devoted to it. Most studies were focused on the experience of captivity, aided by a flourishing of memoir activity. The publication of the best-selling *War Diaries of Weary Dunlop: Java and the Burma–Thailand Railway 1942–1945*, in 1986, followed a highly publicised Weary Dunlop Tour, which culminated at Kanchanaburi on Anzac Day 1985. At that time the return of POW memory was in its early days; RAAF

Butterworth sent up a few buglers for the occasion as a gesture of support. When Dunlop's ashes were buried there nearly a decade later, Australia sent its Prime Minister to officiate.

This emphasis on the history of military imprisonment, when contrasted with my childhood awareness of the fate of women and children in the British empire during the war, prompted me in the late 1990s and into the 2000s to research and write *Australia's Forgotten Prisoners: Civilians Interned by the Japanese in World War Two* (2007). That project relied upon the papers of the Civilian Internees' Trust Fund, an organisation that distributed small cash grants to Australian civilians who had been interned by Japan in the Second World War. The grant application forms, untouched for over fifty years in the National Archives of Australia, provided rich testimony of the wartime experiences of civilian internees and their struggles to adjust to postwar life. Unable to confine their responses to the printed foolscap forms, which asked about war experiences and ongoing disadvantage, many former civilian internees entered a long correspondence with the fund, detailing their postwar rehabilitation, their frustrations and their views of captivity.

My return to Kanchanaburi prompted me to think more carefully about exactly why POWs had become a subject of interest to the Australian public in the late-twentieth century. Having written about the people who had been forgotten in this process – civilian internees – I now wanted to concentrate more carefully on the palpable presence of POWs. How had previous generations, and the government itself, responded to POWs before the 1980s? In what ways had POWs influenced Australia's relationship with its former enemy Japan and its regional neighbours in the postwar period?

This book is the result of that journey along the remains of the railway, which led me back into the archive to explore how the Australian government and people have responded to POWs. Recalling the richness of the Civilian Internees' Trust Fund, I wondered if something similar had been created for military POWs. Indeed it had: the Prisoners of War Trust Fund received over 7000 applications for grants. The vast majority of the documents had not been consulted since the day they were filed away. All former POWs who received a service pension have a repatriation file, currently in the possession of the Department of Veterans' Affairs. That archive remains closed to the public. The Prisoners of War Trust Fund is therefore the best archival source currently available for a study of former POWs.

A discretionary fund, controlled by government-appointed trustees (several of whom were themselves former prisoners), the Prisoners of War Trust Fund was in operation for a quarter of a century, from 1952 to 1977. Applications to the fund now provide astonishing insight into the lives, experiences and perceptions of people not usually given to recording or in any event keeping such records of their feelings about the impact of imprisonment. The applicants to the fund were, by and large, from the 'other ranks': men of limited education who often had menial jobs and sometimes lives blighted by alcoholism, depression, marriage breakdown or loneliness. Yet many of them took the opportunity, in shaky handwriting or in bold, capital letters, to make known their views about the treatment meted out to former prisoners, their family troubles and their struggles to rehabilitate.

The fund gave rise to an archive of extraordinary richness and while the letters and forms it contains were composed in the hope of receiving some kind of monetary payment, the themes that recur in the correspondents' pleas suggest common experience rather than collusion. The decisions and actions of the trustees, men distributing public money who applied their own private standards of appropriate behaviour and respectability, reflect the chasm that could exist between social classes in postwar Australia. The documents also flag the disparity of views that existed among former prisoners about mental illness and the significance of imprisonment itself. The applicants to the fund sometimes commented on the government's attitude towards them. More often, they wrote about their personal experiences.

Reading about the struggles of so many former POWs to rehabilitate themselves, to find work and to reintegrate into their family and community, and the remarkable frankness with which these men discussed their problems with sex and with alcohol, made me realise that I could not write a book about the place of former prisoners in postwar Australia without taking account of the personal cost of captivity. Rather than interviewing former POWs about their memories of those postwar years, I have concentrated on how returned POWs wrote and thought about such issues at the time they occurred. Out of respect to the families, in the cases cited in the following pages I have used pseudonyms, in order to maintain relative anonymity. Public figures, in contrast, are almost always referred to by their full names.[3] One applicant's file provided the title for this book, when he pleaded for people to recognise that former POWs were required to overcome a 'battle within' themselves to put the past behind them.

The 'battle within' was national as well as personal: the Australian government had to be persuaded that a defeated soldier was worthy of commemoration and respect. Until the 1980s the Australian Army and the Australian government had a deeply equivocal attitude to former POWs. Just as the papers of the Prisoners of War Trust Fund reward us with their insight into the views of 'ordinary' former prisoners, so the bureaucratic records of the army and the Repatriation Department, which oversaw veterans' access to welfare based on their service, reveal the arguments they were disinclined to make in public.⁴ Here, the ambivalence towards former prisoners ran deep.

❊

Once childhood recedes, the special form of weirdness that is one's own family begins to take on a different shape. Elements that appeared exceptional or unique turn out to reference a world beyond the family impossible for a child to imagine. To my adult mind, and with my historical training, the trip to Kanchanaburi, the amahs and the bachelor great-uncle with the verbal tics come together to form a pattern, shared by others from the mid-twentieth century onwards, of Australian knowledge of Asia mediated by military experiences. So, too, as the Second World War fades from living memory, we can begin to see its history in a different way – as a pathway into Asia, rather than only as evidence of conflict in the region.

The personal link prompted rather than satisfied my curiosity about Australian attitudes to imprisonment in wartime. Just as a visitor to Hellfire Pass can pick out the railway line by glimpsing the sleepers beneath the gravel, as a historian I have dug deep in the archive to reveal the foundations of the POW story in Australian culture. It is tempting to see the current veneration of former POWs as running along clean iron rails, from the past to the present. This book suggests that the sidings were many, that the tracks were buckled and warped, and that the burden of this difficult journey fell most heavily on the people with the least social, cultural and economic resources to carry it.

Introduction

Edward Ernest 'Weary' Dunlop, an Australian surgeon who spent three and a half years in Japanese captivity, died in July 1993. 'Of all Australians he shares a lone eminence of sustained heroism and superb achievement', former Governor-General Ninian Stephen declared at Dunlop's state funeral.[1] Prime Minister Paul Keating was in attendance, as were his predecessors Bob Hawke and Malcolm Fraser. About 15 000 people lined the streets to pay their respects in the middle of a Melbourne winter's day. Dunlop was one of the nation's most distinguished war veterans and certainly its most famous former POW. The star of other former POWs rose with him. By the late 1990s politicians had begun to lionise all POWs as the bearers of national virtue. 'Their story of sacrifice and suffering, of constancy and compassion, illuminates the very essence of the Anzac spirit', Prime Minister John Howard proclaimed on Anzac Day 1998.[2]

The general public rediscovered Dunlop only in the last decade of his life, after a hiatus of almost thirty years.[3] An officer, a non-combatant and a member of Victoria's social elite, he was in many respects a most unrepresentative former POW. Yet in the post-Vietnam era, as Australia's romance with its war history shed its militarist overtones, Dunlop was well placed to assume war hero status. Far from being a battlefield general, he was a medical officer who had nurtured his men in the most abject of conditions. His longstanding involvement with organisations dedicated to building friendship between Australia and Asia also showed a commitment to reconciliation, not recrimination. The veneration of Dunlop in the closing years of the century, however, disguised the more complex history of Australia's response to POWs in the years after 1945.

A broader revival of interest in POWs began in the early 1980s.[4] The amount of memorial activity, popular and academic history and cultural production that subsequently centred on POWs was nothing short of remarkable.[5] The Australian War Memorial commissioned new sculptures, exhibitions and installations dedicated to POWs.[6] The departments of Veterans' Affairs and Defence published elaborate lesson plans for schoolteachers and glossy coffee table books, funded websites and created film archives.[7] Creative interest also blossomed, led by accomplished sons of former POWs, including Jonathan Mills, with his oratorio *Sandakan Threnody* (2001), and Richard Flanagan, whose POW novel, *The Narrow Road to the Deep North*, was published in 2013.[8] An interest in bodily suffering, psychological trauma, the capacity for resilience, cross-cultural relations and the possibilities for reconciliation dominated work from the 1980s onwards. In comparison, most books and films of the late 1940s and early 1950s about POWs appear to have been acts of deliberate deflection. The intonations of these earlier works – ribald humour, plucky determination and ingenuity in adversity – have not entirely disappeared, but they now play second fiddle to a more sombre reckoning with the past.

Interest in POWs, like that in other aspects of Australia's war history, was part of the international memory boom that occurred in many Western liberal democracies during the late-twentieth century. Events deemed painful for individuals or the nation were its hallmark. The Australian War Memorial's ever-expanding exhibits dedicated to POWs illustrated the trend. The Second World War galleries, before redevelopment in the 1990s, had typically devoted only a small section to POWs. These exhibits focused on objects like camp essentials, Samurai swords and ham radios. In 1999 a gallery devoted to the Sandakan death marches opened. It referenced the fate of 2700 Allied POWs shipped from Singapore to Borneo of whom only six Australians survived, most others having perished during forced marches from Sandakan to Ranau in the early months of 1945.[9] Row upon row of rectangular head-shots of men in army uniform paper the walls in a dizzying geometry of loss. The images that commemorate this event at once individualise the suffering and emphasise its extent. The gallery resembles nothing so much as the haunting portraits associated with the Tuol Sleng Genocide Museum in Cambodia. While any kind of equivalence with genocide is too long a bow to draw, the visual allusion nevertheless links Australian POWs with regional experiences of crimes against humanity and with the international trend to memorialise war's victims.

As this book will show, POWs were not always so memorialised, feted or praised. The almost-universal sympathy that existed for former POWs by the late-twentieth century was notable precisely because it was unprecedented. The central task of this book is to examine the earlier, more ambivalent, status of POWs and to explore how it reflected the approach of the government, repatriation authorities and general public towards them. Sympathy was not the defining or the only response to former POWs in the immediate postwar period. A secondary aim of this book is to explain why by the 1980s a new sensibility, attuned to captivity as a potentially traumatic experience, had become the dominant mode of response. Once this shift had occurred, POWs assumed iconic status in veteran ranks. The changing public reception of POWs therefore also provides a compelling study of how, in the late-twentieth century, the traumatised survivor became a key figure who renewed cultural interest in the history of war.

Popular knowledge about Australians' wartime captivity is centred on POWs of Japan, despite the best efforts of historians to make earlier and contemporaneous experiences of captivity better known.[10] In the First World War, Turkey and Germany captured 4070 Australians, among whom the subsequent overall death rate was 9 per cent. In the Second World War, 8591 men were taken prisoner by either Germany or Italy in the European and North African theatres, with the loss of 265 lives, or 3 per cent of the total figure. A further 22 376 members of the 2nd Australian Imperial Force (AIF) became POWs of Japan in 1942, following the British and Dutch surrenders to the Imperial Japanese Army. The death toll was significant: 8031, or over 36 per cent, of those prisoners perished.[11] As a consequence of these differential survival rates, however, over one-third of all former POWs in postwar Australia had in fact been held prisoner in Europe. This significant minority was not reflected in the public debate over POWs, which focused to a large extent on the experiences of POWs captured by Japan.

The overall death rate of one in three prisoners detained by Japan conceals the considerable diversity in the conditions and burdens of captivity. As Joan Beaumont has argued, 'captivity was mediated through rank'.[12] The death rate among commissioned officers was close to 10 per cent, compared with almost 37 per cent in the 'other ranks'.[13] Within a few months of capture, the most senior officers were transferred to Formosa (Taiwan), then later to Manchuria, and thereafter spent the war years segregated from most other prisoners. The officers who remained behind in larger camps had separate accommodation, received higher rates of pay and in many cases were not required to perform manual work. Such privileges, often in environments where medicines and adequate quantities of nutritious food were in short supply and conditions of labour were demanding and harsh, could make the difference to the men's chances of survival. These were distinctions between officers and the 'other ranks' that were not easily forgotten when the survivors returned to Australia.

Almost everywhere throughout Japan's Greater East Asia Co-Prosperity Sphere, the name Japan preferred for the Asian and Pacific territories it occupied during the Second World War, the quantity and quality of food and medicines in prison and internment camps were inadequate. The high mortality rates led subsequent researchers, both within Australia and internationally, to declare that among former POWs of Japan there was a 'survivor effect': only the fittest survived, making it difficult to interpret subsequent data on the long-term health effects of imprisonment.[14] Even those who survived the Darwinian crucible of the camps emerged with infestations of parasites in their stomachs and bowels, tropical ulcers, beri-beri, tuberculosis, skin conditions, a host of other tropical diseases and the after-effects of malnutrition. The psychological implications of a long captivity were even more difficult to divine in prisoners held in either the European or the Pacific theatres, and remained a point of contention for a long while.

This book begins where many studies of POWs conclude: when the camp gates were thrown open. Most POW memoirs end at the point of liberation too, as if the real point of interest in that particular life could only be the war, not its aftermath. There are also numerous studies of the place of POWs in contemporary memories of the Second World War, but the period between return and remembrance is less well understood.[15] A similar situation exists in relation to Allied POWs more generally. Camp life and the commemoration of POWs from the 1980s are well covered, but the individual and collective responses to the issues raised by captivity in the period 1945–90, including rehabilitation, reintegration to families and community and the attitudes of governments, are less often the focus of research.[16] While Australian involvement in the First World War has generated an extensive literature on its political, social, cultural and individual legacies, the impact of the Second World War is still a scholarship in its relative infancy.[17]

As the Second World War drew to a close, over 22 000 former POWs returned home to Australia. Grief about the lives that had been lost was matched by an uncertainty about how to respond to those who had survived: what did it mean in a country so attached to Anzac, a legend of battlefield prowess, to have spent the war as a prisoner? In the era of White Australia was there further shame attached to imprisonment by an Asian captor? Should POWs from both the European and the Pacific theatres receive compensation for their suffering, or should preference be given to those detained by Japan? Were POWs more likely to be psychologically disturbed than other returning service personnel? How would the experience of being a POW impact on opportunities for employment, marriage and family life? What did the imprisonment of large numbers of Australians in the Asia-Pacific mean for the future of regional relationships in an era when Japan emerged as Australia's major trading partner?

※※

When Robert came back from the war, the sight of him nearly broke his mother's heart. Robert, who had been a POW, was so ill that he spent nine months as a patient at Sydney's Repatriation General Hospital, Concord. Still in his early thirties, he could not return to his prewar occupation as a bricklayer, repairing furnaces for a large steel-manufacturing firm. Like most of his fellow former POWs, Robert had been part of the 'other ranks' of the Australian Army, those who did not hold commissions as officers. Most had been in blue-collar jobs before the war, some more secure than others. In that sense, they were representative of Australia's interwar working class where limited educational opportunities, modest circumstances and restricted horizons were the norm. A war spent as a captive in places as far afield as Germany, Java, Thailand and Japan set them apart from families who had rarely even travelled interstate but restricted their ability to capitalise on worldliness, because it had been gained at such cost. 'How was I to stand up to hot furnace work after dysentery, fever, starvation???', Robert asked. Instead, he was forced to take work as a publishing hand at one of Sydney's daily newspapers. Less well paid than bricklaying, his new job involved a lot of night shifts.

The shift work and the struggle to readjust to civilian life placed pressure on the relationship between Robert and his wife. Two children had been born before the war and his wife gave birth to a baby boy after their reunion. 'Then came trouble', Robert later recalled. He could not perform 'the ordinary husbandly duties'. Robert was not alone in his belief that there was a connection between his impotence and a war spent as a prisoner. 'Through my experiences as a P.O.W. I had lost the urge or the desire to have sexual relations with my wife. Naturally arguments started, but I just couldn't do what was expected of me.' Although some former POWs remained bitter about unfaithful wives, there were many others, like Robert, who experienced the guilt of returning as changed men. Robert blamed himself and his 'sleepless & sexless state' when his wife attempted suicide in 1950. 'My wife left me because of my nervous state & my yelling etc at night', he later reflected. 'Who can blame her? My war experiences were driving her mad, & I could not relax at night although I tried & tried hard.'

In 1958 Robert considered that all his troubles – personal and financial – stemmed from the fact that he had been a POW. 'I will never be able to forget our treatment by the Japs & I still have nightmares & walk the Floor trying to sleep ... It has taken me all these years to get accustomed to Routine Civilian ways of life', he wrote, '& even to-day I want to go scrub'. If it were not for the children, he would have disappeared years earlier. Robert's desire to be on his own, to get away from it all, to avoid company, was a common refrain among former prisoners. Asked to describe his problems in 1973, Robert declared, 'Head-aches. Dizziness. Can't sleep. Bad dreams (never have been released). No relaxation'. 'The rice jungle had some compensation to some of us', he reflected with some sadness, 'who just don't seem to make a success of our return'.

The homecoming of Arthur Seaforth 'Blackie' Blackburn (1892–1960) was a rather more public affair, in keeping with his prewar social status in South Australia. His military seniority ensured that his return was also elaborate. The Australian Army required Blackburn, who was General Officer Commanding of the AIF in Java before his capture, to report immediately upon his repatriation to its headquarters in Melbourne. A return to his hometown of Adelaide had to wait. Blackburn was required personally to deliver his official documents and war diaries, preserved throughout his captivity in a wooden box with a secret compartment. That job completed, he went alone to wait for his wife Rose and two daughters at Melbourne's Spencer Street railway station.

Impatient with the delayed reunion after three and a half years of anxiety and waiting, the Blackburn women had decided to catch the overnight train from Adelaide to Melbourne. 'Nothing had prepared us for the sight of him', daughter Rosemary later recalled. Blackburn, 175 centimetres tall, 'weighed just over

Introduction

40 kilos and looked like a skeleton, the bones in his face very prominent and his body bent like an old man's'.[18] Watched by press photographers, the women rushed to greet Blackburn. They linked arms 'as much to give each other physical support as anything'.[19]

As the fragility of Blackburn's health became evident, the family were inclined to close ranks and shelter him. But as a Victoria Cross winner from the First World War, a former state parliamentarian, past President of the South Australian RSL and city coroner, Blackburn accepted a public welcome home at a reception hosted by the Lord Mayor of Adelaide.[20] He used this platform to encourage Australians to be mindful of the fragile psychological state of returning prisoners. 'Nearly every man returning from camps in the Pacific is a neurosis case', Blackburn declared. They would require immediate treatment, separate from that of other soldiers undergoing repatriation and demobilisation.[21]

Blackburn had articulated a common fear. From the very first moment of the prisoners' liberation, there had been intense speculation in the press and around the kitchen tables of many suburban homes about how those who had been held captive for three and a half years, many of them in conditions of appalling misery and privation, would adjust to civilian life. Young people had scavenged, stolen and schemed to survive; how would they stand up to the rigours of employment and the demands of family life? Older returned prisoners might be permanently ruined, their health never to recover from years of deprivation, untreated injuries and diseases.

Despite his early warning, Blackburn soon became concerned that there was too much emphasis on the potential psychiatric difficulties of returned prisoners. By 1949 he felt that all the talk of neurosis had been exaggerated and 'was getting some chaps down'.[22] Like others of his class and position, Blackburn felt that there were too many returned men open to the power of suggestion; a former officer, he remained alert to the possibility of malingering. He carried this revised attitude into a number of high-profile appointments to non-statutory bodies associated with ex-service personnel, among them the chairmanship of the federal Prisoners of War Trust Fund. In that capacity, he read, commented upon and judged the cases of men such as Robert, who applied for financial assistance in the face of ongoing hardship.

Blackburn and Robert shared the wartime experience of captivity, but their postwar lives could not have been more different. In 1958 Robert appealed to Blackburn and other trustees of the fund. 'Sirs, I beg of you to agree that my troubles and debts were all caused through my P.O.W. days my failure to give a woman happiness & what she wanted & a failure to give the children a mother and a home … I did my job as a soldier & a prisoner of war and now I am asking you as Representatives of the Prisoner of War Trust Fund to help me.' Although Robert on an earlier occasion had received £100 from the fund, his ongoing struggle caused sympathy to wear thin. 'I don't think we can get him out of his jam', Blackburn concluded.

Robert and Arthur Blackburn represent the two main groups of former POWs who appear throughout this book. Robert was more typical, at least in terms of his social class, his war experience as a member of the 'other ranks' and the kind of employment he was able to find on return. Blackburn, as a member of the establishment and with a powerful voice in matters that affected returned service personnel, occupied a very different part of the social order. He belonged to a group of former officers whose influence in matters to do with POWs outweighed their mere numbers, as they were elected to public office, were appointed to key government boards or assumed leadership positions in the veteran community. Their activities in these roles formed part of the public debate about issues concerning former POWs.

While in some respects analysing the views of POWs from the 'other ranks' is an act of historical recovery, in the pages that follow it also allows for consideration of the dynamic of class in the postwar POW community. The privileges accorded to officers that rankled in the camps carried forth into the civilian world. The differences of education, opportunity and wealth that divided former POWs were of longer term consequence than the experience of captivity that united them. In the decades after the war former officers like Blackburn had the ear of the federal government and repatriation authorities when it came to determining policy about former POWs. While they were ostensibly representing expertise on matters relating to the legacy of imprisonment, their views about respectability, morality and responsibility were as likely to be determined by their class position as by their wartime experience, if not more so.

This book considers the 'battle within', at both the individual and the collective level, to comprehend the meaning and impact of imprisonment, through four levels of analysis. First, it examines responses to POWs in relation to broader national mythologies about the performance of Australians in war, specifically the Anzac legend, in order to trace how the former prisoner was received with ambivalence. Second, the book investigates the attitudes of the government, the military and the repatriation authorities towards the treatment of POWs. It demonstrates how decisions about compensation and strategies around rehabilitation accorded with contemporary views about war neurosis and anxiety to compound an already-equivocal attitude towards former POWs. Third, individual postwar experiences of male prisoners, in relation to health, employment, and social and sexual relationships, show how contemporary understandings about masculinity and work shaped and challenged prisoners' own subjectivity. The impact of captivity is also considered in relation to the extent that earlier experiences – of family, work and education – helped or hindered capacity for resilience and rehabilitation. Finally, public activity in relation to one former enemy, Japan, and to other Asian groups who had assisted Australian prisoners in their time of need revealed POWs' receptivity to the new languages of reconciliation and regional relationships that ultimately reshaped their place in the commemorative landscape. By the 1980s, when trauma and victimhood assumed a central place in the memory of war – both internationally and within Australia itself – POWs had emerged as objects of sympathy and subjects of commemoration in their own right.

Part I

Official attitudes to POWs

I
A matter of dishonour?

> He was sufficiently certain of his own courage
> to believe that in the ordinary circumstances of
> the soldier's life he would, given the chance, have
> acquitted himself in a quite superlative way. He had
> spent his youth studying to be noble. But the world
> he was in now was a mystery to him. You do not
> prepare yourself for shame.
>
> *David Malouf, 1990*[1]

The 30 000 Australian men and small number of women who became POWs in the Second World War represented a cross-section of the nation's population in the early 1940s. Their number included athletes who had represented Australia, a prime minister's grandson, and the son of Ethel Turner, whose novel *Seven Little Australians* (1894) had entertained generations of schoolchildren.[2] Highly decorated soldiers from the First World War were imprisoned alongside men who had joined the AIF less than six months earlier. The civilian professions of POWs ranged from those requiring skills that were also useful in a camp environment, such as hairdressing, carpentry and nursing, to others with less relevance, like professional golfing, jockeying and shearing. Almost everyone in Australia knew of a family or community member so ominously absent.

Throughout the war there was public and private concern about POWs in enemy hands. Hundreds of POWs from the European theatre were repatriated or exchanged in 1943 and 1944, but there was no interest from Japan in military prisoner exchange.[3] Information about POWs of Japan was patchy, at best. Unlike Germany and Italy, Japan had not ratified the 1929 Convention Relative to the Treatment of Prisoners of War, known as the Geneva Convention, and did not provide the Red Cross with complete lists of the people it had captured.[4] Relatives and friends turned to support organisations and donated to charities in an effort to salve their anxiety. POW relatives' associations were established in almost every state.[5] Fundraising campaigns such as the Red Cross' This Street Supports an Australian Prisoner of War ultimately raised over £4 million.[6] Encouraging place-based giving was an astute move by the Red Cross, as the 2nd AIF was largely composed of battalions drawn from particular regions.

Despite the groundswell of public sympathy for POWs, the highest echelons of the Australian Army took a different view. In 1943 General Sir Thomas Blamey (1884–1951), Commander-in-Chief of the Australian Military Forces, confessed to Frank Forde, Minister for the Army, that the question of POWs had 'always been a delicate one'. 'It must be held foremost in mind', Blamey insisted, 'that surrender to the enemy on the part of the soldier in preference to death is dishonourable'. In principle, the government and the army ought to regard surrender as a 'matter of dishonour'. In relation to POWs, Blamey warned against 'any tendency to extol them unduly or give them privileges greater than soldiers who have not surrendered'.[7] Ambivalence towards returned male prisoners – towards their capability as soldiers, their part in the war effort and, in the end, their masculinity – started at the top.

Surrender and captivity

Most prisoners entered captivity once a decision to surrender to enemy forces had been taken by a senior or commanding officer. During Axis offensives in 1941 and 1942, Germany and Italy captured over 7000 Australian troops from the 2nd AIF in North Africa, the Middle East, Greece and Crete. A further 1476 airmen were taken prisoner individually or in small groups as a consequence of bailing from planes that crashed during bombing raids over mainland Europe. After a period in rudimentary transit or holding camps, most POWs were eventually accommodated in more permanent camps in Germany and Italy. After Italy surrendered in 1943, Allied POWs under Italian control (including Australians) were sent to Germany, Austria and Poland. Almost 600 Australian POWs were able to escape from German or Italian captivity, given their capacity to pass in the company of white Europeans.[8] Somewhat paradoxically, this was not an option for those who were imprisoned rather closer to home, where White Australia meant ready identification as an escapee among predominantly Asian populations. Scholars at the AWM are currently researching if the small numbers of Aboriginal POWs, which cannot be easily identified through service records, had a particular captivity experience.

The Imperial Japanese Army captured over 22 000 Australians in various locations throughout the Asia-Pacific. Almost 20 000 members of the 8th Division, including medical staff from general hospitals, field ambulance and casualty clearing stations, were deployed in Malaya from February 1941 as part of the Australian commitment to Britain's empire in the 'Far East'.[9] There were smaller concentrations of Australian forces engaged in the defence of the Dutch empire in the Dutch East Indies (present-day Indonesia). Gull Force was on the island of Ambon, and, likewise, several thousand members of the 7th Division were diverted to Java on their return from the Middle East in early 1942. Australia also had its own external territory to defend: Lark Force was sent to guard New Guinea, specifically the islands of New Britain and New Ireland, which Australia held under mandate from the League of Nations.

In February 1942 the fall of Singapore came as an enormous shock to the Australian government and its citizens, who had at once underestimated Japan and overestimated the capacity of the British to defend their colonies in the event of war in both Europe and Asia. Naval and air defences in Malaya and Singapore were far too rudimentary to withstand the Japanese offensive launched in December 1941. Within weeks, British forces in Malaya (which included Australia's 8th Division) surrendered to the Imperial Japanese Army. The Dutch East Indies did not hold out much longer and was under Japanese control by March 1942. As a consequence, Arthur Blackburn's Blackforce was taken prisoner by Japan. Perhaps mindful of the Australian Army's view of prisoners, in March 1942 Blackburn issued an order to his troops stating that 'this surrender was not my choice … The Commander in Chief of the NEI [Netherlands, or Dutch, East Indies] has *ordered* us to surrender'.[10] During the Japanese offensive in the Asia-Pacific in 1941–42 there were over 4000 Australian casualties; after the surrender, those remaining in Japanese-occupied territories became POWs.

Being taken prisoner by the Imperial Japanese Army was among the most dangerous experiences a member of the AIF might encounter in the Second World War, equivalent in its high death rate only to serving in Bomber Command, flying air raids over Europe. POW deaths accounted for 20 per cent of all Australian deaths in the Second World War.[11] There were particular episodes and experiences linked to this dramatic loss of life. Movement from one location to another could be perilous. Almost 1000 people died when a US submarine torpedoed the *Montevideo Maru*, the Japanese ship transporting them from New Britain to Hainan Island, in June 1942.[12] Selection to join a labour force, on projects ranging from the Thai–Burma Railway and an airstrip on Borneo to Japan's coal mines, also increased risk of death, disease and injury. Almost 100 000 *romusha* and 12 000 Allied prisoners, including 2700 Australians, died in Japan's quest to build an inland railway, at record speed through mountainous and difficult terrain, to connect supply lines between Thailand and Burma. At least 13 000 Australians were transferred from Singapore, Java and Timor to Thailand and Burma in 1942–43 to work on the Thai–Burma Railway.[13] Some work parties suffered higher death rates than others. The different locations of the camps, their susceptibility to diseases like cholera, the capacities of medical officers and the nature of the work performed meant that even working on the railway was not a uniform experience.[14]

The 8th Division, to the chagrin of some of its surviving members, became synonymous with captivity in a way that prisoners captured by the Germans and Italians did not.[15] Fifteen years and more after the war ended, John, who had spent time on the Thai–Burma Railway, was still bitter about the way people responded to the knowledge that he had been a POW. A fisherman from Tweed Heads, New South Wales, John had returned to Australia to find that his marriage was over and he went to live on Bribie Island, off the coast of Queensland. He did not remarry and had no children. In 1960 he reflected, 'It occasionally comes out, never directly but by innuendo that because one was a POW that a man must have given himself up instead of seeing it out'. John complained that men from other divisions 'looked down on the 8th for being captured … although we did all that was asked of us [and] I feel bitter about surrender'.

John's was not an isolated case. There were plenty of other former prisoners and senior 8th Division officers who complained about the attitudes they encountered. One man, already in his forties when taken prisoner, claimed, 'Other service-men seem to think we should of made a better show in Malaya and a lot of them look down on us'. James, who had suffered gunshot wounds to his legs and shoulders during the battle for Malaya, often ended up arguing with people about his war service. In the early 1950s, he claimed to have met 'many people (especially work mates)' who were of the opinion that 'Singapore with its great defences should not have fallen'.

The Commander of the 8th Division Lieutenant General Henry Gordon Bennett (1887–1962) retained lifelong bitterness about public criticism of his decision to leave Singapore during surrender negotiations and escape to Australia by boat. He justified this as being a strategic ploy to deliver knowledge about Japan's tactics, but a later royal commission disagreed and found that Bennett's actions had been unjustified.[16]

Suspicion about the soldiering capabilities of their men was an attitude that infuriated the senior ranks of the 8th Division. Lieutenant Colonel Albert E Coates (1895–1977), senior surgeon on the Thai–Burma Railway, remarked, 'Nothing has angered me more than to hear from time to time of soldiers who had fought courageously in the Middle East and in New Guinea, speak in a slighting manner about the men in the Eighth division ... This lie should be nailed'.[17] Brigadier Frederick 'Black Jack' Galleghan (1897–1971), the authoritarian and stern Commander of Allied troops in Changi prison, refused to join an ex-POW association in the postwar years, determined as he was to preserve the memory of the men in his battalion as soldiers, not prisoners. 'You are not going home as prisoners', he had told them at the end of the war. 'You will march down Australian streets as soldiers.'[18] One youthful member of Galleghan's battalion, Stanley 'Stan' Arneil (1918–92), who was a driving force in its association in the postwar years, always declared, 'We were soldiers in captivity not prisoners of war who surrendered voluntarily to look for some place where they weren't going to be killed'.[19]

The army itself exhibited a deeply ambivalent relationship to its soldiers who had been taken captive. There was an initial reluctance to allow any fanfare to accompany the return of POWs and a desire to shield such men from public view. The first prisoners returning from the European theatre were given no welcoming reception on the docks and were whisked away to private rooms for family reunions. Internal army correspondence made clear that, rather than being a protective measure, such reticence existed because senior figures in the military were reluctant to make 'heroes' of these men.[20] The army was fixated on the distinction between captivity and active service: the Adjutant-General was determined that the experiences of POWs should not be promoted over those of the soldiers who had 'borne the whole load'.[21] Upon his liberation Stan Arneil complained about the 'shocking maladministration of the Australian Army', which treated released POWs such as himself as 'an embarrassment'. Food, clothing and beer were in poor supply, and men who had endured a long captivity were given extensive duties on the ship that transported them back to Australia. 'Our stop at Darwin was a disgrace to the Australian Government', Arneil insisted. 'We think now that the only welcome we are likely to receive in Australia will be from our own homes.'[22]

Masculinity and shame

It was incontrovertible that Australian forces had surrendered as a consequence of decisions made by British and Dutch commanders-in-chief; hence, no individual blame was appropriate. While there were former prisoners who resented being 'looked down upon' as the result of a calamity not of their own making, others had internalised the view that surrender was dishonourable, and they felt the sting of failure. 'I feel inferior to a soldier who was not taken P.O.W.', one man confessed in the late 1960s. Stan Arneil described the command to lay down arms as 'the biggest blow' he had endured in the war.[23] 'Although we had no option but to be taken prisoners,' another recalled, 'I have never liked the term P.O.W. ... it seems to infer you were a burden and not an asset to the country'. A grocer from Adelaide had been taken prisoner a few weeks short of his twenty-first birthday. He stated, 'Up until the time of our capture, apart from being happy and self-assured I was proud of myself as a soldier and of the whole Australian Army ... The main thing those years of captivity did was to destroy my confidence'. A full fifteen years after the war had ended another admitted that he was 'ashamed of the fact of being a POW'.

Some historians have detected lingering self-doubt among former prisoners. Joan Beaumont argued that many POWs were concerned that they had proved to be 'second-class soldiers'.[24] Robin Gerster identified 'a keen sense of personal shame' permeating POW memoirs, books that were so different in style and content from their 'big-noting' antecedents.[25] Stigma and shame were responses that reflected the way in which war had marked Western culture. Not only were prisoners physically removed from the front, but they also made a symbolic journey away from the masculine world of the battlefield. War is an arena of action and aggression, and historically its main players have been male warriors, whose fighting qualities have included heroism, courage and valour. The language of the battlefield, of the front, is saturated with the vocabulary of masculinity. A concern with manhood, manliness, virility and brotherhood structures many accounts of combat. The implicit contrast, the other half of the equation, is the home front, a supposedly more feminine world, where there is an environment supportive of the main war effort and an atmosphere of nurture for those who return.[26] Prisoners were in limbo: the camp, neither battlefield nor hearth, was an inherently ambiguous zone.[27]

Fuelling the ambiguity, women were also taken prisoner. Military nurses were stationed in Malaya and at Rabaul in the Australian Mandated Territory of New Guinea; some of them did not escape the invading Japanese forces. Six members of the Australian Army Nursing Service captured in New Britain were transported to Japan in mid-1942 and survived their captivity. A further sixty-five who attempted to flee Singapore by ship in early February 1942 had a more perilous journey. Twelve members of this group were lost at sea when Japanese bombers strafed and sank their ship, the *Vyner Brooke*. A Japanese battalion then executed a further twenty-one, who had been washed up on Bangka Island, off the coast of Sumatra. One nurse, Lieutenant Colonel Vivian Bullwinkel (1915–2000), survived the Bangka Island massacre and joined thirty-one others from her unit who had struggled ashore after the shipwreck. Together, they spent the next three years as POWs in a series of camps on Sumatra and surrounding islands. A combination of malnutrition, disease and unhygienic conditions in the camps meant that a quarter of the nurses did not survive their captivity.[28] The Matron-in-Chief of the Australian Army Nursing Service Annie Sage (1895–1969), who joined the rescue mission that searched for the nurses at the end of the war, was incredulous when those who had survived were finally located on Sumatra: 'Why, where are the rest of you?'[29] Frederick Galleghan, Commander of AIF prisoners in Changi, said the same thing when the troops, or what was left of them, returned from working on the Thai–Burma Railway.[30]

The massacre of the women and the mistreatment of those who survived it attracted intense public outrage. Rohan Rivett (1917–77), a journalist who had himself been a prisoner of the Japanese and went on to write the immensely popular memoir *Behind Bamboo* (1946), commented, 'No incident among the thousands which have befallen those in Japanese hands has aroused such fury among the Australian prisoners as this cold-blooded and senseless murder'.[31] As medical personnel and prisoners, the nurses were entitled to protection under the terms of the Geneva Convention.[32] Furthermore, in the unwritten gender norms of war, women ought to have been shielded from its horrors. As prisoners, however, the women had been subjected to hard physical labour in the camps, starvation conditions and inadequate medical care. Just as imprisonment was potentially emasculating for soldiers, by confining them and rendering them passive, the femininity of the nurses had been imperilled by their exposure to war's worst horrors.[33]

Guilt about the failure to prevent the suffering of women intensified the sense of outrage about their experiences. Major Henry 'Harry' Windsor (1914–87), the doctor who accompanied the rescue mission, was so overwhelmed by the sight of the surviving nurses that he declared any Japanese associated with their imprisonment should be 'forthwith slowly and painfully butchered'.[34] Michael McKernan, a historian who knew Windsor in later life, was astonished to learn that such a gentle and cultured person could have been moved to such sentiment. 'The passion, the grinding anger, is entirely at odds with everything I knew of this man.'[35] One AIF Sergeant wept when he saw the rescued nurses, emaciated and ill, as they were helped from the plane that had transported them back to Singapore. When the nurses, barely able to walk, 'some human skeletons', arrived at the hospital, their male compatriots cried, 'Give us guns. Let us at those dirty b[astards]!' Released male prisoners, themselves hospitalised after years of neglect, 'became hysterical and had to be controlled'.[36] The desire for retribution, tears, hysteria: this was shame. Australian men felt that they had not adequately protected 'their' women from the ravages of the enemy. Almost a decade afterwards, a reviewer of nurse Betty Jeffrey's *White Coolies* (1954), a popular diary-like account of the Australian nurses' years of internment, recalled that the treatment of the nurses was a 'painful subject' and 'a blow in the face to our national pride'. The treatment of the male prisoners had been 'bad enough', but the suffering of the women had possessed 'the character of a deadly insult'.[37]

Imprisonment by the enemy, then, unsettled the logic of the battle front and the home front and the appropriate roles of men and women in relation to both. In certain respects, the focus in daily newspapers in 1945 on the experiences of the nurses, shocking as they had been, served to deflect attention away from some of the more troubling aspects about the imprisonment of much larger numbers of men. Even though conditions in many camps had been manifestly criminal, and were confirmed as such by war crimes tribunals in the following years, captivity also presented a challenge to masculine identity. A war spent as a prisoner sat in awkward tension with the Anzac legend, the key national context for interpreting and understanding the behaviour of Australian soldiers in wartime. Deriving its name from the First World War's Australian and New Zealand Army Corps (ANZAC), the Anzac legend centred on bravery, battlefield prowess and physical strength. These characteristics were given a racial spin: they were proof that the Anglo-Saxon race had thrived in the Antipodes. The 2nd AIF was set to reinvigorate this tradition as citizen soldiers who carried forth the strength of the people.

The surrender of the 'sons of Anzac' to an Asian enemy, the slave-like conditions to which they were subjected and their physical and psychological emasculation were insults to all that had been held dear.[38] Liberated prisoners were the emaciated opposite of the sturdy Anzacs who had beckoned from recruitment posters throughout the war. 'Three and a half years ago they were strong young men and fine fighting soldiers', *The Age*'s war correspondent reported from a Sumatran POW camp. Imprisonment and ill-treatment had rendered them wretched, weak and sick. Bearded, bare-foot, wearing loin-cloths, the men were 'physical wrecks', so light that 'I could have almost carried one on each arm'.[39]

The images published alongside stories about the prisoners' release conveyed much of what the men had lost. Photographs showing emaciated, semi-naked men, lying prone on bamboo racks, appeared in all the major daily newspapers. These liberation images were highly unusual, not only for their subject matter, which was unprecedented in the history of Australians at war, but in the way they presented the male body. The few culturally available photographic images of naked Western men had not usually suggested passivity. Indeed, they had connoted the smooth strength possessed by the statues of classical antiquity. Most recently the physical culture movements of the 1930s had spawned an array of photographic images of the male body that emphasised sport, fitness and racial purity.[40] That kind of physique had animated wartime recruitment posters. The newspaper articles that accompanied the POW photographs struggled to say that the suffering of these men contradicted the male warrior ideal, but the photographs stated it unequivocally. Not only were the gaunt physiques of the prisoners exposed to the camera; they were frequently photographed lying down, a pose that further emphasised their passivity and weakness.

Race and the POW

Captivity held the potential to compromise a soldier's masculinity. For POWs of Japan, defeat and imprisonment also challenged some of the assumptions about race that had held sway prior to the Second World War.[41] Wartime propaganda emphasised the physical strength of Australian soldiers, in a context where the enemy was depicted as small, short-sighted, simian and Asian. Despite the denigration of Japan's forces in such terms, the fact remained that Japan had conquered the United States in the Philippines, the British (and Australians) in Malaya, Singapore and Hong Kong, and the Dutch and Australians in the Dutch East Indies. Defeat cast a shadow over the 8th Division's fighting skill, one lengthened by the audacity and competence of an enemy who had long been constructed as racially inferior. Depictions of the Japanese enemy shifted in the wake of military success. The representation of Japan as a huge, ape-like character underscored at once the nation's elevation to a significant foe and the implication that, despite its victories, it was a barbaric, uncivilised enemy.[42]

The humiliation of Japan's success was tempered by constructing it as an unnatural and temporary inversion of racial hierarchy. A colloquial refrain was that prisoners had been treated like 'white coolies'. In common parlance 'coolies' were understood to be Indian or Chinese indentured labourers who worked for minimal wages, often under the control of white overseers. Such indentured labour had become a feature in the British imperial world after the abolition of slavery and was also used in the United States and Australia. The word had become synonymous with Asian labour and with exploitation. When POWs were compelled to undertake manual labour under the control of Japanese, Korean, Sikh and other Indian guards, the tensions over labour, race and hierarchy that had always adhered to the 'coolie' question could not be contained.[43]

Labelling POWs as 'white coolies' won currency as an oxymoron precisely because it articulated a reversal of the racial order: in the 1940s it was anathema for white people to undertake manual labour for Asian overseers. Stan Arneil, imprisoned in Changi and sent to work on the railway, felt that the Japanese had treated the prisoners as 'coolie slaves'. 'It is a queer sight', he noted in his journal in 1943, 'to see twenty men bronzed like natives, bent almost double as they strain and sweat to pull loads of wood up to two and a half tons up long hills'. Arneil recast shame as a victory for moral courage: 'Even though it should disgust any sane person it gives me a thrill to see such sights and know that our morale is still exceptionally high'. Nevertheless, after months on the railway Arneil was yearning not just for his freedom but for a return to 'white man's conditions'.[44] When victory and liberation came, a war correspondent declared, there would be 'rejoicing in many homes throughout Australia' that their male relatives were 'now safely under the protection of Empire forces and … no longer white coolies within the power of cruel Korean guards'.[45] When Reg Mahoney, who had been a prisoner in Changi and on the railway, first wrote to his brother after release, he anticipated that he and his fellow ex-POWs would shortly be 'living like white men once again'. He continued, 'We are sweating now for more mail, papers and evidence of a white man's world'.[46] Lest we forget the centrality of whiteness to Australian identity in the 1940s, the life of Changi Commander Frederick 'Black Jack' Galleghan contains a salutary reminder. Black Jack was thus named for his dark skin tones, which he inherited from his nineteenth-century Jamaican forebears. Arneil, who became Galleghan's biographer, claimed that Black Jack, who did marry, had no children because he did not want them to suffer the ignominy of being black skinned in White Australia.[47]

Not only did the experiences of POWs of Japan challenge long-held racial ideologies about the superiority of whites; for Australians, they also referenced an aspect of their nation's history considered best forgotten. One of the achievements of the original Anzacs had been to prove that Australia had overcome its unpromising convict origins. The 'convict stain' had been erased at Gallipoli. Had it emerged again, as it were, in the camps of East and South-East Asia? For a country that still in the 1940s had an awkward relationship to its convict past as a source of shame or embarrassment, the imprisonment of large numbers of its soldiers had some unsettling parallels. In a cartoon image published in the *Sydney Morning Herald* in 1945, of an imprisoned soldier bleeding from the lash, a symbol of convict punishment was transposed to the Japanese prison camp (although beating with a bamboo stick would more likely have been the norm in the latter case). The cartoon established the physical might of the liberating digger but in its focus on the scarred and bleeding back of the POW, it contained some eerie reminders of the brutality of the convict era.

In 1945 the war correspondent and later novelist George Johnston (1912–70) reported on the feelings of liberated prisoners, who worried that 'they were going back home "like a pack of convicts and cowards"'. 'It is tragic to see these emaciated, sometimes tearful, men', Johnston wrote, 'men who for three years … have suffered beneath the feeling of stigma of disgrace and shame'.[48] 'It has left a stain that won't come out', one returning prisoner told a journalist, unwittingly doubling the reminder of a convict past and the fear of emasculation: 'It has robbed us of decent manhood'.[49]

There was one group not tarnished by the fear of emasculation or the stain of captivity. Medical officers and surgeons attached to the 7th and 8th divisions in captivity were able to continue the work for which they had been trained, albeit in restricted and difficult circumstances. The most revered became household names in postwar Australia. Albert Coates, a surgeon from Ballarat, was hailed as 'Coates of Thailand' for the mighty job he performed on the Thai–Burma Railway. Edward Dunlop was similarly feted. Upon release Arthur Blackburn wrote to Dunlop, 'I have heard from dozens and dozens of men of all nationalities, Americans, British, Dutch and Australians, and in all places from Calcutta to Colombo back to Australia, of the magnificent work which you and the other medicos did in looking after the P.O.W.s during those awful years'.[50] 'I've taken this war seriously like a life on its own', Dunlop told his fiancée Helen, 'and just poured everything into it as if five years were one's mortal span'.[51]

Within a year of the POWs' return, there was a sense within some ex-service circles that the Australian public had already forgotten, or insufficiently appreciated, the suffering those former prisoners had endured. In spring 1946 the Victorian RSL's magazine *Mufti* published a series of articles by 'Selarang' about the experiences of men in Changi. The articles were designed 'to inform the people of Australia of the privations endured by servicemen while in captivity', which had to be restated so that men who had continued to suffer from the effects of their ill-treatment might 'have the sympathy and the understanding of the general public'.[52]

By the early 1950s former POWs were reporting that they encountered indifferent attitudes and sometimes hostility in the workplace. Employers regarded them as possessing 'doubtful reliability and stability', according to a man with a reasonable level of education who could only find work driving a taxi. Those who still required treatment for ongoing health issues could be subject to cutting asides. One manager remarked of the frequent visits of a former POW to the repatriation hospital 'such as, what again? How long are you being the guinea pig?' Another former POW, who worked for the post office in Tasmania, complained in the early 1950s that the Post Master had taken 'a couple of "shots"' at him over the time he had been 'off work through War Disabilities'. On one occasion, after this man had made an unsuccessful application to have his war service pension entitlements increased, the Post Master had quipped, 'I should think so. You jokers go away to these wars and come back and expect the world. I've been paying into the superannuation fund for years and if the Department goes taking broken down crocks like you into the service all of my money will be going to you blokes'.

In further illustration of the RSL's concerns about eroding sympathy for POWs, in 1952 historian and journalist Malcolm Ellis (1890–1969), publishing under his Hindi-inspired pseudonym, 'Ek Dum', penned a scathing review of Russell Braddon's memoir of captivity, *The Naked Island* (1952).[53] Known as a forthright anti-communist and a conservative, Ellis was called 'Dumb Hec' by the labour movement.[54] Leading with the title 'Naked island and naked souls', Ellis considered the current generation of prisoners undignified in their desire to recount their experiences in captivity. Traditionally, Ellis suggested, the British soldier had preferred not to advertise the fact either that he had been forced to surrender 'or that he had been at the beck and call of some Oriental, to have his face slapped and to be ordered around in the course of thoroughly menial work'. Recalling the imprisonment of British soldiers during the Second Anglo-Mysore War in southern India during the late-eighteenth century, and in the Anglo-Afghan wars of the nineteenth, Ellis approved of their 'silent fortitude' and contempt of the enemy. In contrast, Australians captured in the mid-twentieth century had felt compelled to write about their experiences, indeed were 'becoming addicted' to doing so. These books begged for pity and their message might be summed up in a sentence: 'I was a p.o.w. Oh, how I suffered'.[55]

The troubled status of former prisoners became even clearer as their long battles to rehabilitate themselves and to lobby for compensation began. Ellis was a divisive figure whose writing was designed to court controversy, yet in some ways his overstatements captured a raw truth. While few people were likely to share his extreme reaction to the 'self-pitying' former prisoners, there was ample evidence that in some circles returned prisoners were greeted with ambivalence, at best. Increasingly, former POWs relied on ex-service organisations, their own associations and high-profile doctors and politicians who had spent the war years as POWs to press for a more sympathetic view of their captivity.

Some felt that service personnel who had been POWs had special needs and therefore required an organisation focused on their cause. Former POWs were entitled to join the largest ex-service association in Australia, the RSL. But by September 1946 the battalion associations connected with the former 8th Division formalised their links and sent delegates to the newly formed 8th Division and AIF Malaya Council.[56] The primary concerns of the Council of the 8th Division, as it became known, were the welfare and entitlements of former POWs of the Japanese. Notwithstanding the RSL and the Council of the 8th Division, each state also had its own independent ex-POW association, which represented POWs held in all theatres.[57] These groups added their voices to emerging concerns about former POWs in the postwar period, in a climate in which the government and the military retained a more ambivalent view.

2
A bit queer

> I think it is in the back of every fellow's mind that he might be a bit queer.
> *Brigadier Arthur Blackburn, 1945*[1]

On the last Saturday in September 1945 it was only a little over six weeks since Japan had surrendered and the Second World War had come to an end. The city of Adelaide prepared for one of its rituals, the South Australian National Football League Grand Final. The league had decided to mark the end of the war by asking the state Governor, Sir Charles Willoughby Norrie, to welcome home returning POWs. Three hundred former prisoners and their families, invited as special guests to the match, were seated in a separate enclosure. The Governor proposed three cheers for the POWs and the crowd enthusiastically complied. Brigadier Arthur Blackburn, known as 'Blackie' to the men he had commanded in the Middle East and then on Java, replied on their behalf. He thanked the Governor and declared that POWs simply wished 'to become ordinary citizens' again then moved to join the men seated in their cordoned-off zone. But Blackburn had made a mistake: he was to join the official party. He was escorted back to the stands. Press reports described the 'underlying camaraderie' of the returned POWs, who looked and acted like other spectators despite the 'subtle differences' that set them apart. 'There were the silent grips on the shoulder as one man passed another, which said more than any words could.'[2]

The spectacle in Adelaide on that springtime afternoon summed up the well-meaning but awkward response to returning POWs: welcomed home, at one with, yet apart from, their community. The incident epitomised Stephen Garton's observation that returned prisoners were caught in a conflict between the normal and the exceptional.[3] Even Blackburn seemed at sea – insisting on normality, then heading off in the wrong direction from the podium. 'I think it is in the back of every fellow's mind that he might be a bit queer', Blackburn had confessed at his public welcome, employing the word 'queer' in its contemporary sense of 'odd' or 'strange'. 'We had no way of telling. So when they come back, don't treat them as anything but the good fellows that they are.'[4] This was a confusing message from a respected public figure. Yet Blackburn spoke from the heart. Only the previous week, his wife Rose had comforted him every night as he woke, screaming, from the force of his nightmares.[5]

Other families also noticed the changes in returned prisoners. There were the ongoing physical ailments that stemmed from a long period with inadequate food and poor medical facilities: tuberculosis, malaria, irreparable damage to teeth and eyes, tropical ulcers, and bacterial and parasitical infections of the stomach and bowel. The mental health of returned POWs was of equal, if not greater, concern. Some former prisoners seemed more neurotic than before, anxious, hostile to authority or antisocial. The experiences of shell-shocked soldiers from the First World War were still within living memory, but returned POWs seemed to exhibit a different set of neurotic symptoms. Could it be that imprisonment constituted a specific type of war experience, one which demanded specialised treatment and recognition of its particularity? These were questions asked not just within families and organisations devoted to the welfare of former POWs; they formed part of a broader public conversation about the best way to respond to released prisoners. For the government, the relationship between captivity and its psychological consequences was also situated within a pressing financial context: war-caused disabilities, physical or mental, were the basis of pension claims.

Barbed-wire disease

Responses to POWs from the First World War provided little guidance. In Australia, as in Britain, repatriation authorities had made no special provisions for returning POWs. British and German psychiatrists had concluded that captivity, which removed men from the battle front, had insulated prisoners from developing shell shock.[6] In contrast, Adolf Vischer, a Swiss physician who had visited various POW and internment camps, had argued that neurotic symptoms were commonplace within them.[7] Vischer had described the susceptibility of the POW to 'barbed-wire disease' – irritability, suspicion, trouble with concentration and memory, restlessness and depression – as a consequence of the indefinite nature of captivity, lack of privacy, disruption to routine, sexual deprivation and, 'above everything else, the barbed wire', which wound 'like a red thread through his mental processes'.[8] Vischer had conducted no follow-up studies of this group, but the concept of barbed-wire disease had lingered as short-hand for the psychological implications of captivity.

In the interwar period governments and psychiatrists had abandoned shell shock as a useful way of understanding the psychiatric casualties of war. A conference convened in 1939 to advise the Minister of Pensions in Great Britain about the principles for dealing with what was then referred to as 'nervous breakdown' in the current war had ruled that the term 'shell shock' had been 'a gross and costly misnomer and should be eliminated entirely from our nomenclature'.[9] In Australia the Minister for the Army had followed this lead and insisted that 'neurosis' was the word to use when discussing nervous conditions.[10] Adoption of the term 'neurosis' more accurately reflected the assumption in medical circles that only people predisposed through existing weakness would succumb to mental health problems and that concussion from the blast of a bomb or poisoning from gasses had nothing to do with it. As the British conference had concluded, 'Nervous disorders arising during the war differed in no material way from those well known in civil life'.[11] Therefore, the implication of a physical cause for psychological responses was by the beginning of the Second World War considered not just erroneous but also an expensive mistake, particularly in light of the number of First World War veterans who had claimed a pension for psychiatric conditions.

If battle itself was no longer considered a trigger for neurotic response, what of imprisonment and Vischer's quarter-century-old theory about barbed-wire disease? As the end of the Second World War approached, with literally millions of people around the world in captivity and awaiting release, attention again turned to the psychological implications of imprisonment. Among Britain and its Allies, prisoner exchanges with Germany in the early 1940s had reopened the debate. When officers repatriated from German captivity had begun to display signs of dysfunction, the British Army had instituted a series of rehabilitation studies, programs and units designed to smooth the return of former captives to their battalions and, ultimately, after the war had ended, to civil society.[12] Drawing on studies conducted at these facilities, the British Army had concluded that most returned POWs were not prone to neurosis and the tiny minority who were mainly struggled to adjust to the changed conditions on the home front.

In 1944 Major PH Newman, both a surgeon and a repatriated prisoner, revisited Vischer's idea of barbed-wire disease and suggested that it was a mental condition that could continue after release. He considered it common during the repatriation period for prisoners to experience 'restlessness, irritability, disrespect for discipline and authority, irresponsibility and even dishonesty'.[13] Only a small minority of prisoners, he thought, would go on to develop more serious neurotic symptoms.

Similar debates occurred within Australia about the potential for returning POWs to exhibit neurosis. The war correspondent Kenneth Slessor brought a poet's sensibility to the issue when writing in 1944 about the problems returning POWs might face. 'Peacetime living,' he wrote, 'with its industrial jungles, its machine-gun fire of economic necessity', would be particularly difficult for POWs returning from German and Japanese prison camps. 'These are the psychologically wounded men with stumps of broken lives, men trying to bridge the gap between oblivion and normality, men unbalanced or sometimes warped by "barbed-wire disease".'[14] Unlike its British counterpart, the Australian Army refused to countenance the idea of separate treatment or rehabilitation for the POW. It would have no truck with the theory of barbed-wire disease. It advised demobilisation and repatriation teams that the liberated prisoner 'should not be encouraged to regard himself as a palpably abnormal person, with a spirit scarred, a mind warped or a body weakened by his experiences'.[15] In November 1945 a meeting of all branches of the armed services and the Red Cross agreed that there should be very little publicity given to returning prisoners: it 'would probably retard rather than hasten their return to normal civilian life' if a perception developed that they were 'different'.[16]

By the late 1940s years of case work with returned POWs had led the Red Cross to believe that this had been the wrong approach and that it was important to develop a specific response to them. Some doctors who were also returned POWs, who exercised an inordinate influence on the government's approach to former prisoners, begged to differ. For them the growing public debate about the neurotic former POW was a self-perpetuating myth, and they insisted that the vast majority of neurosis cases could be put down to a bad infestation of worms. This divergence between medical orthodoxy about the impact of captivity and community views on its legacies and appropriate responses to them continued until at least the 1970s.

Dominating doctors

The government body responsible for dealing with the welfare and entitlements of veterans, including POWs, was Repatriation. Sir George Wootten (1893–1970), a Gallipoli veteran who had served with distinction in both wars, was Chairman of the Repatriation Commission between 1945 and 1958.[17] As General Officer Commanding of the AIF's 9th Division in 1943–45, Wootten had been involved in the liberation of POW camps on Borneo. Newsreels had captured the moment and broadcast memorable footage of the stark contrast between the portly physique of Wootten, who weighed 127 kilograms, and the emaciated frames of the released POWs whom he greeted. Wootten's own son had been killed in an accident while on active service with the Royal Australian Air Force. Liberation had come too late for his nephew, who had perished on Borneo as part of the Sandakan–Ranau death marches.

Wootten was inclined to consult medical men who had themselves been POWs for their opinions about the repatriation needs of others. Albert Coates and Edward Dunlop became key advisers. Both country boys, who had by dint of hard work and

A bit queer

determination put themselves through medical school, Coates and Dunlop had a common touch that appealed to the 'other ranks' of the Australian Army. They also had the education, military seniority and social standing to gain access to the higher echelons of the bureaucracy associated with the health and welfare of veterans.

Another former POW doctor, Walter Edward 'Ted' Fisher (1901–65), developed a particularly influential voice in Repatriation's handling of the POW issue. Fisher and Coates had shared a hut on the Thai–Burma Railway and became friends. After the war, the Sydney-based Fisher and his mother stayed with the Coates family when they visited Melbourne. Fisher was less of a people's hero than either Coates or Dunlop and did not inspire the same devotion or accolades for his work on the Thai–Burma Railway. Nevertheless, he had a high profile in the veteran community as President of the Council of the 8th Division from its inception until his death in 1965. He also donated vast amounts of time and energy to Sydney hospitals in visiting and honorary capacities and was the pre-eminent physician at the Repatriation General Hospital at Concord.

By most accounts Fisher was an aloof and temperamental man, intellectual, and intolerant of ignorance and foolhardiness. Rohan Rivett claimed that his 'biting tongue and dictatorial manner' had earned him the nickname 'the Fuehrer'.[18] With movie-star good looks and immaculate attire, Fisher was an only child who never married. One obituary declared that his 'real and only love' was his mother, with whom he lived for most of his adult life, except for the period when he was away at war.[19] He was a single man with a cultivated taste for theatre and the classics; his personal life and interests were worlds away from those of most of the people he chose to represent. This did not prepare him well to give an empathetic response to those facing the challenges of less secure professional lives or with responsibilities to provide for wives and children.

The Repatriation Commission's practices contradicted its policy that former POWs should not be distinguished from other veterans. The guiding philosophy in relation to returned POWs was that they should not be considered as a 'class apart', yet this co-existed with a preference for POWs to be treated by doctors who had themselves spent the war in captivity.[20] 'There is an affinity between ex-prisoners of war,' Wootten explained in 1949, 'and it is felt that a doctor who has himself shared similar privations is able to discuss with greater understanding and sympathy the physical and mental problems of an applicant'.[21] Former POW doctors also believed this to be true. As one of them, Colonel Alfred Derham (1891–1962), suggested to Dunlop in 1950, some of the medical officers employed by Repatriation were uncaring, 'lazy and fed up'; he added that 'of course they [didn't] *know*' what it was like to experience captivity.[22] Furthermore, Wootten was also committed to using the services of doctors like Coates, Dunlop and Fisher to develop policy responses to the health needs of returned POWs.

The former POW medical specialists had a very particular view about how to manage the needs of returned prisoners, which was at variance both with a small but growing international medical literature on the impact of captivity and with the views of many other former POWs. Research emerging in Britain and the United States suggested that there were indeed psychological problems among former prisoners, even if this was based on the assumption that only those predisposed to neurosis, through weakness or pre-existing frailty, would succumb to it.[23] The response of Repatriation to the welfare and health needs of former POWs was rather more determined by a fear of distinguishing prisoners from other veterans and thereby of encouraging a culture of entitlement. In that regard, there was alignment between the army's determination to avoid giving privileges to POWs greater than those provided to soldiers who had not surrendered and Repatriation's view that they should not be treated as a 'class apart'. Australia had one of the world's most extensive repatriation systems, but this did not correspond with a sympathetic response to returned prisoners. Prominent former POW doctors and Repatriation were especially determined to put paid to the idea that prisoners were more likely to be susceptible to war neurosis than any other group of returned service personnel. Ted Fisher had a favourite phrase for that kind of talk: 'sob stuff'.[24]

In its dependence on the advice of POW doctors, Repatriation built a conflict of interest into the very heart of repatriation policy for returned POWs. Even though they were surgeons, doctors and specialists first, and former POWs second, this group of men had a vested interest in maintaining a view that imprisonment had no long-term legacy in rehabilitation. No one thought to question the wisdom of the department's relying so heavily on the advice of men who had themselves endured a harrowing war. In retrospect, the practice seems akin to asking the doctors, did *you* return as a changed man? Was your competence, your identity as a doctor or your mental health compromised by years of imprisonment and seeing many people die a needless or painful death?

Rehabilitating released POWs

The period immediately following return to Australia was a bewildering time for both released POWs and their families. What was the most appropriate response to people who had been through such an experience? Would it be better to encourage reflection or to get on with the business of living? Some war correspondents explicitly contested the advice of government-endorsed specialists who told relatives to 'humour them, agree with everything they say, discourage any conversation which will recall what they thought about in captivity'. 'If you do not show interest', one critic claimed, 'they are going to feel that somehow you are ashamed of them'.[25] POWs of the Germans published a flurry of advice for the families of people released from Japanese captivity. 'Nerve-wracked P.O.W.s need understanding', one pleaded.[26] John Newman-Morris, national Chairman of the Australian Red Cross Society, visited POW reception camps in Singapore and elsewhere in September 1945. He too emphasised the need for caution and had a blunt warning for concerned relatives: the period of elation experienced by POWs on their release would soon pass, many men were fearful about return, and they could be subject to depression once they arrived.[27]

In keeping with its view that to surrender was a 'matter of dishonour', the Australian Army evinced little interest in providing any distinctive treatment for released POWs. After a perfunctory medical inspection, and sometimes not even that, POWs were allowed to return to their families. Those who required ongoing treatment and hospitalisation were placed together with defence forces personnel returned from other theatres and military operations. The assumption in both cases was that it was not in the interests of released POWs to encourage them to think that their health issues or disabilities were any different from those of others.

The army was equally disinclined to dwell on the psychological after-effects of captivity. Given the refusal to distinguish between released POWs and other personnel, more general practice in relation to mental health for returned veterans prevailed. Neither the defence forces nor Repatriation devised a specific program to assist with the transition from captivity to freedom. Contemporary views about the link between pre-existing frailty and vulnerability to neurosis, and a growing belief that granting a pension could aggravate neurosis and impede recovery, produced an equivocal attitude to returned service personnel who presented as anxious or neurotic. Acute cases of psychosis, depression and debilitating anxiety were admitted to repatriation hospitals, but the pressure on these services was immense, and insufficient beds meant a reliance on state psychiatric hospitals to accommodate veterans with mental health conditions.[28] In an environment where the predisposition theory held sway, further problems arose when medical officers were required to rule whether or not a mental illness or neurosis was 'war caused'. The Commonwealth was not responsible for providing ongoing support in the form of a pension to those veterans whose mental illness was not deemed to be war caused, and the link between service (including captivity) and psychiatric problems could be especially difficult to prove if the latter emerged after discharge. Mindful of a looming pension bill, the Commonwealth encouraged a rigorous approach to applicants that crossed over into suspicion and hostility. A handbook prepared to help doctors employed by the Repatriation Commission to determine whether or not mental health conditions were war caused described any applicant as a 'potential exaggerator' and warned assessors that he was more likely to be a 'malingerer ... rather than neurotic'.[29]

By the late 1940s there was a great deal of public controversy about Repatriation's response to the needs of war neurosis cases in general. Administrative processes were slow to develop. It took two years from the end of the war for the department to appoint as its consultant psychiatrist British-born Dr Alan Stoller (1911–2007), who had been working at Perth's Claremont Mental Hospital before enlisting as a medical officer in the AIF.

The RSL regularly petitioned the Minister for Repatriation with resolutions passed at its Federal Executive urging that more be done for returned service personnel suffering from war neurosis. In April 1947 the RSL took matters into its own hands and opened a Worry Centre in central Sydney, which served over 600 cases in its first few weeks of operation.[30] Parliamentarians regularly questioned the Minister about the methods adopted for treating neurosis cases, implying that the issue had been mishandled. Yet Repatriation continued to believe that neurosis was 'largely a social problem': once the housing shortage eased and returned men could settle properly with their wives and families, it presumed, there would be a marked decline in neurosis cases.[31] By the end of 1949 almost 12 000 Second World War veterans were in receipt of a pension for various forms of war neurosis, although returned service organisations claimed that the number of unsuccessful applicants was far greater.[32]

There was a further public perception that returned POWs were especially prone to psychological problems. Ex-service and POW organisations wrote regularly to the Minister for Repatriation outlining their concerns. Former prisoners were having difficulty re-establishing themselves in civilian life, and the care of this group fell most heavily on families and private and voluntary bodies.[33] The Red Cross in particular was responsible for thousands of cases.[34] It had several convalescent homes, such as Rockingham in Melbourne, where hundreds of former POWs sought refuge in their struggle to reintegrate into families, workplaces and communities. Alongside these residential facilities, the Red Cross also employed a team of social workers who visited former prisoners in their homes and worked with their families. By 1947 sixty-one social workers were employed by the organisation.[35]

Considering the inadequacy of state-sponsored mental health services, the Red Cross was therefore well placed to report on the readjustment problems faced by POWs. It was unequivocal that there was a persistent core of former POWs who had failed to make a successful transition to freedom. 'Many find it hard to remain in one job,' the Red Cross insisted in 1947, 'and they become worried about their ability to support their families, about their health, their work, their personal adjustment difficulties'. 'Even though they are alright for a time', it continued, very few former POWs made a 'permanent adjustment', and many were prone to 'personality problems'.[36]

A body of broken men?

Doctors who had also been POWs were determined to quash what they saw as a growing public myth about the neurotic former prisoner. In 1947 Albert Coates declared, at a closed meeting of government and private bodies dealing with the question of returned POWs, that the greatest disability facing former prisoners was the prejudice 'that they must necessarily, because of their humiliations and their physical sufferings be a body of broken men'. 'This false-hood,' Coates continued, 'whispered in the market-place, printed in the newspaper, spoken in Parliament … has tended to act detrimentally'. There was an 'obnoxious pre-conception' that the returned prisoner was a damaged man. Of course there were a few 'whingers and whiners', but most had rehabilitated successfully and returned to civilian life. The vast majority of former POWs had no desire to be treated differently from other ex-servicemen; nor did they exhibit any greater rate of neurosis. 'They are not ashamed and their tribulations, physical and mental, in the majority of cases have rendered them even better men than they were before.'[37]

A few months earlier, in April 1947, Coates had convened a meeting to discuss what he considered to be the irresponsible reporting in the press of POWs' health problems. This group ultimately became Repatriation's chief advisory body on ex-POW health policy. Five doctors who had spent the war in captivity – four as prisoners of Japan (Coates himself, Alfred Derham, Edward Dunlop and J Glyn White) and one of Germany (AG Carter) – comprised the committee. Alan Stoller, the department's newly appointed consultant psychiatrist, was the final member. Chairman George Wootten invited the group, constituted as the Repatriation Committee on Repatriated Prisoners of War, to determine the nature of the problems facing POWs and to propose solutions to them. During its deliberations the committee sought further assistance from at least thirteen former POWs, including Arthur Blackburn, Ted Fisher and nine other doctors.

The committee concluded that prisoners of the Japanese (but not those held in Europe) suffered from 'an indefinite malaise or "feeling out of sorts" together with an undue tendency to fatigue'. This was sometimes accompanied by symptoms of emotional or psychological disturbance. Unlike studies in Britain, and the Minister for Repatriation's only public statements on the matter, which had concluded that changed conditions on the home front accounted for most cases of disquiet, this inquiry found untreated diseases to be the major culprits. Explicitly disputing the suggestion that a state of mind associated with captivity, such as anxiety, fear or humiliation, might have ongoing consequences, the committee argued that the root cause of melancholy in returned POWs was most likely to be the continuing effects of bacterial or parasitic infections. Many diseases contracted in captivity remained undiagnosed and could account for the vast majority of cases of despondency. Problems of neurosis did exist, of course, but this was no different from the proportion of neurosis cases among all members of the forces who had seen active service in the war. The existing programs and facilities run by Repatriation would be sufficient to handle the needs of returned prisoners. Indeed, the committee specifically warned against placing any stress on psychological factors in investigating and handling the returned prisoner, as it might 'affect him adversely'.[38]

The committee members were also determined to prove that there was a misconception that returned prisoners, particularly those held by Japan, were worse off than any other returned personnel. With this aim in mind, from that point forward, Repatriation focused any work performed in relation to returned POWs on those held by Japan, rather than on the significant minority of POWs who had been held prisoner in Europe. In the late 1940s the department ordered two surveys to investigate the health and readjustment of POWs of the Japanese. In private internal correspondence it was made clear that the surveys had been designed, in part, to counter the constant barrage of letters from ex-service organisations about the ongoing difficulties faced by former POWs.[39] The surveys also embodied the determination of Repatriation and the army to discourage former POWs from believing themselves to be special, different or entitled to any specific treatment.

The first survey, undertaken in 1947 and entitled Survey of Selected Groups of Those Who Served in the 1939–45 War, compared 10 per cent of returned POWs of Japan with a control group of men who had served in the South West Pacific Area but had not been taken prisoner. It was run after hours in the offices of the Commonwealth Employment Services to avoid creating an impression in the minds of the former prisoners that they were being considered for any special medical treatment or particular type of pension.[40] Despite the Minister for Repatriation making a public statement that the 'ten per cent survey' revealed that former prisoners 'had adjusted themselves a little more readily to civilian life than other Servicemen', this was a case of gilding the lily.[41] Reports from doctors around the country who participated in the survey exhibited some common themes: concern about the men aged twenty to forty years who did not seem to have the mental resilience of the older cohort and a perception that it was difficult for uneducated and working-class men to return to the occupations in which they had worked prior to enlistment, owing to ongoing physical problems. There were plenty of former prisoners who participated in the survey and were subsequently referred for further medical examination, not having previously availed themselves of Repatriation's services. As a consequence, it was decided to contact all returned POWs of Japan and conduct a full medical survey, known as the Ex Prisoner of War [J] Survey.

When the Ex Prisoner of War [J] Survey was initiated, in 1949, Repatriation tried to keep it quiet, in line with its policy of not drawing attention to POWs, although this was a predictably impossible task in light of the 12 000 people invited to take part. Participants were told that they might be experiencing 'latent physical disabilities' that had not manifested at the time of discharge, that there was no objective other than identifying 'disabilities due to war service' and that every effort would be made for examinations to be conducted by ex-POW doctors, who would have 'a sympathetic understanding' of their cases. This would be followed by a final examination before a medical board, at which a doctor who had also been a POW would be present.[42]

Ted Fisher ultimately used the data generated by the first survey to bolster his views, shared with Albert Coates, that the psychological consequences of captivity had been exaggerated and that far too many pensions were being granted to former POWs for specious anxiety states. Fisher received licence to share this view with doctors throughout the country when Repatriation commissioned him to write a pamphlet, *Some Aspects of Medical Investigation and Treatment* (1947), to guide medical practitioners and physicians treating returned POWs. The subjects of the pamphlet deliberately received no mention in its title, in keeping with Repatriation's policy about POWs 'that there should be complete avoidance of any publicity concerning them'.[43] Fisher editorialised in the pamphlet, insisting that there had been an unhelpful 'preconceived idea' throughout the English-speaking world that repatriated prisoners would present with 'grave psychological problems'. Belief in the incidence of psychological suffering among returned prisoners had created a self-fulfilling prophecy. According to Fisher, psychiatric problems stemming from captivity had become a popular cliché in the press and within the medical profession. Moreover, anxiety state and war neurosis were on the rise as 'excessively fashionable' diagnoses. Fisher advised that the incidence of neurosis among returned prisoners was no greater than that among other returned service personnel and, indeed, the former might well have lower rates of neurosis. Like Coates, he resorted to the message of strength through hardship as his clinching argument. Adopting an industrial metaphor to describe the tenacity of former POWs in the face of adversity, the pamphlet concluded: 'Blows on metal, if they do not break, may toughen it'.[44] For Coates and Fisher, survival as a prisoner depended on traits of masculine robustness, a deliberate counterpoint to an alternative equation between captivity and passivity.

Behind closed doors Fisher complained vociferously about the predilection of doctors and psychiatrists to grant pension entitlements to prisoners suffering from anxiety state. His own view was that amoebiasis (a gastrointestinal infection caused by a parasite) could account for the majority of neurosis cases. 'Some of these cases got to the psychiatrist before stool examination had been reported', he complained. 'Psychiatrists should be told that anxiety state entitlement was not to be decided until investigations for infestation had been completed.' If Fisher could have his way, men complaining of anxiety, stress and panic should have their excrement tested before they were allowed anywhere near a psychiatrist.[45]

When the results of the full medical survey came in, Fisher felt they confirmed that 'far too many ex P.O.W. – J[apan] were labelled in the first year or so after discharge "anxiety state" or its equivalent'. It was a 'grave error' to diagnose anxiety too hastily: the label would attach forever and might 'prove a handicap to employment'. Thenceforth, all patients would have their stools tested before seeing a psychiatrist, an amendment to advice in the original pamphlet that the other doctors on the Repatriation Committee, including Alfred Derham and Edward Dunlop, thought to be 'excellent'.[46]

Despite the clear message from the department that the psychological problems of former POWs had been overstated, public disquiet continued. One of the men Coates would have considered a 'whinger' was Norman Cohen, the Secretary of the NSW Ex-Prisoners of War Association. Cohen was tireless in his efforts to promote the needs of former prisoners, and this set him on a collision course with those doctors who subscribed to the view that prisoners were no different from other returned servicemen. An exchange in 1949 between Fisher and Cohen published by *Smith's Weekly*, a journal always vociferous in its support of veterans, encapsulated the different views:

> Mr. Cohen: The idea that human beings can go through three years of hell in a prison camp and then return to ordinary life and adjust themselves automatically has been exploded.

Dr. Fisher: This is completely wrong. One of the things we pride ourselves on is that p.o.w. of the Japs have come back better balanced very often than when they went away. They had seen a good deal of the stripping off of veneer. They came back determined they could rehabilitate themselves. The community as well has done its best to assist them.

Mr. Cohen: These torments have left their mark. Minds as well as bodies cracked under the strain.

Dr. Fisher: This is completely false. One of the striking things about p.o.w. life was that men had no neurotic manifestations. They had no barbed-wire psychoses.

Mr. Cohen: Lack of resistance and the will to fight life's battles is the greatest loss these men have suffered.

Dr. Fisher: Absolutely untrue.

Mr. Cohen: More than a dozen men have come to me for help, whose problem is that they would dearly love to become fathers. Because of their sufferings their potency has been impaired.

Dr. Fisher: I don't believe for one minute that having been a prisoner of war of the Japs has anything to do with the sterility of the few. It is criminal to put the idea into p.o.w. heads that they will be sterile because of the deprivations they suffered in prison.[47]

Cohen's views, although anathema to doctors like Fisher and Coates, were beginning to have some traction in the psychiatric community. In 1947 Alan Stoller had sensed an opportunity to do some further research on the question of 'sex activity' in the first POW survey. Fisher gave his suggestion short shrift, but the request itself was a sign of a different approach.[48] A final comment at the end of Fisher's pamphlet prepared by Stoller and another psychiatrist who had been a POW also gave a note of caution. John Cade (1912–80) had spent a lifetime among psychiatric patients: as the son of a medical superintendent, he had during his childhood resided at several prominent Victorian mental hospitals and had subsequently trained as a psychiatrist. He had enlisted in the army as a medical officer (but not in his capacity as a psychiatrist), only to spend his war at Changi prison camp. Cade conceded that imprisonment might well have strengthened POWs' resistance to stress but described as a 'general impression' the view that psychiatric disorders among them were not unduly common. Physical disorders might still possess a psychiatric component, and it was important to consider the patient in toto. Cade and Stoller were concerned to have it noted that in former POWs 'the incidence of psychiatric disorder [was] by no means yet finally determined'.[49]

As the new decade began there continued to be unease in the community about the health of former prisoners and the official attitude towards them. Betty Armstrong, the Secretary of the Katoomba Leura Repatriation Local Committee, wrote to the Minister for Repatriation in October 1953 suggesting that the health of prisoners held by the Japanese appeared to be getting worse, not better, with the passing of time. 'They are confused and disheartened in their mental approach to the problems which confront them', she insisted.[50]

The findings of the Repatriation surveys had done little to shake a broader public belief that prisoners of the Japanese, in particular, had undergone enormous hardship in the war and that the health of some of them had been irreparably damaged as a consequence. As an *Argus* feature writer, himself a former POW, put it in 1952, 'So the majority have fought their way back to standards approaching good health. But there is still the minority who will never have erased from mind or body the mark of the Japanese'.[51]

3
Three bob a day

> Despite all the natural instincts in my heart to recompense the men who suffered so much as P.O.W., and particularly those men in the hands of the Japs for 3½ years, logic and reason forbid me accepting a solution based on payment for suffering endured as a P.O.W. My intimate knowledge of war, obtained in all ranks from Private to Superior Commander, my personal experience of suffering and hardship, and my understanding of Troops, lead me to the conclusion that the granting of this Claim will be interpreted by men of weaker fibre as a premium on surrender, which they cannot expect as a right.
>
> *Lieutenant General Stanley Savige, 1950*[1]

In the immediate postwar years one issue revealed the ambivalent attitude towards former POWs more than any other: the subsistence allowance campaign. Supporters argued that former POWs ought to receive three shillings, or 'bob', for each day of their captivity. The money would be an allowance in addition to their normal salary, which had continued to accrue during the period of imprisonment. For a time the subsistence allowance campaign directed towards the Australian government eclipsed efforts to win from the captor powers compensation for POWs.[2] Refused by Ben Chifley's Labor government, the 'three bob a day' claim had gained sufficient public profile by 1949 for Robert Menzies, the Liberal prime ministerial hopeful, to make it an issue at that year's federal election. Yet, as Menzies later discovered, the Australian Army was far from convinced that an impartial settlement was possible in an issue that turned on the question of surrender. The fate of the 'three bob a day' claim demonstrated that a view of imprisonment as a 'matter of dishonour' continued to hold sway in the highest echelons of the Australian Army.

The subsistence allowance

The campaign for a subsistence allowance, which commenced in 1946, heralded the arrival of the voice of former POWs in federal politics. There was already one sitting Member who had spent the war as a POW of Japan: Adair 'Chill' Blain (1894–1983), the Member for the Northern Territory, had been a parliamentarian in absentia while he was a POW.[3] He returned, thin and grey haired, to the House of Representatives in September 1945 in full military dress and was cheered to his seat by his parliamentary colleagues. 'My mind feels very much in splints', he confessed after taking the oath; he promptly returned to hospital for a further two months to aid his recovery.[4] It was not until the following year that a by-election in the rural Victorian seat of Wimmera delivered Blain another former POW as a parliamentary colleague. Winton Turnbull (1899–1980), on joining the House of Representatives, immediately launched the subsistence allowance claim. An auctioneer who had made several tilts at a parliamentary career before the war, he had campaigned for his parliamentary seat in uniform, complete with slouch hat.[5] Still gaunt from his years in captivity at Changi, and having been discharged from the army only the previous week, Turnbull advanced the idea of the allowance in his first speech, pointing to his own body as evidence of the havoc wreaked by malnourishment. 'I have gained 4 stone in weight since I returned to this country,' he declared, 'and there is not much of me yet'. With proper food during their imprisonment, to the value of about three shillings a day, many men might have avoided such malnutrition.[6] When Blain returned to the House after his recuperation, he became a constant supporter of Turnbull's campaign and was in regular contact with ex-POW organisations about its progress.

The subsistence allowance became a common cause for ex-service organisations and their parliamentary supporters. Turnbull advanced the basis of the claim later in 1946: 'The Army was not called upon, during that time [the term of POWs' imprisonment], to feed and clothe them'.[7] He was particularly concerned with POWs of Japan, who, he believed all Australians knew, 'suffered more hardships during World War II than did any other Australians'.[8] The RSL supported the initiative by passing a resolution at its Federal Executive a few months later, arguing that subsistence conditions for POWs had not conformed to the 1929 Geneva Convention and requesting that the government grant a 'compassionate allowance'.[9]

The RSL was careful in this and subsequent resolutions to insist that the sum be paid to 'all prisoners of war from all theatres'.[10] The subsistence claim had the potential to divide the ex-POW community along the lines of the different captor powers. Turnbull was insistent that POWs of Japan had suffered the most; others wondered if the claim ought to be extended. POWs of the Germans and Italians wrote to returned service journals claiming that those detained in Europe had suffered great hardships and should also be entitled to an allowance.[11] The exclusive nature of the claim was raised in parliament too, with several Members mentioning that it was impossible to distinguish between degrees of suffering for prisoners in different theatres of the war.[12] In its own deliberations the government was inclined to agree, noting in an internal document that prisoners of the Germans had also received inadequate rations.[13]

Supporters of the claim were especially vexed by what they saw as the privileging of POW officers over the 'other ranks' in matters of pay and entitlements. Officers remained entitled to, and received as back pay, their 'field allowance' – an extra payment of three shillings a day to all officers serving outside Australia.[14] This was, Turnbull argued, 'nothing more than a subsistence allowance under a different name'.[15] The RSL agreed, forwarding a resolution to the Prime Minister in late 1946 insisting that the 'other ranks' had been 'neglected in this matter'.[16] It was also incontrovertible in the case of POWs of Japan that officers had survived in far greater proportions than the 'other ranks'. Granting a subsistence allowance would redress a perception that those who had suffered most had received the least recompense.[17]

The question of differential treatment was an aspect of the subsistence allowance claim of greatest relevance to POWs of Japan. In the final reckoning, POW officers in Japanese captivity received more cash entitlements than those detained in Europe. Under the terms of the Geneva Convention, the detaining power was required to make advances of pay to POW officers, commonly known as 'convention pay'.[18] The normal practice was that these amounts were then debited from the pay and allowances accruing in an officer's home accounts, a protocol followed in relation to Australian POW officers in Europe.[19] In the case of officers held by Japan, however, the government determined that, with the amounts received from Japan being so unreliable and the purchasing power so negligible, and owing to 'the terrible privations generally suffered', the officers would have nothing debited from their accounts. Officers who were POWs of Japan therefore received a field allowance, any convention pay and the standard salary for the entire period of their captivity.[20]

Throughout the late 1940s the Federal Executive of the RSL, the Council of the 8th Division and ex-POW associations lobbied the government about the subsistence allowance.[21] The Council of the 8th Division, in particular, constructed the allowance as a matter of justice and entitlement, informing the Prime Minister that its own policy was 'definitely against the sob-stuff type of publicity regarding the present state of ex prisoners of war'.[22] Reference to 'sob stuff' revealed the hand of the council's President, Ted Fisher. Individuals, too, pressured their local Members over the subsistence claim, with one former POW urging that these were not his sentiments alone; they were 'those of thousands of people ... too heartbroken to do anything on this matter'.[23]

Government refusal of the subsistence claim

Despite the many voices urging settlement of the claim, the government remained adamant that subsistence was an implicit part of the pay of the 'other ranks' and could not be singled out or reimbursed if rations were deemed insufficient. The argument had been tried, and failed, once before. In the First World War, there had been a claim that the troops who had fought at Gallipoli should receive an extra allowance of two shillings a day, owing to the paucity of rations during the campaign. The army had decided then that when members joined the forces the subsistence to which they were entitled was that which it was possible to provide at the time.[24] It would in fact constitute a breach of protocol, and an unwarranted 'special privilege', if such an allowance were now paid to POWs.

Moreover, other members of the Australian forces had gone without while on active service in the Second World War, it being impossible to provision them properly when military conditions did not permit. In parliament, to prove his point, Minister for the Army Frank Forde quoted a communiqué received during fighting in Papua describing the paucity of rations that the troops had received. 'But they never grumbled', the text concluded. 'On the contrary, they carried on with that spirit of self-sacrifice which has always distinguished our Australian soldier.'[25] The contrast between complaining, defeated POWs and the stoic active service of others was hard to miss. These remarks, a POW spokesman later complained, were an 'indecent attempt to split the ranks of ex-servicemen'.[26]

Public pressure eventually prompted the Minister for the Army to prepare a confidential internal report on the matter. The likely cost if all POWs, including those detained by the Germans and Italians, received the allowance, was £4 million. All members of the forces, including POWs, had already been paid a war gratuity of two shillings and sixpence for each day of overseas service, in 'recognition of the arduous and hazardous periods … generally associated with such service'.[27] The Minister advised against the payment of a subsistence allowance on the grounds that there were many members of the forces who could claim to have received inadequate rations and that they had all been duly compensated through the payment of the war gratuity. The three service chiefs, particularly the army Chief of Staff, also made clear to Prime Minister Ben Chifley that they opposed the allowance.[28] When the Labor Cabinet considered the matter in March and April 1947, it therefore ruled a subsistence allowance for POWs to be out of the question.[29]

There was widespread criticism of the government's decision. Arthur Blackburn described it as an 'utter disgrace'.[30] An officer himself, he was sympathetic to the charge that his class had been unduly favoured. RSL state branches urged their Federal

Executive to continue the fight. A plea from Western Australia was typical in this regard. 'Many of the unfortunate ex-POW are still suffering', the Secretary wrote, 'and will probably never be able to forget their harrowing experiences, and therefore what is considered as a legitimate payment to them should be honoured'.[31] The Victorian RSL explicitly contested the argument that it would be inequitable to compensate POWs in light of the sacrifices also made by those on active duty. Rather than being resentful, other servicemen 'would applaud any generous gesture' for the prisoners who had suffered so much. 'Those who saw the prisoners return from Japanese hands after the war will always remember with horror the grisly evidence presented of the fiendish cruelty of the Japanese.'[32]

While the government may have been concerned about the cost of awarding a subsistence payment, the military was more worried about such a payment's ethical and strategic implications as encouragement to surrender. In 1947 Reg Pollard, Minister for Commerce and Agriculture, mentioned the elephant in the room during a debate on the floor of the House of Representatives. 'We may be involved in another war at some later time and if this proposal be agreed to it may constitute an inducement in the eyes of the military authorities …' Harold Holt, a future prime minister, almost choked as he interjected: 'That is a terrible thing to say'.[33] Given that the Labor Cabinet had debated the issue, and the Prime Minister had sought the service chiefs' views on the matter, it is unlikely that Pollard was mistaken about what those views were. Equating compensation with an incentive to surrender was an unpalatable public reflection of the military's position.

Pollard's views may have been insulting, but they can hardly have come as a surprise. POWs were acutely aware that there were people in the military and the broader community who had little sympathy for their plight. The response to POWs in the

First World War had been similarly ambivalent. The Victorian RSL recalled that POWs from that conflict had been 'sometimes looked at askance and regarded as men who had perhaps caved in when they should have continued fighting, and who enjoyed good security and reasonably good food for the rest of the war period'. Despite acknowledging this was 'mostly an unfair view', even mentioning it was evidence of a perspective that held at least some traction.[34] In the wake of the Second World War, POWs from the European theatre in particular continued to struggle against community perceptions that their captivity had been less burdensome than the experiences either of those who had fought on or of POWs of Japan. The question of officers' convention pay had been a case in point.

Ex-POW organisations were incensed by what they felt to be a blight on their members' reputation in the federal parliament. Pollard's remarks made front-page news around the country. The NSW Ex-Prisoners of War Association wrote to Pollard accusing him of 'gross insult'. The association insisted that the 'gross inefficiency and unpreparedness on the part of the higher authorities' had sealed the POWs' fate, not a lack of fighting spirit or a willingness to surrender. 'We say that no finer or braver body of men existed', it thundered. 'These men, both in the front line and as prisoners, exhibited the greatest courage and upheld the honour of the country continually.'[35] Pollard's remarks had exposed the fault lines of POW sensitivity about perceptions of surrender and service. They also demonstrated to the astute that it was not just the financial considerations of a cash-strapped postwar government that prevented the payment of the subsistence allowance. There now appeared to be high-level resistance from within the military itself.

Subsistence claim revisited

Developments in the United States had reignited the Australian campaign by 1949. The 1948 US War Claims Act created a War Claims Commission, which entitled POWs to a lump sum payment of US$1 per day of captivity if they could prove they had been denied the quality and quantity of food stipulated in the Geneva Convention.[36] The American Legion forwarded to its Australian ex-service colleagues all the relevant legislation and documentation.[37] One dollar a day was almost twice the rate of subsistence that had been sought by Australian POWs. The RSL immediately relaunched its campaign. This was a long-awaited breakthrough. The US government was the first of the Allies to award significant financial compensation to its former POWs. In recent years Prime Minister Ben Chifley had been fond of pointing to the fact that no other Allied government had thought it necessary to award subsistence to its former POWs. Now one of them had.

News about the US payment to its POWs coincided with a federal election year in Australia and gave the issue more oxygen. Robert Menzies, leader of the Liberal Party, had previously declared that a parliamentary or independent committee should make a full investigation of the matter.[38] Indeed, Menzies reproduced a 1947 speech to parliament on this matter in the joint Liberal–Country Party policy handbook for the 1949 election. It is little wonder that ex-POWs were hopeful. Under the heading 'Prisoner of war claims', Menzies reiterated, 'I have no doubt that a very powerful case can be made out for prisoners of war in all theatres'. A 'full, impartial and authoritative' inquiry into the matter, which would do 'justice to the enormous, human issues involved', was now officially an election promise.[39]

The subsistence allowance campaign benefited from the leadership of former POWs who already enjoyed a high public profile and maintained postwar connections through their work for Repatriation. An alliance of former POW doctors, Ted Fisher in his capacity as President of the Council of the 8th Division and Edward Dunlop in his as President of the Ex-Prisoners of War and Relatives Association of Victoria, formed the nucleus of a new, coordinated campaign. Each candidate in the federal election of 1949, apart from the communists, received a letter asking them to support the 'three bob a day' campaign.[40] Both Menzies and Arthur Fadden, leader of the Country Party, had responded promising the appointment of an inquiry to investigate the matter 'on the basis of humanity, and not purely economics'.[41]

Dunlop's Victorian ex-POW organisation had been the driving force behind a contemporaneous campaign to keep the plight of POWs in the public spotlight. Cast as a fundraising effort, the appeal was in fact a weapon in the ongoing war to win the subsistence allowance. Fisher would have considered the appeal 'sob stuff', but it had a powerful effect in galvanising public support. In September 1949 the Lord Mayor of Melbourne launched a £10 000 appeal for funds to aid the widows of POWs, needy former POWs and their families. Three former POWs from Changi set up a bamboo and palm leaf hut in Collins Street, Melbourne, to attract attention to the appeal. Stories about former POWs still in hospital, suffering the ongoing legacy of captivity, were printed in the daily newspapers. Five years after the conclusion of hostilities, readers were told, 'their war isn't over yet'. The publicity was, however, careful to present the former POWs in a self-deprecating light: all the highlighted cases insisted that there were 'other blokes' worse off than themselves.[42] In the official letter sent to solicit donations, Dunlop claimed that a significant proportion of ex-POWs were still suffering from tropical diseases, nervous disorders, tuberculosis and the after-effects of malnutrition. Funds were required until those men were given 'the necessary treatment and financial aid by the appropriate organisations and Government departments'.[43]

Responses to the appeal demonstrated the complexity of feeling in the community about returned POWs. Even though there were times when former POWs encountered prejudice about their soldiering capacities, or hostility from employers who doubted their fitness for work, there was a bedrock of belief that veterans of any hue should receive adequate health care from the state. The Australasian Meat Industry Employees' Union forwarded Dunlop's letter to the Prime Minister and made a pointed remark about the shame of former POWs 'depending on charity'.[44] 'It is surely scandalous that the Federal Government has not made adequate provision for those whose lives and prospects have been grievously wrecked by war service', a Melbourne daily paper declared; these men and their relatives should not have to 'depend upon the rattle of collection boxes in the street'.[45] One worker who sold badges on behalf of the appeal wrote to the Minister for the Army claiming that he had never heard 'such biting criticism – very many people emphatically stated that it was a standing disgrace to any Government that such an appeal should be necessary'. Too many former POWs were in a bad way: it was 'the duty of the government to stand by them' and to grant the subsistence claim.[46]

Those who pressed for the subsistence allowance claim were jubilant at Menzies' electoral victory in December 1949, which they saw as next to guaranteeing its positive settlement. As a bonus, seven former POWs had been elected to the federal parliament, all but one of them for the coalition.[47] Fisher sought to capitalise on the cooperation that had typified the months prior to the election and to position himself or, at the very least, his organisation at the forefront of any kind of inquiry that might be established. Assuring the RSL that he had no problem with pursuing a claim for all POWs, of both the European and the Japanese theatres, he insisted that the Council of the 8th Division was 'particularly competent to advise and lead in collaboration'.[48] The Federal Executive of the RSL had other ideas and perceived Fisher as a thorn in their side and a man primarily concerned with the welfare of Japanese prisoners. They were uninterested in any kind of shared authority in the matter.[49]

The Menzies government moved quickly to establish a tribunal to inquire into the question of subsistence payments. The army prepared an extensive briefing document outlining all of the well-rehearsed reasons why the allowance was a bad idea.[50] On 8 February 1950 the Vice Chief of the General Staff, one of the most senior officers in the Australian Army, considered the matter and deemed that any consideration of a subsistence payment would set an unwelcome precedent in future wars. It was army practice to instil in the soldier a will to fight on, and the prospect of compensation would weaken it. He concluded,

> One cannot be unaware of the terrific hardships inflicted on prisoners at the hands of the Japanese. Many of those that have survived have suffered irreparable damage to their health and have been granted war pensions on the same scale as soldiers who suffered in health as a result of active service. This is very fit and proper, but it cannot be conceded that a soldier who becomes a prisoner of war should be given financial payments that are not available to the soldier who continues to fight on and who, as a result, may be killed or maimed for life. A decision to do so would be prejudicial to our success in future wars.[51]

All of this information was forwarded to Menzies, who now knew, even if he had not before, that the army was opposed to the payment of a subsistence allowance. Given its election promise, the new government had no choice but to press on and establish a tribunal to inquire into the issue.[52]

The Owen Committee

The tribunal, which became known as the Owen Committee, comprised three middle-aged men, all with military service. In the chair was Justice William Owen (1899–1972), who had run away from his elite private school to enlist in the first AIF. He had been a judge of the NSW Supreme Court since the 1930s and later in the 1950s chaired a much more famous inquiry: the Royal Commission on Espionage. The military officer was Lieutenant General Sir Stanley Savige (1890–1954), who had served with distinction in the First World War and whose friendship with General Sir Thomas Blamey had led many to believe he had been promoted above his competence in the Second. Nevertheless, Savige was known for his people skills and compassion, and he had founded Legacy, a charity for the families of men who had sacrificed their lives, in the immediate aftermath of the First World War.[53] The final member was Ted Fisher in his capacity as President of the Council of the 8th Division and presumably as a prominent former POW of Japan. The RSL, which had been asked to nominate a candidate but had then been overlooked, was livid.

The RSL's submission to the Owen Committee revealed a host of contemporary views about the surrendered soldier and confirmed, despite the best of intentions, that a stigma was attached to those who had spent the war as POWs. It lamented the popular view that a soldier was 'less of a soldier' if he had 'surrendered to the enemy'. Granting a subsistence allowance to former prisoners would assist the RSL 'in its effort to educate the community towards the adoption of a more favourable attitude'. If the subsistence claim were granted, it would be 'official recognition that no stigma attached to any man' who had surrendered and that the government viewed ex-POWs 'as men who did their duty valiantly, in a manner worthy of the AIF'.[54]

When it came to discussing POWs of Japan, the RSL invoked racial understandings as a way of generating support for the subsistence cause. There was a 'difference between the standard of living of the Japanese, and that of the white race', and prisoners ought to be compensated for being thus short changed.[55] In addition, no men who had enlisted in the AIF had 'expected that they would have to live on "coolie" rations for long periods'.[56]

The preliminary public sitting of the committee took place at the Commonwealth Arbitration Court in Sydney on 14 June 1950. Virtually all ex-service organisations, from the Partially Blinded Soldiers' Association to the Limbless Soldiers' Association, were represented. The various state-based ex-POW associations also had a presence, among them the Chair of the Victorian branch, Edward Dunlop. Large organisations like the RSL, the Council of the 8th Division and the Australian Legion of Ex-Servicemen and Women were also present. Fearful that the committee might be overwhelmed with voluminous reports and gory detail, Owen insisted on brevity. He told the gathering that the committee was 'prepared to accept as a notorious fact that most prisoners of war underwent much and frequently extreme hardship'. He also articulated the common belief that POWs of Japan 'suffered greater hardships than those in other theatres of war'. The primary considerations of the committee were, first, to decide whether a special allowance to POWs was warranted and, if so, what form it ought to take.[57] Some supporters were extremely confident. The Secretary of the Ex-Prisoners of War and Relatives Association of Western Australia flew home to Perth and declared, 'It's in the bag'.[58]

The report of the Owen Committee, published in September 1950, delivered a bitter blow. The optimism that had accompanied the election of the Menzies government had proved ill founded. Fisher had done his best for his men, but he was unable to convince either Owen or Savige of the wisdom of supporting a payment to POWs. Owen and Savige published a majority report rejecting the claim. Despite his reputation in the ex-service community for welfare work, Savige would not countenance the payment of a subsistence allowance. 'My intimate knowledge of war,' he wrote, when drafting the final report, 'my personal experience of suffering and hardship, and my understanding of Troops, lead me to the conclusion that the granting of this Claim will be interpreted by men of weaker fibre as a premium on surrender, which they can expect as a right'.[59] Winton Turnbull later reflected that he should have objected to Savige's membership of the committee: 'If a rank-and-file ex-prisoner of war had been appointed to the committee instead of a high-ranking military officer, the result might have been a little different'.[60] Ever conscious of the divide between officers and the 'other ranks', Turnbull felt that Savige had fallen in behind the most senior military officers in the country, who had opposed the allowance. He was right. The committee had indeed sought the opinion of the three services, all of which had endorsed the views expressed in February 1950 by the army's Vice Chief of the General Staff and passed by the Military Board: POWs should not be privileged with an allowance additional to that given to men who had chosen to 'fight on', and such an allowance would be prejudicial to the nation's interest in any future war.

The Owen Committee did not deliver the vindication former prisoners had desired. Its ultimate conclusion reminded them instead of the debt they owed to those on active service and contained an implicit criticism of surrender. 'In bald terms', Owen and Savige argued, they had been asked to decide whether a 'moral obligation' rested upon the Commonwealth government to make a monetary payment to prisoners

> in excess of that made to the members of its Forces who remained in the field and by whose efforts … the defeat of the enemy and the release of its captives was brought about … In our opinion it is impossible to find a just or logical basis for such a claim, and to concede it might set a precedent fraught with possible danger should the nation again become engaged in war … We believe that it would be unsound and contrary to the national interest if any proposal were adopted which might, now or in the future and to a later generation, carry with it an implication that a 'monetary premium' was being placed upon becoming and remaining a prisoner of war.[61]

Fisher was so enraged that he refused to sign the majority report and instead produced a dissenting statement. He exposed the defence forces as the main stumbling block to the success of the claim. While he conceded in theory that there should be no reward for surrender, in practice he felt that the 'abnormal' captivity of POWs of the Japanese had rendered such objections null and void. Fisher pointed to the high death rates in Japanese captivity: 'Few potential prisoners of a barbarian captor in the future are likely to regard captivity as the easier way'. He recommended that the payment 'be made forthwith'. Ultimately, however, Fisher fudged the question of who should be responsible for it. While acknowledging that there was insufficient money under the terms of the Australian *Trading with the Enemy Act 1939*, he recommended relentless pursuit of compensation during peace treaty negotiations and, failing that, ultimate Commonwealth responsibility.[62]

While POWs of both theatres had been denied a payment, the committee's report cemented an understanding that POWs of Japan had endured the greater wrong. There were points of agreement between the final published majority report and Fisher's dissenting judgment which ultimately enshrined the primacy of POWs of Japan in perceptions of suffering. Both found that Germany and Japan had not conformed to the provisions of the Geneva Convention and that POWs in both theatres had suffered 'excessive and undue hardships'. Although sympathetic to European prisoners, Owen, Savige and Fisher felt that their experiences 'pale[d] into insignificance when set against those endured by the servicemen who fell into the hands of Japan'. Owen and Savige's language reflected a struggle to assimilate the evidence they had read. It was 'difficult to describe' the 'full horrors' of this captivity; the hardships and privations were 'so great, in many cases, as to be almost beyond belief'. They concluded, 'We think it sufficient to say [that] prisoners in Japanese hands were treated by their captors throughout the long period of their captivity, with a brutality and inhumanity incapable of imagination by a civilized people'.[63] Like the RSL, the Owen Committee perceived captivity by the Japanese through the lens of race: this had been an inversion of hierarchy with disastrous consequences and sadistic overtones. 'The captor,' the report concluded, 'by every means which malevolent ingenuity could suggest, endeavoured to degrade his white captive and to break his spirit'.[64]

When the report of the Owen Committee was made public, its clear articulation of the often-subliminal ambivalence towards POWs caused a sensation. Prime Minister Robert Menzies accepted the majority report and tabled it in parliament in October 1950. During the ensuing debate, Labor Member of Parliament Leslie Haylen (1898–1977) urged the adoption of Fisher's minority report. The author of an anti-war play, *Two Minutes' Silence* (1930), performed in Sydney at the height of the Depression, Haylen was sensitive to the impact of war on former POWs.[65] He was astounded at the implication that compensation might set a dangerous precedent. 'Is it not a scorching and awful condemnation of a prisoner of war,' he asked, 'and an insult to every prisoner of war?' He also deplored the representations of the army, navy and air force and objected to their opinion that an allowance might compromise the desire to fight on. 'If that is not scandalous,' he argued, 'I have never heard scandal in my life'.[66]

Haylen was outraged about the way POWs' soldiering capacities had been impugned, but he shared the committee's views on the racial inversions of captivity and crafted some insults of his own. He contrasted the Australian government's attitude towards postwar social welfare measures in Europe and Asia and its approach to returned POWs. He pointed to the £19 million that Australia had donated to the United Nations Relief and Rehabilitation Administration. 'Caught up in a resurgence of humanitarian feeling after the end of a major war, we were willing to help everybody!' he recalled, reminding his listeners that the nation had 'poured a great deal of money into Asia'. His own first-hand experience on a tour of China had suggested that some of this had been wasted. He considered it a generous donation 'made to our neighbours and our allies, people who are outside the ambit of our own national family circle. But we have been peculiarly mean and pernickety about making payments to our own people … We have to find £18 000 000 for a "Spender plan" in Asia. Surely we can provide £6 000 000 for the men who saved us from Asia'.[67]

Former POWs and their organisations were devastated by the committee's report and experienced it as a personal slight. The Victorian RSL described the result as 'insulting': 'Australian servicemen are renowned all over the world for their gallantry and courage; it has remained for an Australian committee to doubt them'.[68] William Yeo, the President of the NSW branch of the RSL, described the suggestion that an allowance might encourage surrender as 'one of the most dastardly allegations' he had ever encountered.[69] The Council of the 8th Division wrote to all Members of Parliament urging them to overturn the findings of the report. A year later, the RSL continued to write to the Prime Minister, asking him to make a 'public retraction' of the 'slurs cast ... on the moral character of Australian servicemen' by the Owen Committee.[70] More publicly, it focused on winning compensation from Japan for POWs via the mechanism of the peace treaty then being negotiated.[71]

Compensation

After the failure of the subsistence allowance claim, efforts at compensation focused on POWs of Japan. The Owen Committee's report argued that any compensation forthcoming to POWs ought to be paid by Japan, not by the Australian government. After the Treaty of Peace with Japan was signed in 1951 (see chapter 7), Australia did gain access to two potential sources of Japanese money: seized Japanese assets held in Australia under the terms of the wartime *Trading with the Enemy Act 1939* and Australia's share of Japanese assets held in countries that had been neutral from or at war with the Allies, which were to be transferred to the International Committee of the Red Cross for the benefit of members of the Allied armed forces who had 'suffered undue hardship'.[72] The Australian government decided to divide equally the proceeds of all assets thus realised among former POWs of the Japanese.[73]

Announcing the first payments from these sources at the annual dinner of the Council of the 8th Division in 1952, Ted Fisher claimed that 'even one-sixth of a loaf is better than no bread'. On a newsreel, he called for the government to 'put an end to this long period of frustration', to pay the balance to POWs straightaway and to recoup its costs from the Japanese later.[74] The request was refused. Labor Member of Parliament Les Haylen described the payments as the 'pawnshop technique' and derided them as inadequate.[75] Senator Justin O'Byrne (1912–93), a former prisoner of the Germans, quipped that the payments provided 'about enough money to buy a new suit'.[76]

By the late 1950s all former POWs of the Japanese had received some compensation money, although they considered it a poor substitute for the more substantial amount that a successful subsistence claim would have delivered. Unlike the United States and Canada, which controlled vast sums of money derived from the sale of Japanese assets in their respective territories, Australia had far more modest means at its disposal. In the United States alone, the amount realised from liquidated Japanese assets was US$228 million.[77] In contrast, by 1957 Australia had realised £810 000 through the sale of Japanese assets and had received £969 000 from the International Committee of the Red Cross and a further £75 000 in proceeds from the sale of the Thai–Burma Railway to the Thai government.[78] These asset sales and distributions resulted in two major payments to all former POWs, of £32 in 1953 and £54 in 1957. All monies from asset sales were distributed by 1963, by which time surviving Australian prisoners of the Japanese had each received a total of £102.[79] This was approximately half of the amount of the original subsistence claim. Canadian ex-POWs, in contrast, received a relatively handsome sum, equivalent to £650.[80]

The drawn-out series of small payments from the realisation of Japanese assets, both within Australia and under the terms of the peace treaty, did little to assuage former POWs' feelings of being slighted and overlooked. The 'three bob a day' campaign which had begun with such confidence of a positive resolution had brought into the public sphere the thorny issue of POWs' status as defeated soldiers. The army's opposition to the subsistence claim made public, in the most painful and controversial way, its view that POWs were failed soldiers. It was not so much state parsimony as disapproval of surrender that prevented a Commonwealth-funded settlement of the claim. Its failure left bitterness among the 'other ranks', in particular, a sense that their sacrifice had been sullied. Apart from resentment about ongoing and subtle reminders that to surrender had been shameful, there was a growing feeling in the ex-POW community that captivity had caused a series of physical and psychological problems that the government was reluctant to address.

Brigadier Arthur Blackburn (right), just released from captivity, at the Melbourne home of General Sir Thomas Blamey, Commander-in-Chief, Allied Land Forces, South West Pacific Area, September 1945.

AWM 115466

Above Join the AIF. This Is Serious!, by James Northfield, Australian Commonwealth Military Forces recruitment poster, published by Director-General of Recruiting, c. 1939–42.

AWM ARTV06723

Top right We Must Wipe Off That Smile, by John Frith, *Sydney Morning Herald*, 1 September 1945, p. 2.

Courtesy of Jeffrey Frith

Below right Private Robert Harvey Gill, QX10305, upon release from Changi POW camp, c. September 1945.

AWM 019195

WE MUST WIPE OFF THAT SMILE

News Item: Marines who occupied the Yokosuka naval and air base found that without exception the Japanese were friendly and helpful. They smiled often and brightly—and apparently without guile.

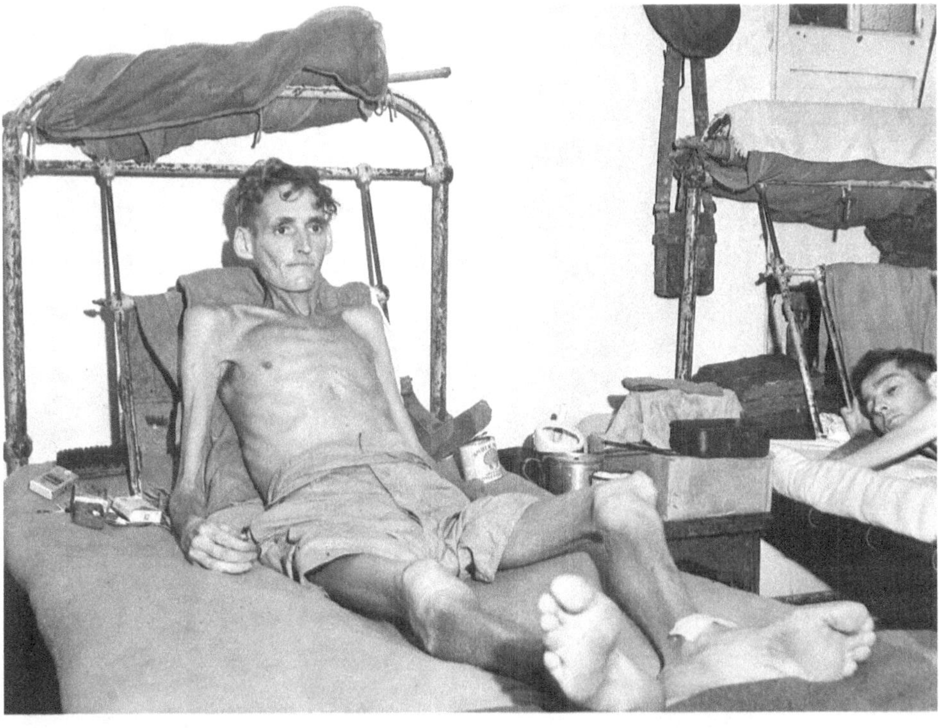

Major General George Frederick Wootten, General Officer Commanding, 9th Division, speaking to Australian, British and Indian ex-POWs of the Japanese during his visit to Kuching POW and Internee Camp, Sarawak, September 1945. In the postwar period Wootten was Chairman of the Repatriation Commission.

AWM 118308

Lieutenant Colonel Albert E Coates, Chief Medical Officer, Nakom Paton POW Hospital (left) and Lieutenant Colonel Edward E Dunlop, Commanding Officer, 2/2nd Casualty Clearing Station, outside their office at the Medical Headquarters, Recovered Allied Prisoner of War and Internees Unit, at the Chinese College, Bangkok, Thailand, September 1945. Coates and Dunlop became influential figures in the postwar discussion about the health of returned POWs.

AWM 117362

Left Major Walter Edward ('Ted') Fisher, a member of the Australian Army Medical Corps, before his departure with the 8th Division for Malaya, c. 1940. Fisher spent most of the war working in hospital camps for POWs in Thailand. He was the founding President of the 8th Division Council on his return to Australia and held this office until his death, in 1965.

AWM P02330.001

Below Lieutenant Colonel Vivian Bullwinkel giving evidence at the International Military Tribunal for the Far East, Tokyo, 1946. Photograph: United States Army Signal Corps.

AWM P04585.003

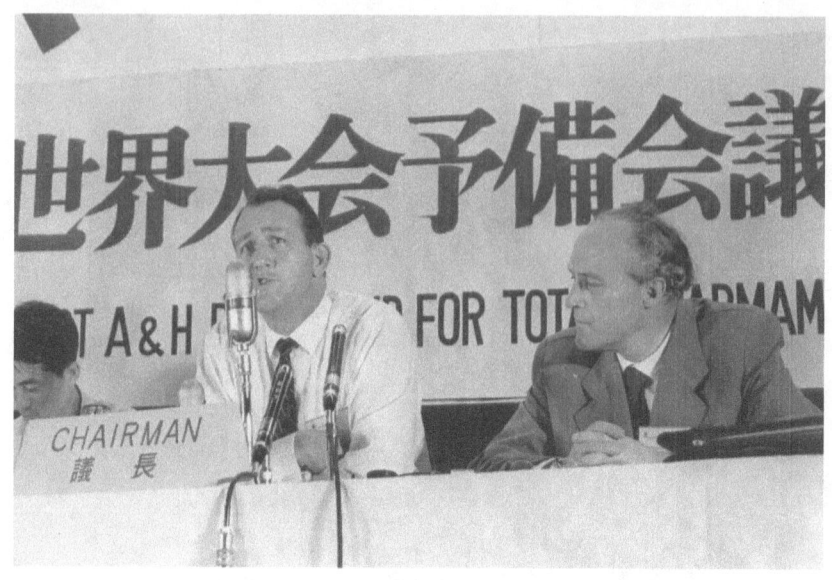

Tom Uren, federal Labor Member of Parliament and former POW, delivering the opening plenary address at the Sixth World Conference Against Atomic and Hydrogen Bombs and for Total Disarmament, Tokyo, August 1960.

National Library of Australia, MS 6055, box 28, series 5, file 9

Dolls not soldiers: 'An exhibition of Japanese arts and crafts which was originally intended to be exhibited in Australian cities for four months will soon be concluded in Brisbane, 12 months after it began. Father Tony Glynn corrects two Australian school girls' ideas of Japan'. Photograph by R Reeves, 1959.

National Archives of Australia, A1501, A1855/3

Japanese Prime Minister Nobusuke Kishi (left), visiting the AWM, December 1957.

National Archives of Australia, A1671, JPM3/13

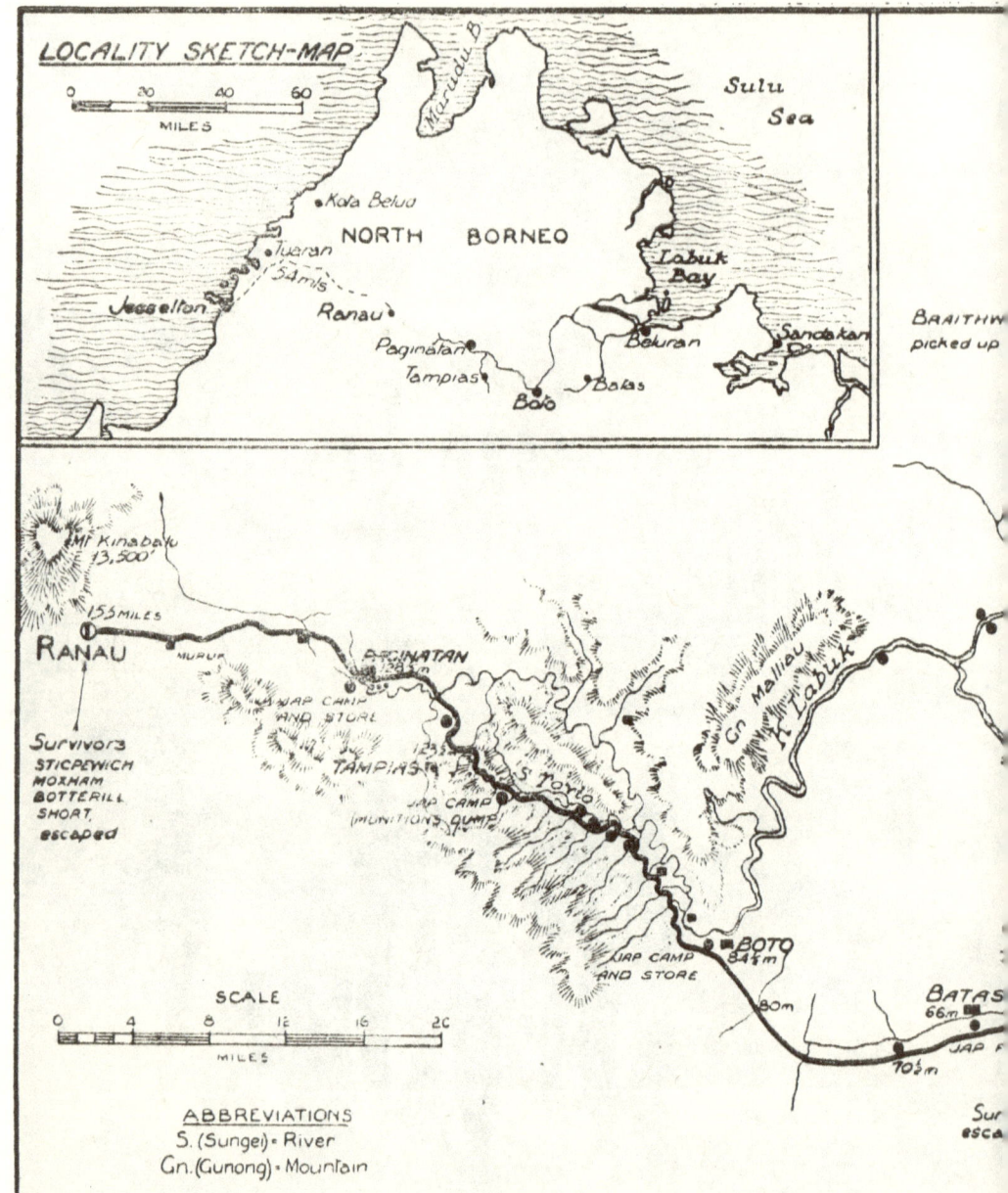

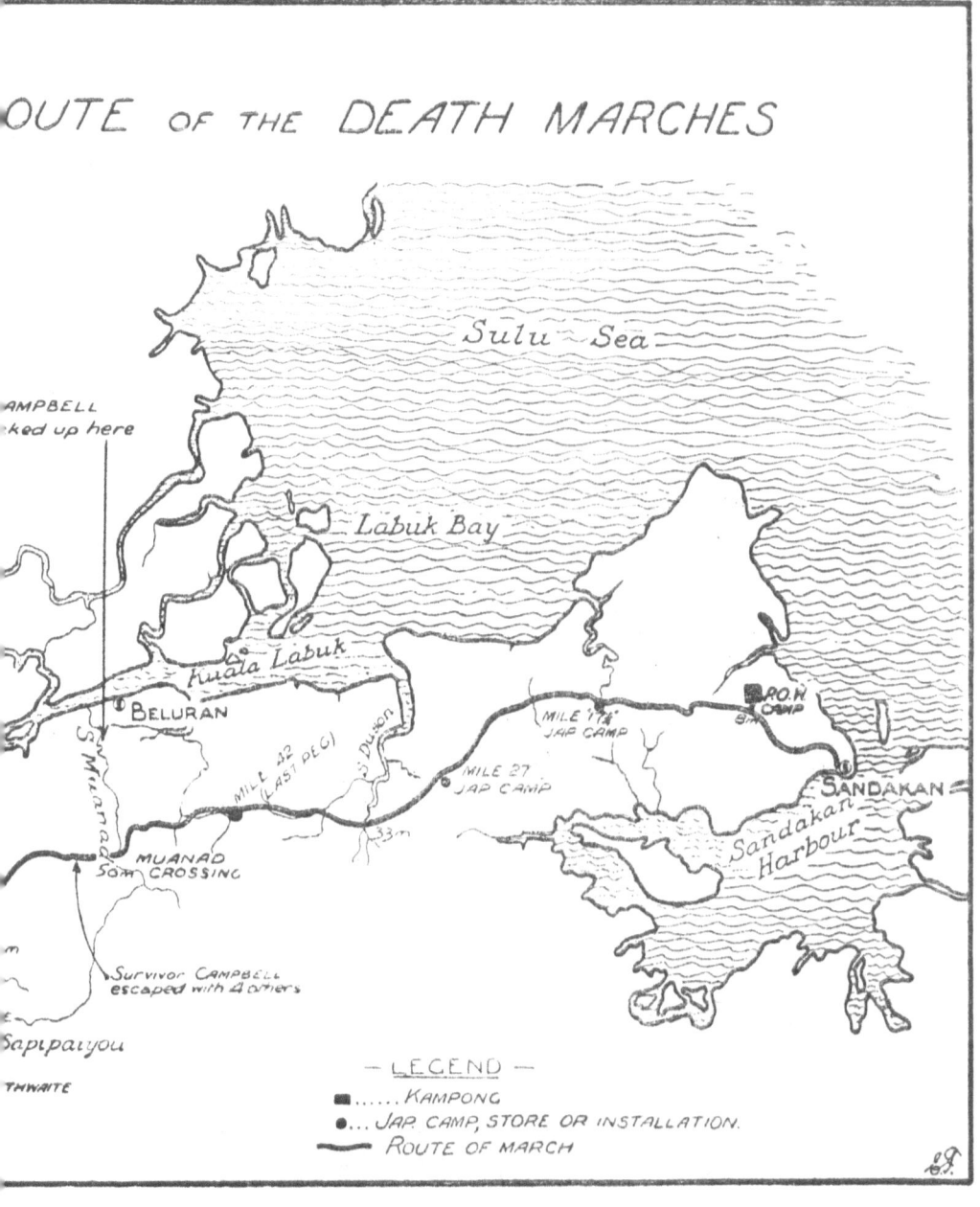

'Route of the death marches', from Colin Simpson, *Six from Borneo: Documentary Drama of the Death Marches*, transcript, ABC, Sydney, [194–].

Courtesy of ABC Library Sales

Members of the Australian–British Reward Mission team in Borneo, 1946–47. *Opposite top left*: Warrant Officer William Sticpewich, one of the six survivors of the Sandakan–Ranau death marches; *opposite bottom left* 'Major Jackson interviews widow and daughter of Borneo native who valiantly aided POWs of Sandakan and was executed by Japs'; *this page top* Major Henry 'Harry' Jackson (left) and Major Roy Dyce interviewing Barigah, 'a native of the Ranau district', who found the escaped POWs Keith Botterill, Bill Moxham, Nelson Short and Andy Anderson after their escape from Ranau camp; *above* Colin Simpson, ABC writer.

Top row and bottom right: National Library of Australia, MS 5253, Folder 258, Box 89; bottom left: AWM 042562

Major Henry 'Harry' Jackson returned to Borneo in 1950 to distribute further rewards. He is photographed here with men from the village of Sapi who assisted Australian POWs and were responsible for the rescue of Dick Braithwaite, one of the six from Borneo who survived the Sandakan–Ranau death marches, 7 August 1950. Left to right: Aliudin, Mangulong, Roy Parsons, Sapan, Harry Jackson, Orang Tuan Onchi, Amit and Sagan.

AWM P02492.031

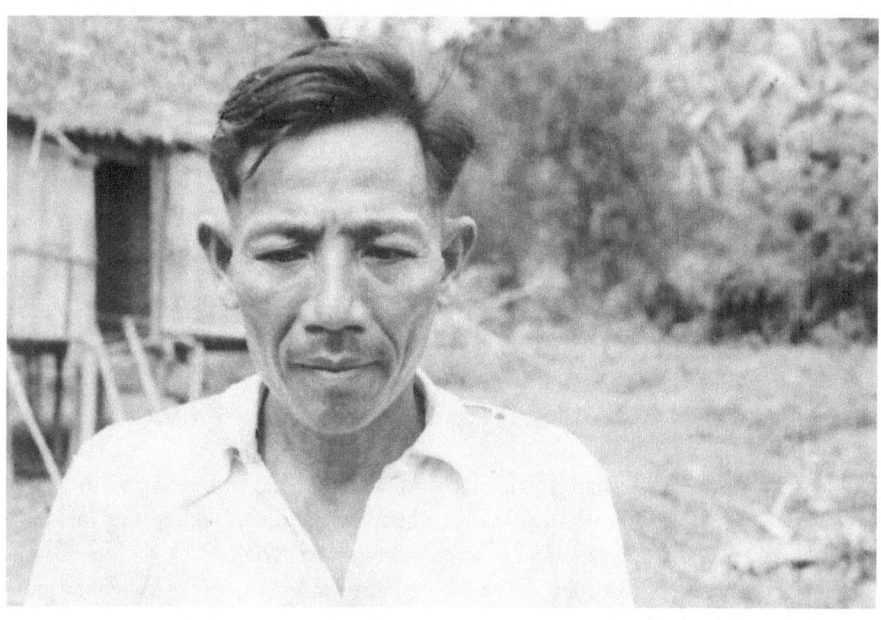

Orang Tuan Kulang, Dusun headman of Kampong Maunad and a wartime member of the Australian Services Reconnaissance Department, 13 December 1946. Kulang helped reunite POW Owen Campbell with Australian forces and later received a grant from the Australian–British Reward Mission.

AWM 042512

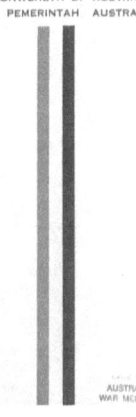

COMMONWEALTH OF AUSTRALIA

DEPARTMENT OF THE ARMY
MELBOURNE, AUSTRALIA

No. 158   1st March 1951

To   SURAT MIN,
of   MILE 11, SANDAKAN,
    NORTH BORNEO.

The Minister for the Army of the Commonwealth of Australia desires to recognize your valuable assistance to Australian soldiers during the War with Japan, 1941-1945, and extends to you, on behalf of the Commonwealth and the next-of-kin, most sincere thanks for services rendered.

MINISTER FOR THE ARMY

Issued at MELBOURNE
Countersigned   Major-General,
             ADJUTANT-GENERAL.

DARI PEMERINTAH AUSTRALIA

KEMENTERIAN KETENTARAAN
MELBOURNE, AUSTRALIA

Nomor 158   1st March tahun 1951

Kepada   SURAT MIN,
dari   MILE 11, SANDAKAN,
         NORTH BORNEO.

Menteri Ketentaraan dari Pemerintah Australia dengan ini mengakui segala bantuan yang berharga yang telah tuan berikan pada pasukan-pasukan Australia sewaktu perang melawan Jepun dalam tahun 1941-1945.

Atas namanya Pemerintah Australia dan keluarga dari pasukan-pasukan Australia itu, Menteri tersebut menguchapkan dengan sungguh-sungguh hati terima kasinya atas bantuan yang telah tuan berikan.

MENTERI KETENTARAAN

Diberikan di MELBOURNE
Disaksikan oleh   Major-General,
             ADJUTANT-GENERAL.

Commonwealth of Australia, Department of the Army, Certificate of Commendation for assistance rendered to Australian soldiers during the war. The certificate was created in 1947 on the recommendation of Major Henry 'Harry' Jackson, who claimed that people he met in Borneo asked for a 'letter of good name' and that a testimonial or certificate 'assumed the proportion of a family heirloom'.

AWM EXDOC098

Chang Siew Ha, Sandakan, North Borneo, September 1950, the widow of Soh Kim Sing, who died in prison during the Japanese occupation while serving a sentence for assistance he had provided to Australian POWs. Chang Siew Ha received a grant from the Australian–British Reward Mission for her children's education needs.

AWM P02492.023

Alice Chia and Ooi Soh Im, the first two AIF Malayan Nursing Scholarship recipients, c. 1948.

University of Melbourne Archives, NO39, 2016.0061

Singapore, Straits Settlements, 20 September 1945. Officers and men of the 2/29th Battalion of the Australian Infantry Battalion, ex-prisoners of war of the Japanese, chatting with Chinese women coolies who gave them so much assistance during their period of captivity by the Japanese.

AWM 117129

Fit for Work. Left to right: NX4417 Bruce Pearce, NX47506 Oscar 'Ossie' Jackson (both of 2/30th Battalion) and an unidentified POW, Shimo Sonkurai No. 1 Camp, Burma–Thailand Railway, c. 1943. Photograph: George Aspinall. This photograph was used in publicity for the 1980s Radio National documentary series, POW: Australians Under Nippon.

AWM P02560.192

4
The Prisoners of War Trust Fund

> Give the £250000 to the Federal Members. It may help them to pay their Income Tax. It may also entice some of them to join up next time. LEST WE FORGET.
>
> *Ex-POW, 1955*

> I remember when I enlisted in the AIF we were acclaimed as great fellows, we were told that nothing was too good for us. I feel now that there was not a lot in that. If we got nothing it would still be too good for us. Promised the world & get nothing. Australia expects every man to do his duty. Australia should also see that every man should get compensation for his duty.
>
> *Ex-POW, 1955*

Robert Menzies' government had moved quickly to devise a solution to appease the large numbers of people disappointed in the failure of the subsistence allowance claim. Member of Parliament Sir Thomas White (1888–1957), who had been taken prisoner by Turkey in the First World War, had some thoughts on the matter. He had a personal connection with the POWs of the Second World War: his nephew Rohan Rivett had been imprisoned by the Japanese and afterwards published a book that became a classic in the POW genre, *Behind Bamboo* (1946). For over twenty years White had been interested in the 'human issues' that stemmed from imprisonment, and he took a long view. He had battled Repatriation officials on behalf of First World War POWs, who experienced trouble having their injuries recognised as war caused, owing to a lack of documentation. White had suggested that it was a difficult road back to health and civil society for men who had spent so long in captivity. Acknowledging that equality of sacrifice was a fraught concept, he had instead proposed a board that would 'assess hardship' of former prisoners on a case-by-case basis. 'The Minister for the Army should not be afraid to try something new', White had insisted in 1947. 'Do not let us be static, and believe that a method which was good enough after World War I is equally suitable now.'[1]

In October 1950 Menzies announced the formation of the Prisoners of War Trust Fund, open to former POWs from both the Pacific and the European theatres of the Second World War. While former POWs, like all returned service personnel, were entitled to apply for a pension through the repatriation system, this new fund was premised on the assumption that imprisonment in war might lead to 'cases of special disability or hardship ... not common to other members of the services'.[2] The Repatriation Commission held the line that POWs were not to be treated as a 'class apart' from other ex-service personnel, and the defence forces, having been instrumental in the subsistence allowance's defeat, were resolute in their opposition to any broad-based allowance claim. But the government was subject to constant political pressure from ex-service organisations and parliamentarians to take some action in relation to the fate of former POWs.

The Prisoners of War Trust Fund

Government officials were aware that any compensation payments due to Australian POWs under the terms of the Treaty of Peace with Japan would be piecemeal, paltry and slow. The Prisoners of War Trust Fund therefore emerged as the government's compromise solution to the demands of its competing constituencies. The special hardships suffered by POWs would be acknowledged, but there would be no automatic entitlement to a payment from the fund. Indeed, despite its dependence on government funding, a grant from the Prisoners of War Trust Fund most resembled a gift distributed by a private charity. There was rigorous vetting of applicants – assessment of ongoing disadvantage and hardship, and a means test – and no avenue of appeal existed for those who were unsuccessful. Opened in 1952 with an initial endowment of £250 000, the fund received further government grants during the 1960s and 1970s and had distributed almost $1 million by the time of its closure in 1977.[3] Over the course of its quarter-century operation, about one in three former prisoners applied to the fund. The applicants were overwhelmingly male: only seven of the 30 returned women prisoners applied and they were not inclined to be verbose. In order to determine the success or failure of claims the government created a board of trustees, which assessed all applications and retained absolute discretion over the award of payments. One of the first appointees to the board was a man who had plenty to say about the rehabilitation of former prisoners: Dr Ted Fisher. If former prisoners were hopeful of a sympathetic hearing, they were to be sorely disappointed.

When it became apparent that the money available via the fund was to be allocated in a discretionary fashion, rather than equally among all former POWs, the ex-POW and other service organisations were enormously frustrated. 'This is grossly unfair to the great majority of ex-prisoners who have had a tough postwar fight to rehabilitate themselves physically and economically', one spokesman claimed.[4] Further disquiet in the ex-POW community about the terms of the fund centred on the invasive application form and the implication that some cases were more deserving than others. The operation of the fund carried forward the ambivalence that had defeated the subsistence allowance claim and exposed applicants to an assessment regime premised on judgments about their respectability, morality and worthiness. Rejections often came as a surprise to those who had anticipated a successful claim and revealed that there was not universal agreement about the entitlements of former POWs.

The workings of the fund and the correspondence to it offer a rare insight into how the 'other ranks', in particular, thought about their right to compensation in the immediate postwar decades. These men, many of them unaccustomed to expressing themselves on the page, took an uncommon opportunity to articulate their understandings about service and sacrifice. Former POWs saw themselves as entitled to some compensation from the state for their suffering beyond the standard repatriation benefits available to all veterans who had served the nation in wartime. Given that the government had created a trust fund specifically for POWs, this was not an unreasonable expectation. Through the colourful vernacular of the applicants and the po-faced responses of the trustees, we glimpse the chasm of experience and perception that separated their worlds. The descriptions of jobs, houses, cars, furnishings and clothes in the ex-POWs' correspondence to the fund, encouraged in part by the latter's need for details of the postwar impacts of captivity, evoke the modest existence of many Australians in the 1950s and 1960s. The very terms used to describe those lives conjure a vanished world: 'fibro', 'linoleum', 'hire purchase', accounts at 'the butcher's'. There is also the parlance of a different age: 'going crook' at people in authority, the denigration of 'urgers' and 'cadgers', and the fear of being considered a 'bludger'.

Charles, a private from the south coast of New South Wales, had been in his early twenties when he was taken POW and sent to Selarang Barracks in Singapore. Beforehand, during the fighting in Malaya, he had been shot in the wrist and as a consequence of nerve damage his fingers on one hand were permanently disfigured. Charles described the result as a 'claw hand'. By the early 1950s he was married with two children and received a 40 per cent war pension for his condition from Repatriation. Charles had been furious about the failure of the subsistence allowance claim. In 1952 in an application to the Prisoners of War Trust Fund he told the trustees, '[I am] crooked on our rotten Government for not giving us the 3/- per day sustenance'. In response to a question asking why he needed money he stated, 'All I require is my fair and right share of all POW fund monies – the POW Fund should be equally divided even if each person only gets 10/- each'.

The trustees

There was a significant class difference between the majority of claimants on the Prisoners of War Trust Fund and the men who administered it. The trustees, two of whom were senior public servants employed by Treasury, were joined by three former POWs, all men from the officer class. In its first decade of operation the fund had Brigadier Arthur Blackburn in the chair. Blackburn was not a sentimental man and was inclined to be tough but fair. Ted Fisher held his position as a trustee from the formation of the fund until his death in 1965. While Fisher championed the compensation cause of former POWs in public, he could be a dour and harsh judge of applicants to the fund, an attitude in keeping with his views about the negligible psychological impact of captivity. The final ex-service trustee was Colonel Allan Spowers (1892–1968), a former POW of the Germans who had been captured in Egypt. Spowers had spent his childhood at Toorak House, a former Victorian governor's residence, and was part of Melbourne's wealthy elite. In 1957 he offered his opinion that the trustees 'should take a broad & generous view' of their position and 'make grants where obvious good would be done'. The rub was in the definition of 'obvious good', which turned on the trustees' own assessments of applicants' worthiness. In its 25-year operation the fund had only three chairs: Blackburn (1952–60), who died in office; Spowers (1961–68), who succeeded him and also died in office; and Edward Dunlop, who first joined the fund in 1961 and took over as Chair after Spowers' death in 1968. Dunlop was Chairman until the fund wound up in 1977.

Blackburn, like all the other non-government trustees, was appointed for his deep links with existing charity and welfare bodies and with Repatriation (and hence familiarity with veterans' health issues). He was also Chairman of the Services Canteens Trust Fund, a government body responsible for distributing welfare to ex-servicemen and their dependants. A fund with such an obscure title is hardly remembered today, but from the late 1940s until the 1970s it was a major distributor of welfare relief and education schemes to Australian former service personnel and their families.[5] It was created in 1947 with a budget of £4.5 million; the money came from the unexpectedly large profit remaining at the end of the war from canteens that sold items like beer, tobacco and food at reduced prices to serving members of the forces. The fund was a body with significant resources and absolute discretion. By the time it finally closed, in 1986, it had distributed $11 million to almost 200 000 people.[6] It had regional committees in all states, and the Menzies Cabinet assumed that it would have records of those people most likely to apply to the Prisoners of War Trust Fund. More to the point, the government was hopeful that this information would be shared between the two funds to allow both to benefit from 'investigations already made' and to prevent payments to unworthy cases. Since Blackburn had acquitted himself well as Chairman of the Services Canteens Trust Fund, the government was keen for him to share his insight and knowledge about potentially troublesome applicants with the trustees of the POW fund.[7]

The other ex-POW trustees also had useful networks. Fisher practised at numerous repatriation hospitals around New South Wales and was a frequent consultant to Repatriation about POWs' postwar health and welfare. Dunlop was similarly placed and had extensive links in the ex-POW community, owing to his position as President of the Ex-Prisoners of War and Relatives Association of Victoria. Spowers was Chair of the Victorian division of the Red Cross and was a ready conduit to other Red Cross divisions around the country. All of these connections proved useful when the POW fund trustees were making decisions about grants.

Charity in its most insulting form

The first circular letter, in 1952, from the Secretary of the Prisoners of War Trust Fund to all known former prisoners set an adversarial tone. It announced that an equal division of the £250 000 among all ex-POWs 'would obviously do little good'. Hence, only 'genuine cases of hardship and distress' that were 'directly referable to the period of captivity' would be supported. 'Often the most deserving dislike "asking for charity"', the letter continued, warning that 'the least deserving' might be 'the most forthcoming'.[8]

In an era when the foundations of the postwar welfare state were being laid, this language, with its implication that those most likely to seek financial help were somehow to blame for their own predicaments, echoed older understandings about assistance. Assumptions that had guided the operation of private philanthropy for much of the nineteenth century, among them the idea that charities needed to guard against imposition, co-existed with newer understandings about the origins of disadvantage. One of the lessons of the Depression had been that sometimes poverty and unemployment were consequences of structural factors and not merely evidence of moral failing or an unrespectable life. The two world wars had created a new category of entitlement, based on service to the nation. Yet the suspicion that not every claim was genuine lingered on, as did the perception that to be a supplicant carried a certain degree of shame. The circular letter to former POWs included a capitalised exhortation to potential applicants: 'DO NOT HAMPER THE ACTIVITIES OF THE TRUST BY CLAIMS FOR CONDITIONS THAT ARE MINOR OR WELL ADJUSTED'. It went on to say that the trustees would only consider claims from a former prisoner who

> (a) suffers distress or hardship as a result of any major disability (physical or mental) directly referable to the conditions of captivity, or as a result of any material prejudice directly referable to such conditions
>
> (b) is in need of such payments to overcome such distress or hardship.[9]

It was not an auspicious beginning. There were complaints about the tone of fund correspondence and the application form, which looked to some like a questionnaire for unemployed workers. The extent of questioning – about family structure, income, assets, mortgages and debts – caused enormous offence. The RSL Federal Executive asked the trustees to redesign the form after members became aggrieved about its 'inquisitorial nature'.[10] One branch thought that the form implied that POWs had to be 'in the gutter' if they were to be considered, and another that the form was 'insulting, obnoxious and humiliating'.[11] Charles, the former POW with a 'claw hand', was particularly scathing: 'P.S. In your personal questions you forgot to ask: what kind of toothpaste we use, do we suffer from constipation, and can we afford to wear a hat on Sunday afternoon'. 'One's financial position', another applicant chided when refusing to provide particulars, 'did not appear to carry much weight in POW camps'. The questions were 'unnecessary and damned impertinent'. George, who had already been middle aged when forced to work on the Thai–Burma Railway, was especially bitter. He defaced the form and wrote large, angry slogans in key sections. Along the top he declared, 'FED UP'. Under 'Places of imprisonment' he wrote, 'A Bashing in every camp'. Albert, after crossing through every question on the form, declared in his supporting statement, 'give what you damn well like I'll take it out of the first Jap that comes to Brisbane'. In conclusion he demanded an amount equivalent to the failed subsistence claim as a 'right not a charity'.

Outrage about the form stemmed from a perception that it replicated the working practices of charity organisations, rather than offering former POWs any sort of entitlement for their suffering. The Victorian branch of the RSL insisted that the form 'implie[d] charity in its worst and most obnoxious form'.[12] Labor Member of Parliament Les Haylen had seen it coming. When the discretionary fund had been first announced in parliament, in 1950, he had commented, 'Many ex-servicemen who now live in the back blocks and the suburbs would rather die than crawl up those marble steps in order to ask for a hand-out. We do not want to have any more dole depots in this country'.[13] The Depression had bitten hard and deep in Australia and in 1950 the memories were fresh and reminders of its miseries unwelcome.

Bitterness about the defeat of the subsistence claim persisted in the early years of the fund's operation, and there were applicants besides Charles who insisted that the money be shared, rather than judged on a case-by-case basis. Joseph, who had survived the bombing of the ship which transported him to Japan and had been 'bashed many times' and subject 'to the usual starvation', informed the trustees, 'I like most other P.O.W.s am disgusted with the way this compensation is to be distributed. I feel that every POW regardless of Rank or anything else should share equally'. Such views were usually coupled with an insistence that war service was a contract of citizenship and that imprisonment, rather than undermining entitlement, enhanced it, due to the extreme suffering it caused. Richard, fifty-seven years old and of 'no fixed place' of residence when he applied for a grant in the early 1950s, wrote, 'I have done my duty to Australia (2 Wars). Do I get anything? I think I am entitled … I have done my duty to my country & expect a little for my service'.

Applicants who were particularly rude or objectionable did themselves few favours. Charles could not confine himself to acerbic remarks about the failure of the subsistence claim or the suggestion that the trustees should inquire if he suffered from constipation; he also surmised that 'of course' not much money would remain 'after all the Committees and hangers-on [got] their expenses paid'. This provoked Arthur Blackburn, during a trustees meeting, to reflect that they 'should ignore all comments or "dictation" by applicants', and he turned down Charles' claim. When one man took his form to a legal firm for completion, the trustees were outraged. 'I don't think much of this form as filled in by solicitors', one remarked, in apparent disregard of the nature of the form itself, which asked applicants to divulge a great deal of personal and financial information. Additional comment on the nature of the application form was equally unwelcome. People like Russell, who was in receipt of a pension from Repatriation, nevertheless failed to qualify for a grant from the Prisoners of War Trust Fund after he defaced his form, warned that the fund could be 'swallowed up by administration costs & no hopers' and told the trustees to return the £250 000 to federal parliamentarians, who might then be enticed to 'join up next time. LEST WE FORGET'.

Yet for every angry applicant determined to make a point about the parsimony, ingratitude and temerity of the trustees or the questions posed by their form, there was another who felt the sting of supplication. It is difficult to determine the extent to which those who expressed reluctance or embarrassment about applying to the fund had internalised the shame associated with charitable relief. Perhaps the disgrace of seeking help compounded the indignity that their sense of masculinity had already suffered as a consequence of imprisonment itself. Edward, who by 1959 was working as a truck driver and was responsible for a wife and two children, had suffered from 'nervous dyspepsia' – problems with digestion assumed to be of psychological origin – since his return from Changi and the Thai–Burma Railway. 'I do not like this Begging because that's what it is and I am ashamed to do it', he told the trustees, asking them to avoid telling his wife about the application. Another confessed that he had left his initial application form sitting on his mantelpiece for months, before throwing it in the fire. 'Call it pride if you will, from our standpoint it's a fear of being bludgers.'

There seemed to be more an element of performance in Thomas' 1952 application, when he assured the trustees, 'as God above knows I've never asked for charity but I'm up against it, trying to get a home & a decent living for my wife and child'. After detailing three interstate moves, his difficulty in getting along with people ('Since I came home I cannot keep a friend'), his constant sickness, his inability to play sport and his struggle to furnish his home, Thomas concluded, 'It's hard to write to you about these things but it kindles a hope that at least someone is still a bit decent to us'. Although the Repatriation doctor had remarked in 1950 that Thomas was 'basically unstable and immature psychologically', the trustees regarded him as 'one of the few genuine anxiety states'. They agreed that he appeared 'quite open and honest in his letter', and Thomas was given a relatively generous grant of £120 as 'encouragement'. In contrast, Douglas, on a higher rate of pension but uninterested in making obsequious statements to the trustees, was given short shrift: he had 'more of a grievance than a hardship'. Meanwhile Harvey insisted, 'My case is one of the many … who gave our best for what we thought was our duty to our country & now find living Impossible. But who cares?'

Determining a claim

These complaints pointed to the power vested in the trustees to determine the success or failure of claims. There was no accountability for the decisions they made, no transparency in the logic they employed. It was not even clear to applicants that the trustees in fact had no authority to check the financial and assets details that they requested; nor did they ever seek to do so.

The minute books of the trustee meetings reveal that there was a small number of guiding assumptions. The trustees considered information held by Repatriation to be essential to the effective functioning of the fund. Although they vetoed Repatriation's request to examine the fund application and determine its eligibility, the trustees did request, and receive, pension details for each claimant.[14] They were also in possession of the results of the large-scale medical survey of ex-POWs of Japan, conducted by Repatriation in 1949–50, with reports on individuals frequently attached to their application forms. This was despite the fact that when POWs had participated in the survey, they had been expressly reassured that its results would remain confidential. Furthermore, the trustees sometimes received detailed psychiatric assessments of applicants that had been conducted in repatriation hospitals. This information effectively allowed for confirmation of the disabilities claimed by each applicant and made the trustees aware of the Repatriation doctors' assessment of their significance and impact.

The trustees used the Repatriation assessments as guides for their own decisions. A pension from Repatriation was not an all-or-nothing situation: there were plenty of returned service personnel on pensions ranging from 10 per cent to a ruling of 'totally and permanently incapacitated', or TPI. The trustees decided that any applicant deemed totally and permanently incapacitated would be automatically entitled to a grant. Conversely, any applicant not in receipt of a pension for war-caused disabilities was scrutinised very closely and unlikely to receive a grant. This left the vast range of cases which fell between these two extremes as matters for debate and deliberation. The maximum grant, which could be accumulated over a number of separate applications, was £250 ($500 after the move to decimal currency). To give some indication of the value of a grant, in 1958, a household might purchase a new washing machine for around £200, but a new Holden was worth more in the order of £1000.[15] The maximum grant was therefore a substantial but not a life-changing amount of money for most applicants.

While there were people who argued that entitlement rather

than discretion should be the modus operandi of the fund, others saw the information that was gathered in order to make a decision as imprecise, imperfect and ultimately subjective. There was certainly no clarity around what purpose the intricate financial details requested would serve: was this to means test applicants, identify the thrifty, assess levels of need or punish the dissolute? Albert, whose financial history and steady employment suggested a relatively smooth transition to post-captivity life, objected. 'I am astonished that the Commonwealth government is virtually applying a "means test" in consideration of claims by ex-POWs against Japan. I receive a small pension from a "grateful country", but how does that compensate for loss of vision in one eye, a damaged shoulder, as well as the ineradicable scars left on the mind after over 3½ years imprisonment by the Japanese?' There were many others who pointed out that if there were some kind of means test applied, the prudent were more likely to be disadvantaged than the degenerate. Eric argued that there were 'trials and tribulations' of postwar life that could be just as demanding as the more visible disability of losing an arm or leg. And what to do with the man who 'came home feeling sorry for himself, drank every penny he had, and abused himself so much' that all he eventually had was 'nothing but a wreck of manhood to show for himself'? Eric concluded, 'Surely those of us who won the battle within ourselves, settled down to a decent home life and used our hard earned savings for a good purpose are just as entitled to some help, if not more, than quite a fair percentage'. Ted Fisher described the letter as 'quite one of the most memorial incidents of our experience with claims' but still refused the application. Others put Eric's distinctions in more crude terms. Charles again provided one of the most colourful complaints: 'The fellow who wasted his money on the horses and can put over a good story will get some dough and the blokes who didn't waste the money and are not quite stone broke will get nothing'.

Those in straitened circumstances eagerly detailed their indebtedness, thereby inadvertently creating an impression of fecklessness, but the struggling middle were just as likely to undermine their own claims through honesty. Joseph was a case in point. On a 50 per cent pension in 1953, with a wife and two children, he worked in a timber yard. He confessed to a bank balance of almost £500, which was the result of his war gratuity and the army wages that had accumulated when he was a prisoner. 'I think I am as much entitled to help as those that have lost theirs at races hotels gambling etc.' Yet his bank balance did tell against him. 'I think £50 is ample for a man with £499 in the bank', a trustee noted. Harold had contracted tuberculosis during his imprisonment. Although he was temporarily totally incapacitated, or TTI, when making his first application, in 1952, he was unmarried and owned a property worth £1000 (with a £500 mortgage). Initially refused a grant, Harold complained, 'One wonders if it pays to tell the truth when submitting an application such as this, but I have always been taught to tell the truth … I am not trying to be petty or rude in any way, but I do consider that I am entitled to any benefit that is payable'. Others were more canny and simply ignored the financial part of the form. Perhaps they realised that the trustees were not actually invested with any power to check the financial details (apart from pension entitlements) of applicants. A portfolio of shares, substantial cash on hand or property ownership could be easily concealed from trustees, merely by avoiding its mention.

The trustees did not always agree about the distribution of money. Treasury officials wanted to limit the award of grants to applicants in dire financial circumstances. Blackburn, Spowers and Fisher insisted on making a 'wider interpretation' of the fund's terms and used their discretion in each case.[16] This sometimes meant that the disadvantaged went without, while respectable men fallen on rough times received preferential treatment. Word travelled around ex-POW circles about who had, and who had not, received a grant. It led to tension and resentment. Archibald, who worked as a truck driver in the early 1950s, stated that he knew of people who had told 'a very convincing pack of lies and therefore succeeded beyond even their wildest imagination'. Disappointed at the denial of his own claim, he complained that 'known urgers and Charity bums' were able to 'get unlimited funds to carry out Hotels and so-called clubs', while he received nothing.

Applicants who worked the land received the most favourable treatment and reflected the longevity of the attachment to the idea that Australia rode on the sheep's back. Rupert, a country boy from rural New South Wales, was the type of man the trustees were keen to assist. When he returned from captivity, he learned that his father had been unwell and had let the farm run down into a shocking state of disrepair. There was no stock or farming plant on the property and about £900 owing to the Rural Bank. Rupert had used his war gratuity to partially pay for a tractor and a few sheep but wanted the Prisoners of War Trust Fund to assist him to purchase fencing, fertiliser and more stock. He was also responsible for the support of his wife and now-widowed mother: his father had died in 1948. Rupert did not mention it in his application, but local newspapers had reported that his father had committed suicide in a shed on the property. Rupert had found the body. In the interconnected worlds of the ex-service community, it is possible that the trustees knew about this family tragedy. They were certainly inclined to be generous to Rupert, who provided no pension details or evidence of ongoing disability from captivity. It was rather his position as a farmer determined to restore the property that made the trustees vote in his

The Prisoners of War Trust Fund

favour: 'I think this man has suffered "material prejudice" thro' captivity in that his farm went to pieces during his absence thro' his father's sickness. Had he not been in captivity he most probably would have been recalled from service to work the property. I would make him a grant.' The other trustees agreed and in 1952 provided Rupert with the relatively generous sum of £100.

A slide down the social scale, often euphemistically referred to as 'reduced status', was another situation that might provoke a positive reaction from the trustees. A bank accountant who had become a farm labourer owing to an impaired memory – the result of imprisonment and torture by the Japanese *Kempeitai* (secret police) – was awarded £150 in the early 1950s on the grounds that he had suffered 'serious loss of status'. Similarly, a former farmer who had tried his hand at a transport business owing to ill-health was forced to give that up as well and take employment as a caretaker at a bowling green in country Queensland. His loss of status was also considered grounds for a grant. Alan, another applicant, was a former officer who had quit university to enlist in the army. He had found work as a guard on the Queensland railways when he returned. When his health proved unequal to the task, Alan joined the public service and attempted (unsuccessfully) to return to tertiary study. A series of nervous breakdowns led his Repatriation doctor to describe Alan as a 'nervous young man', 'very introspective', with a 'big functional overlay in all his disabilities'. While there were few medical grounds to support Alan's application – he was on a 10 per cent pension – Allan Spowers' opinion was that a 'broad and generous view' ought to be taken of his case. Another trustee agreed that there had been 'genuine efforts to rehabilitate himself'. Awarded £50, Alan, a man struggling to improve himself through tertiary education, was a recognisable type to the trustees and won over their sympathy.

A more harsh, judgmental attitude was on display when it came to other applicants, whose disabilities and disadvantages seem now to have been at least on a par with those of an officer failing his university courses. The trustees were not averse to drawing on their own familiarity with applicants – 'I know this man' – and offering judgment upon them. The fortunate were typified as, for example, 'an unskilled battler with a string of dependants' or 'a good type now bedridden'. Yet there were more frequent mentions, in the trustees' minutes on application files, to 'low types', 'no hopers', 'cadgers' and people who had a tendency to try it on. 'How can we help this man except by holding his hand for the rest of his life?' one trustee remarked in 1956 of a laundryman who had endured several spells in a psychiatric unit after suffering from psychosis. 'He obviously spent all his deferred pay &c on drink and now has nothing.' In the 1960s a trustee recommended against a grant because he considered the applicant 'a poor type rarely sober [who] would make for the nearest hotel and drink the lot in no time. He wants help re lodgings, clothes and heating. I would recommend that we grant no more than $75 this time. This should fit him out with new clothes and a heater. If he is genuine, this will smarten him up and help him obtain employment'.

Another applicant, a father of seven children on a 70 per cent war pension for a war disability, who was unable to support his large family and manage a crippling, non-war-related disease, was dismissed as a figure akin to a contemporary cartoon magician: 'This POW ... has had more trouble than MANDRAKE, stemming from his POW neurosis and his general improvidence arising from his numerous (7) family when on low wages'. Cutting references to large families on low wages was a code for Catholicism in mid-century Australia, and although sectarianism does not seem to have determined the success or failure of applications, there was little sympathy from these establishment figures for impoverished people who did not limit their family size.

There was extreme scepticism about nervous complaints. Despite many applicants possessing at least a part pension for 'anxiety' disorders – a determination made by doctors employed by Repatriation – the trustees, and psychiatrists and psychologists too, were inclined to be wary. One 42-year-old man described as 'very nervy' since returning home and subject to 'crying fits' was assumed to protest too loudly about his desire, but incapacity, to work. 'It would be unwise to attach too much importance to the patient's "nerves"', one doctor (himself a former prisoner) commented. 'He is a type of man to whom well meant but misplaced sympathy would do a great deal of harm. It is, I think, important that he should be kept at work. Prolonged holidays for any reason are likely to do him more harm than good.'

The trustees retained unshakeable faith in their processes and in their capacity to determine the causes of the postwar fates of former prisoners. In 1953 when Wilfrid Kent Hughes (1895–1970), a former POW and Menzies government Minister, wrote to the trustees on behalf of applicants who felt aggrieved about the operation of the fund, he claimed to be 'horrified' by the way it was being administered. In response, Arthur Blackburn revealed that the trustees themselves had actually shaped the terms of the fund and revised the government's intentions. Menzies' Cabinet had originally directed the trustees to make payments to prisoners who 'suffered special disability not common to other members of the Services and as a direct result of their imprisonment'. Influenced by the views of Repatriation , however, the trustees pointed out that 'medical advice' held that there was 'practically no disability suffered by any P.O.W.' that was not regularly encountered by 'other members of the services to a greater or lesser degree'. This was Ted Fisher's view, stated regularly at

Repatriation meetings and in the press, and one that was ultimately incorporated into the operation of the fund. The original terms of the fund had subsequently been altered and limited to distress or hardship as a consequence of major disability or material prejudice. Blackburn told Kent Hughes that he felt confident that the trustees had, 'in the main, rejected the claims of the "ne'er do well"; the scrounger who merely thought he could pitch a tale and get a grant and the "no-hoper" whose difficulties, if any, had nothing whatever to do with his captivity or any disability arising therefrom'.[17]

The welfare network

Assessments of the applicants, while giving the appearance of being made on a case-by-case basis by a small board of trustees, drew upon a network of knowledge about former POWs. The trustees consulted state ex-POW associations, the RSL, the Red Cross and myriad other welfare organisations about cases they considered potentially problematic or suspicious. In 1969 for instance, a trustee commented that an applicant was 'living in a very fine private hospital' and was 'well cared for'; he gave his opinion that 'any grant would be wasted'. In addition, the applicant received monthly visits and 'cigarettes etc.' from the NSW Ex-Prisoners of War Association's Welfare Officer, who did not recommend giving him a grant. In 1959 a Red Cross social worker at the Repatriation General Hospital, Hollywood, in Perth, was asked her opinion on a man the trustees considered a 'simple soul – but also presumptively a spendthrift', a lonely man with a profound stutter, who received a 100 per cent pension and lived in a boarding house. Fifteen years after returning to Australia, he still had an open ulcer on his leg which was protected by a shin guard. In the view of the social worker, who had spoken to the applicant about his desire to start a business making paper flowers, 'a grant of a large sum' while the man was 'unable to propose any definite scheme for its use might not be very constructive'. The trustees promptly halved the amount they had considered granting him.

On more than one occasion grant money was paid over to the Red Cross for distribution in equal instalments to individual applicants or for settling accounts at local stores for applicants deemed too unstable, given to drink or too untrustworthy to receive money in one lump sum. Despite a trustee declaring that Leslie was a 'wreck – from abdominal operations during captivity' and 'a classical "genuine case"' who would 'never be the same again', Ted Fisher was determined that it was 'not to this man's best advantage' to receive the money in a lump sum. Leslie had wanted the money to purchase a boat in order to assist him in establishing a small fishing business, but the trustees decided to offer him the money in weekly instalments or paid directly to the launch company. When the Red Cross social worker agreed to visit him and try to work out a compromise solution, Leslie made clear that he was unhappy with the grant's being distributed to him in this way, 'as his own brother and several friends of his were given lump sums'. Fisher was adamant that Leslie was 'a pretty poor type' and refused to pay him the grant of £150 directly.

Fisher frequently judged the suitability of applicants to receive grant money and use it wisely. He cannot have known every applicant to the fund, of course, but those who had come on his radar, either during captivity or in the NSW health and repatriation system in the 1950s and 1960s, were at a distinct disadvantage if he did not like or approve of them. Raymond, who was deemed to have a 'psychopathic personality' by the doctor who examined him during the Ex Prisoner of War [J] Survey, in 1949–50, was a constant applicant to the fund from the late 1950s. Repatriation handed over a recent psychiatric report on him in 1958, which declared that he was a 'well-known alcoholic and psychopath' who had assaulted the nurses and had been banned from the local repatriation hospital. The psychiatrist was amazed that Raymond seemed to be able to hold down a job but noted that his work didn't require any particular stability or social graces. The fact remained, however, that Raymond was in receipt of a 30 per cent pension for his war-caused disabilities. Fisher nevertheless managed to persuade the other trustees that the personality issues that so troubled Raymond should preclude him from receiving a grant. 'I know this man well', he insisted, expressing surprise that he hadn't already died because of his lung abscesses. 'He really was at death's door.' Now his main problem was a 'personality defect'. 'If he grasps a causal link between the bodily ailment of captivity and the psychological damage of the post war years, he wants a much larger grant than £30.' But the question remained, Fisher concluded, 'what good would it do him?' When the trustees finally agreed to pay Raymond a direct sum of £100 in 1964 (the Red Cross having organised some clothing for him in 1961), after Repatriation declared him totally and permanently incapacitated, it was too late. Raymond had died the previous month.

Welfare organisations which interacted with POWs, such as the RSL and Red Cross, were not always merely the handmaidens of the Prisoners of War Trust Fund. At times the Red Cross attempted to argue on behalf of its clients and to present their cases to the trustees in more favourable terms. There were also cases of genuine kindness and concern for broken and dysfunctional men. A solicitor in a Victorian country town, who also happened to be a stalwart of the local RSL, took care of 'poor old Jim' and attempted to win some kind of assistance for him. When Jim attempted to complete his form in 1952 all he could say was, 'I cannot share. I cannot settle down to do work. I often try to do light work but I get the shakes'. He suffered blackouts and neurosis. A longer letter from the solicitor explained that the best way to describe Jim was as a 'War-wreck'. Before the war, he had been a 'very hard working farm labourer', and although he had received little formal education he had been proud of his reputation as a 'good Worker: he could lift a bag of Super-phosphate from the ground into the combine'. The war had changed all that. Jim could not even remain present when a rotary hoe backfired as he was planting potatoes: he just walked off and left the machine running until the petrol evaporated. He was now living in a hut down by the river – a new ceiling, a stove and a chimney would assist in making it a home. The trustees were happy to send the money to the solicitor to distribute for Jim's benefit. For his part, Jim was exceedingly grateful, and the £80 he was granted made his hut a little more comfortable before his death, four years later, in 1956, at the age of fifty.

Mobilising the Red Cross to administer grants was the extreme end of a paternalistic attitude towards men perceived as prone to substance abuse and insufficiently reintegrated to familial and community relationships. Most often these were cases in which it was impossible to deny – owing to the pension rate they received – that disadvantage stemmed from a condition referable to captivity. There were other applicants – the majority, in fact – who received a lower rate of pension and for whom success or stability also proved elusive. These were applicants who certainly believed that captivity had blighted their chances and disrupted their capacity to produce, connect properly with other people or settle down and find happiness in work and family life. Whether imprisonment in war caused their problems or merely exacerbated or compounded existing structural disadvantages lay at the heart of deliberations. In many ways, this was an impossible question to answer on the evidence the trustees had before them:

what difference had the war made to these working-class men (for the vast majority of applicants were from the 'other ranks') of limited education who now felt disconnected from their families and communities?

A strict interpretation of the terms of the fund might have been justified if they had been adhered to in all cases. The trustees had no trouble in refusing the applications of men who appeared to be in genuine need – such as those living in homes with dirt floors who requested money for a cot for their new baby or who were separated fathers with four children to support – on the grounds that they did not seem to have conditions referable to captivity. At times the trustees' asides and summations appear harsh. There was one frequent applicant who caused a trustee to quip, 'We should rename him Mr Trouble as he certainly gets it'. This was a former POW with crippling arthritis trying to run a pig farm in New South Wales. He had one child, a profoundly disabled nineteen-year-old daughter, who dirtied the bed every night but whom he refused to put in a home because as he said, 'I know how it is to be put away ... it would be like a POW'.

There were plenty of other applicants who clearly struggled to rehabilitate themselves but exhibited such deference to the fund that the trustees awarded a grant with no strings attached. The compassion shown in such cases hardly seems unwarranted, although it does further demonstrate the biases of class and respectability that appear to have operated in the more measured use of empathy in others. The cases that fell in the grey area of the blighted life could be hard to split, and it would seem that sometimes tone and the capacity to present a believable case made the difference. This was especially so if the trustees, despite their extensive network of contacts, had no personal knowledge of an applicant and could not quash his case with a hastily scrawled remark about a proclivity for beer and horses.

Rejection caused some applicants to question the wisdom of their decision to go to war or to consider that their nation had been ungrateful. 'Only prejudice and unfair treatment has been my reward', Francis complained, 'for my lone fight through Humiliation Sorrow Fear Pain & expense I have suffered due undoubtedly to my POW experience'. The trustees' decision to deny his claim was 'a staggering blow'.

Ralph, married with two children, worked as a surgical bootmaker in Queensland. During the war he had been imprisoned in Changi and sent to work on the railway. Unusually, Ralph described some of his experiences in captivity, including three horrendous 'bashings', which he had not been expected to survive, and a 'miraculous escape' after being tied up and sentenced to be shot. He described himself as having 'mental disability, bad dreams, headaches, eyes, nerves, hernia, many sleepless nights, on edge all time'. Ralph relied on his brother to do much of the work in their business; he was simply ill a lot of the time and 'always very tired & despondent'. 'All the money which we deserve', he concluded, 'cannot repay what we lost in human sufferings in the 3½ years captivity, spent with the mighty Nippon Army'. Others were more bitter. One rejected applicant signed his letter of complaint 'with a resolve never to re-enlist for the sort of country represented by people like you'.

The trustees were most harsh in the earliest, busy years of the fund and were more inclined to be generous as the number of applications declined in the late 1960s and 1970s. In the first round, Norman, who had been shot in the right knee, had a twisted ankle and 'anxiety state, dermatitis and coronary hypertension' and struggled with memories of being bashed by the Japanese, a broken marriage and a desire to avoid company, was considered a 'very doubtful' applicant. He was on a 60 per cent war pension, but the trustees wondered whether the gunshot wound was referable to his captivity and whether his present difficulties had anything to do with being a prisoner. In the early 1960s a trustee complained that it seemed 'just too easy' to receive a handout. 'Everyone can do with a bit of money in their pockets.' Yet in 1968 they were willing to grant one totally and permanently incapacitated pensioner the money for his stepdaughter to attend a ballet school. Even then, some old assumptions remained. When the decision was made to wind up the fund in 1971 the trustees decided against any publicity because it might 'reawaken many of the least deserving', who would reapply for a grant.[18]

The administration of the fund revealed the distance between the worlds of the trustees – men who moved in relatively elite social circles and returned to their prewar occupations – and those of the applicants, who pursued a more modest and precarious existence. Men who had worked as labourers and farm hands before the war, for instance, found difficulty in returning to occupations that often required rude good health. Bureaucrats and former officers were often ungenerous to men who sought some kind of help for their troubles, and many of those so denigrated were inclined to speak back to power and tell those in control exactly what they thought of their imperious or parsimonious attitude. Even though applicants were unwittingly provided with an outlet to vent their frustration, such complaints were usually swatted back with the bland language of administrative process. An examination of the fund documents tells us much about the attitudes towards charity, welfare and entitlement in postwar Australia. It also offers a rare view into the peacetime battles of former POWs in the 1950s and 1960s, men by that time scattered through the cities, country towns and rural regions of Australia. It is to the stories of three of these men in particular that we now turn.

Part II

The POW story

5
Rebuilding a life

24 June 1959

Dear Sir

I wish to make application for financial assistance as I have been unable to pay the costs of my son's funeral since he was buried on 23rd March 1959. My son was twenty years old when he joined up, and served for four years as a prisoner of the Japanese, before he went away he was a good boy but since the war he has been treated for nerves by the Repat for which he was paid a pension of £2:1 per fortnight.

During the last 15 months of his life he became worse & his nerves went to pieces & he was unable to work at all & I had to keep him although my husband is only a working man and very sick at that.

On March 18th my son was so upset that he did not know what he was doing & tried to swim the Yarra in the city at 6 O'clock at night and was drowned[.] [A]s my boy had done his best for his country and I believe eventually gave his life as a result of his service I thought that he should at least have a decent funeral, and that the government through the repat would pay the costs however when I applied for assistance the repat only paid £25 leaving me £76 to pay from I don't know where.

> As it is impossible for me to meet this account I appeal to you to see if you can give me any help not for myself but for my son's sake who gave his life for his country.
>
> Mrs C, Clayton, Victoria.[1]

Before his death in 1959 David said he was suffering from 'anxiety state and also nerves'. He had trouble sleeping and could neither work in factories nor find suitable employment outdoors. His mother firmly believed that his death by drowning, at the age of thirty-eight, when he was 'so upset that he did not know what he was doing', was a consequence of his experiences as a POW. 'Anxiety state' and 'nerves' were common complaints among other prisoners, and accidental death or suicide their most dramatic conclusion. Without access to the repatriation files of Second World War veterans, it is impossible to know just how many former POWs committed suicide. Even then, the blurred line between accident and intention can make identifying suicide a difficult task.

Large-scale studies of the health of former POWs in Australia did not begin until the early 1980s, and their findings confirmed what many people had long suspected. In an explicit rebuttal of the logic that guided discussion at Repatriation in the 1950s, one report argued that there was 'no evidence that organic factors directly accounted' for the high levels of psychiatric illness among former prisoners: Ted Fisher's theory that most neurosis sufferers had a bad case of worms was finally put to rest. The assumption that had guided psychiatrists and psychologists in the immediate postwar period that men who experienced war neurosis were predisposed to it through an existing frailty was also challenged. 'The horrendous and prolonged psychological stress' of captivity was instead proposed as the primary reason that POWs had a rate of clinical psychiatric disorders, most commonly depression and anxiety, almost double that of other ex-service personnel.[2]

There is copious evidence of anxiety disorders and neurosis in the papers of the Prisoners of War Trust Fund. Such complaints are often accompanied by histories of discontinuous work, feelings of inferiority and difficulties in familial and social relationships. Rather than rehearse the myriad variations on these themes, this chapter reconstructs the life histories of three applicants to the fund, drawing on information they provided in correspondence and supplementing it with material available in public records. Owing to the small number and reticence of female applicants to the fund, the focus here is on men. These men's stories present in microcosm some of the difficulties faced by single, divorced and married ex-POWs: the struggles to hold down jobs and the impacts of anxiety and neurosis on health and relationships. The cases also take account of the prisoners' experiences of war itself and their prewar histories as far as possible – their families of origin, employment records and personal relationships. It is not possible at this distance and with the fragmentary nature of, and piecemeal access to, the archival record to make any sound judgments about the mental states of these men before they went to war. The purpose of these mini-biographies is twofold: to demonstrate the impact of captivity on former POWs and to explore to what extent earlier experiences of family, work and education helped or hindered their capacity for resilience and rehabilitation.

There is potential, given family and work histories, to develop some sense of the men's socioeconomic backgrounds. One of the lasting impressions created when reading the applications to the fund is that while applicants acquired war-caused disabilities many of them already carried the injuries of class. Disadvantage in the postwar world was woven from many threads; it is difficult but important to recognise war experience as one element in the complexity of veterans' life histories. Former POWs carried the burden of a long captivity, but they should not be reduced to cardboard-cutout figures, removed from the social and economic contexts of twentieth-century Australian society, which also gave form and shape to their lives.

Ronald

When he was twenty-one Ronald found a job with the National Roads and Motorists' Association. It was the mid-1920s and the increasingly popular motorcar symbolised freedom, leisure and modernity. The association employed roadside guides and patrol men like Ronald to assist motorists in trouble. Ronald loved the work, eventually becoming a qualified motor engineer and spare parts manager. He stayed with the association for thirteen years, stationed variously in Sydney and country New South Wales. 'Prior to enlisting for overseas service', Ronald later reflected, he had enjoyed steady employment and 'had never been in a hospital, or ill other than the usual colds'.

When the war came Ronald enlisted in a motor transport unit. The company comprised men from Queensland and New South Wales aged between thirty-five and forty-five, an older profile than most. The unit was formed to assist with the transport needs of troops defending British possessions in Malaya and Singapore. Ronald fitted the company profile on several counts: born in Queensland, almost thirty-five years old by the time he sailed for Singapore and over a decade's experience working with cars. Many of his fellow army recruits were First World War veterans; Ronald himself had no experience of war and little idea of what to expect.

Rebuilding a life

During its first six months in Malaya the company traversed the peninsula, assisting with transport requirements and working in conjunction with Chinese and Indian troops. At the time when Japan attacked Thailand, in December 1941, Ronald and his company were stationed in northern Malaya and moving supplies, fuel, ammunition and troops in battle. Along with the rest of the British forces, they reversed down the length of Malaya, all the way back to Singapore. The company then received orders, before the capitulation, to board a ship and proceed to Java to assist in the Dutch East Indies. The plan was for it to join reinforcements from the 6th and 7th divisions, which were returning from the Middle East. The company became part of Blackforce, the brigade on Java commanded by Brigadier Arthur Blackburn. In February 1942 Ronald became a POW of Japan. Many men from his company were transferred from Java, via Changi in Singapore, to work on the Thai–Burma Railway; Ronald was spared that experience, at least.

Details of Ronald's imprisonment are scant, but he did witness a horrific attack on a fellow prisoner in No. 1 Cycle Camp on Java that he recounted to war crimes investigators in 1946. He described the Japanese camp Commander, Lieutenant Soni, as 'perfectly dressed, very smart and correct in his movements, about 5'3" [160 centimetres] tall and good build'. He was therefore a full thirty centimetres shorter than Ronald himself. Although of diminutive size, Soni was a man who engaged in random and extreme acts of violence. During a propaganda film night, which Ronald and some of his friends did not attend, the group failed a room inspection. Soni singled out one of their number and beat him relentlessly for fifteen minutes, punching him over a heap of rubbish, slamming him against a tree, throwing him into piles of furniture and continuing to punch the victim until he was almost unconscious.

Ronald did not say whether witnessing such violence had made an impact on his mental state, but this man who had such a settled prewar employment history struggled to reintegrate to Australian society on his return. At discharge in 1946 he was declared medically fit, with no war-caused disabilities or injuries, and he purchased a 'Motor Business' at Coonamble, New South Wales. After only six months recurring bouts of malaria and 'the bad state of my nerves and mental condition' meant that the business was sold. Ronald was irritable. The bouts of depression that had started when he was a POW – although he had not mentioned them at discharge – returned. He sought private help for 'nerves'. Rather than pursuing his own business, Ronald tried to find work in other garages. Letters from employers in the early 1950s regretted that he felt forced to resign owing to his ill-health and attested to his 'honesty, loyalty and a will to help out'. Many other former POWs also complained about their incapacity to return to their prewar jobs. For one man who had worked on the Thai–Burma Railway, a return to his role at the Victorian Railways proved too much. 'It only took a short time for me to realize that I was in no fit state to stand the racket and noise of the continual train movements.'

As a single man in his early forties without the responsibilities of a wife and child and 'unable to settle down', Ronald decided to 'travel & have a good holiday' and so made his way around Australia. This pattern of beginning jobs and businesses and abandoning them owing to ill-health, ennui or 'nerves' emerged among other former POWs as well. A few simply went bush and camped out alone, surviving on odd jobs and rabbits they trapped. The resort to travel or, more commonly, interstate or intercity moves for work, was another frequent element in returned POWs' life histories. Equally prominent was Ronald's lament 'I could not find a place of contentment'.

Rebuilding a life

Many returned POWs complained of 'nerves' and 'anxiety', and a few were prepared to go into more detail about how they experienced them. Most just used the single word 'nerves', which implied either that they assumed people knew what they meant or, conversely, that their mental attitude was so complex it was difficult to articulate. Worry, nausea and sleeplessness were common complaints. Crowds were often cause for concern. The man who could not return to his job on the railways also found being in the city itself difficult. 'I could not stand being caught in a crowd', he explained in the early 1950s. 'Ordinary city street crowds upset me to such an extent that I could not walk in them unless forced to do so by the utmost necessity.'

Perhaps Ronald didn't like crowds either. From Sydney he went to Brisbane, where he had a succession of jobs, then inland to Dalby and further north to Mackay. Again and again, his mental health made the work impossible and he kept moving: Innisfail, Atherton, Cairns. Finally, he found work at Mitchell River Mission on Cape York Peninsula, but he claimed that this was only because the mission was unable to 'get anyone else to do it'. With each move he went further north, back to the tropical environment of his captivity.

Eventually the mental state that became the defining feature of Ronald's postwar life set in: paranoia. He was convinced that employers denied they had vacancies out of a disinclination to take him on. The superintendent at Mitchell River offered him jobs on both the mission and nearby stations and gave him somewhere to live. The accommodation was basic: a 'cabbage tree hut' with a cement floor and a bed. Ronald's work on the stations involved some engineering and book-keeping, but he was unsuccessful in obtaining more secure or permanent employment. Of one occasion he recalled, 'While being interviewed I was so ill I could not retain my self-control & as on several other occasions started crying & could not talk'. Malaria and mental instability continued to plague him, despite the Church of England missionaries attempting to do their best. At one point, he even accepted an invitation from the Bishop of Carpentaria to sail through the Torres Strait Islands. The sea air and sympathetic ears of the missionaries provided some small comfort, but work on the York Peninsula was always punctuated by visits to doctors and spells in psychiatric hospitals back in Brisbane.

Perhaps in desperation for some stability, Ronald decided to give the army another try. By 1950 Australia was at war again in Asia, this time as part of the United Nations forces in South Korea. Ronald tried three times to join up but each time was rejected on the grounds of his ill-health. Frustration with his lack of success and the ultimate insult of being rejected by the army, in whose service he felt he had acquired his disabilities, inflamed his nervous condition. By 1953 Ronald considered that he constantly encountered 'preju[d]ice, lies & apparent hatred'. He was 'very bitter against everyone and everything'.

Ronald felt both in need of full pension entitlements and appalled at the prospect of receiving them. Even though the repatriation system was premised on the idea that service for the nation carried entitlement to financial support for war-caused disability, there were some, like Ronald, who continued to feel that a pension demeaned their independence. Containing these contradictory feelings was psychologically exhausting and fostered an increasingly paranoid attitude. In 1953 Ronald told a psychiatrist at the Repatriation General Hospital at Greenslopes, in Brisbane, that he received 'off hand treatment' from hospitals, doctors and the army. A medical report recorded him as having 'a hidden fear that whenever he goes into a room, people stop talking and say to him that he "looks ill" then say, "of course you receive a pension"'.

Rebuilding a life

When describing his ongoing disabilities from the war, Ronald used a phrase that peppered the language of other former POWs: 'inferiority complex'. Given the relative frequency of this complaint among former prisoners, it is worth considering what was meant by it. Ronald was more prepared than most to go into detail about how 'inferiority' actually felt and possessed uncommon insight into its contradictions and tensions. People avoided him and wouldn't talk to him. Yet the fear of being shunned could be just as acute as, and could even co-exist with, the fear that other people were talking about him and 'running him down' or 'having a shot at him'. Another POW, who had divorced his wife on return from Ambon but had remarried and returned to his employment for the railways, described it in this way:

> I am really ashamed to admit this, but since my return from captivity, on a slight upset I just break up and cry. Prior to my enlistment and captivity I led a social and sporting life, being a keen tennis and squash player, also was treasurer of the Lawn Tennis Club and actively associated with social bodies. Now due to my condition I am unable to partake of any sport, and when with a number of people I cannot enter into any conversation and just tremble in case I am called on to voice an opinion. The result is I just stay at home and very seldom go out, then only to visit close relations.

This man did not have confidence to speak his own mind; Ronald feared being shunned or slighted. Both mental states speak to a sensibility shaped by shame.

Ronald further confessed that he was 'always looking' at what people said to discover if there was 'any hidden meaning in it'. Given that many other prisoners reported this feeling of 'inferiority', it is tempting to see it as a consequence of the ways in which defeat and imprisonment challenged masculine identity. Perhaps it was. Or maybe the awkward status of POWs had to reverberate with other, pre-existing psychological states or proclivities to produce a feeling of inferiority. In Ronald's case, there is only one clue. In 1953 his clinical notes recorded his sense that other people were 'passing comments of a derogatory nature, whether inferring a dependence on Repatriation, or suggesting a sexual perversion'.

The implication of 'sexual perversion', usually in the 1950s a shorthand reference to homosexuality, occurs nowhere else on Ronald's file. It would be drawing rather a long bow to suggest that this lifelong bachelor was a homosexual merely because he never married. We cannot know if a repressed sexuality compounded his troubles. Yet Ronald realised that his suspicions about other people might not always be well founded and once stated that, even though he felt judged and criticised by others, 'the trouble may be in himself'.

Repatriation doctors described Ronald's physique as 'pyknic', a polite way of saying that he was obese. By the early 1950s his weight had ballooned to 133 kilograms, which is heavy even for a man of Ronald's height. Perhaps the weight gain could be attributed to the medications he took to manage his nervous condition. There were also other lifestyle factors that eroded his physique. Loneliness and depression led him to the bottle. He admitted to being reasonably happy and contented during the working week (if he had a job), but he found the weekends 'almost unbearable … stuck out here like a hermit with no friends or entertainment of any sort'. Alcohol made him 'garrulous and euphoric', but the bouts of drinking a bottle of whisky a night when he could get it, or two dozen beers in a sitting, were taking their toll.

Alcoholism was a common complaint in cases that came before the Prisoners of War Trust Fund. While some men tried to deny or downplay their drinking, others were prepared to discuss its impact on their lives. This was especially the case if they had finally managed to control their addiction. Alcoholism was in many ways another form of imprisonment, its utter selfishness isolating men from their families, the dictates of needing a drink controlling their thoughts as well as their actions. One man, finally sober after thirty years of drinking 'and all that goes with it, the degradation, humiliation, lies, cheating, the fear and guilt that the alcoholic life embraces', profoundly regretted the way it had affected his wife and family. 'This is what the war had turned me into,' he remarked of the money wasted on alcohol, 'depriving my family of such little things so I could have my drink'.

Alcoholism exacerbated other physical and mental complaints. In Ronald's case, his blood pressure was at dangerously low levels. He started to have falls in the street, which he attributed to the hypotension rather than the alcohol. In 1961 he fell so awkwardly that he broke his ankle, and his nose was almost torn from his face and had to be sewn back on. The physical complaints compounded his nervous condition, and job interviews became a torture. 'When I go for an interview I get a nervous twitch & sweat & am continually wiping my face with my handkerchief also I have been asked if I was a POW & when I say yes even when I try to get a temperory job also my nervous state in appearance causes me to loose the job.' In this jumbled, almost stream-of-consciousness description, it appears that Ronald assumed that his nervousness and jumpiness would be attributed to his imprisonment, and that once alerted to his status as a former prisoner employers would be even less likely to give him a chance.

Ronald's depression and drinking were matched by bouts of acute mania. He told doctors that his mind raced ahead of what he could say or write, and he developed fantasies about the untapped wealth of his family. He had traced his family 'way back past 648' and had developed a conviction that there was money in the Chancery owing to him. Although he was 'mentally alert and of above average intelligence', the depression and mania led doctors to conclude that he had all the 'classical affective swings of a manic depressive'. Ronald himself, who had rudimentary spelling, always described himself as having 'mania sycosas'. His manic depression was accompanied by a list of other complaints: 'acute fear of the future, fear of the unknown, sweating & shivering at night, not sleeping, unable to eat at times through feeling ill'. There had been two operations for internal bleeding in his stomach, four compounded vertebrae and osteoarthritis.

By the early 1960s Ronald had returned from the far north and was again living in Brisbane. Repatriation had granted him a full pension for his various health conditions, but he remained fearful that it might be rescinded. Indeed, specialists deemed that the topic of the pension had become an obsession for him. Ronald shuttled back and forth between the repatriation hospital and his room in a boarding house, repeatedly applying to the Prisoners of War Trust Fund for the cost of a new suit in case he had to prepare for a job interview. His hat, he said, was stained with hair oil, and he needed a new one.

The trustees were never sympathetic to Ronald's case. They viewed his constant moving through northern Queensland and his complaints about the squalor of the mission station as evidence that he was 'just a bit work shy'. His heartfelt letter was considered 'a long screed', the implication being that it was self-indulgent. Ted Fisher, however, gave him the benefit of the doubt, owing to Repatriation's assessment of his psychiatric condition. He received a small grant in the 1950s and a further £100 in the early 1960s to assist him with the suit but was not trusted to spend it wisely. The Red Cross was called in to pay accounts

Rebuilding a life

at various tailors and department stores to ensure that Ronald spent the money as intended. It is unlikely that he ever attended another job interview. His stints in the repatriation hospital grew longer, his empty room at the boarding house a stark reminder of his postwar rootlessness and solitude. Within a few years Ronald was dead, from a stroke, at the age of sixty-one, his remains cremated and interred in a Brisbane cemetery.

William

William was younger than Ronald – in his late twenties – when he left Australia in 1941. He had been born in a country town but had spent much of his life in the city. His parents lived in the inner suburbs, where his father worked variously as a cook and a carpenter. Even though his parents still lived together when William went off to war, the home had been violent throughout his childhood. When he was only twelve years old, his mother had charged his father with assault at the local courthouse. 'He has assaulted me before', she told the magistrate. 'I am frightened that he will do me harm.'

William was keen to avoid the vicissitudes of insecure work that had dogged his father throughout the Depression. By his early twenties he was a hairdresser, had married Dorothy and lived near to his parents. Before Dorothy had turned twenty, they had two daughters. What, therefore, compelled him to join up? The motivations for enlistment can be difficult to divine. It later became clear that William's marriage was not a happy one. There were other push and pull factors. After the Depression some wanted more secure employment, others a chance to see the world. Patriotism and sense of duty cannot be discounted either. In William's case perhaps it was a chance to vindicate the family's name. His father had unsuccessfully applied to join the first AIF. William, in contrast, was accepted and assigned to a battalion.

William was far from the ideal soldier. After undergoing rudimentary training, his battalion arrived in Malaya in February 1941. During training he had gone absent without leave several times, and when on service in Malaya he ran foul of army discipline by drinking, swearing and brawling. Once the campaign began, the battalion fought in the southern and eastern parts of Malaya and was still fighting in Singapore when the British surrendered. Its members were imprisoned in Changi. Some of them were taken on work parties to the Thai–Burma Railway; William was sent to Korea in August 1942 and spent the rest of the war there. When liberated in 1945 he was suffering from malaria and dysentery. After a month-long stay in hospital on Morotai Island (now part of Indonesia), he finally returned to Australia in November 1945.

Intrigued by the cultures he had encountered as a soldier and a captive, William, who returned to domestic discord, was inspired to return overseas. Unlike many other released prisoners, he did not seek immediate discharge and by May 1946 was serving again, this time as part of the British Commonwealth Occupation Force in Japan, where he remained until late 1947. He later claimed to have been curious to see what Japan looked like 'from the other side of the fence'. Returning to old patterns, he engaged in 'conduct to the prejudice of good order and military discipline' and resumed his pattern of drinking and going absent without leave. During this period he also gave evidence about his Korean camp guards at war crimes trials in Yokohama. As soon as the trials were concluded, he sought to leave the army. Interviewed by journalists who greeted his troopship upon its return to Australia, he said that there were too many restrictions placed on the occupation force's members: 'So much of Japan is

Rebuilding a life

out of bounds for Australians that it is like being back in camp again'. Privately, William applied for discharge on compassionate grounds, because he needed to attend to his marital affairs. Although it had been possible for wives and children to accompany occupation force members to Japan, Dorothy and the girls had stayed behind in Australia.

William's marriage had been troubled before he enlisted. The month he had returned to Australia from captivity, he had begun divorce proceedings. Dorothy had admitted to an affair with a member of the Swedish merchant navy during the war and in any case was uninterested in reuniting with her husband. She had taken out a summons against him for assault before the war, in a sad echo of the violence that had dogged his parents' own relationship. The marriage ended officially in 1949 but had in effect been over for many years before that. William later claimed that he had heard about his wife's infidelity while he was still on active service in Malaya.

After his divorce William struggled to find work and led an unsettled existence. In early 1948 he had told his estranged wife, 'I am trying my hardest to get back to Japan, even if I have to stow away'. He had insisted that a divorce was pressing because he and five other ex-servicemen planned to buy a large diesel launch and start a business in the 'Far East'. It appears to have been the last time William had a concrete plan for employment, and it is telling that returning to Asia as a businessman seems to have been a fantasy. Within months of announcing this plan, William was on the road, and not to Japan. Indeed, the divorce was delayed because neither his mother nor his ex-wife knew of his whereabouts. By 1952 he was able to claim that since his discharge from the army he had 'wandered in every state in the Commonwealth working in some, sometimes one week or a day or maybe 2 months the longest, [and had] not been able to settle down'. He estimated that he was 'working perhaps eight months of the year, sometimes ill, but mainly travelling from state to state'. He added to his long-held record for public drunkenness, with arrests all over the country. Much later, he admitted that all the wandering had been linked to 'not knowing exactly what I wanted'.

Some POWs put instability in employment and frequent moves down to their troubles in relationships with other people. 'Difficulty mixing' was a common phrase used in applications to the Prisoners of War Trust Fund; 'desire to be alone' was another. The more poetic referred to 'wanderlust'. 'Being moody and irritable,' one man confessed, 'I find it difficult to mix with other company at work or at leisure. This condition isolates me to a large extent'. A former tram conductor claimed, 'Before I went away and captivity in my job I was known as Jovial Tom. Now I am morose and want to be on my own. Mentally I cannot suffer to be crossed by anybody. Think the world is against me. Recluse'. One man considered that he had a 'terrific desire for some sort of privacy', which he attributed to his 'confinement whilst a POW'. 'When discharged all I wanted to do was get away from all men', a Queensland farmer stated, adding that he had 'developed into a kind of lone wolf', finding it 'very hard to work or mix with other people'. Even in the 1960s a former prisoner claimed that he couldn't get along with anyone 'without going into violent fits of temper and smashing things up'; after these bouts he was unable to remember what had occurred.

Admitting to random acts of violence was relatively rare, but another common refrain was the challenge of accepting the authority of a workplace superior: 'I can't settle down, or stand being ordered around by a boss'. A South Australian veteran admitted, 'Somehow or other I have become incompatible & cannot get along with employers'. Consequently he had endured long periods of unemployment, because he would 'pick a row' with his superiors. In one job, all had been progressing smoothly until he began to receive instructions. 'These annoyed me very much & my brain seemed to go haywire. I know now that I cannot work under any Boss as a result of my captivity & I'm working for my keep with friends who know me well and will put up with me.' Another former POW who had been only nineteen years old when taken captive claimed, 'Since I have returned home I cannot stand anyone bossing & standing over me, when ever this happens to me, I get that mad that I sometimes lose compleat controll of myself'.

Resentment and anger were common responses to authority; another was fear: 'Since my captivity I have developed an infeirity complex. If spoken to by anyone of authority I shake uncontrollably'. The conflation of boss and captor seems almost inevitable, but very few seem to have made the connection in an overt way. A doctor at a Red Cross residential facility in Melbourne told the wife of a man who had become addicted to prescription drugs as a consequence of his extreme anxiety condition that he was 'completely ORIENTATED to the Japanese POW system'.

William had issues with alcohol and violence before he went to war, and perhaps captivity compromised his capacity for steady employment. There were other facets of his character, too, that were in evidence before his time as a POW and continued to create trouble thereafter. William's first wife was only sixteen when they married, and while this was a legal marriageable age, a predilection for young girls became evident in the postwar years. By the mid-1960s William could claim to have finally found happiness with a 'young girl' he had met at an RSL hostel. 'She is', he wrote, 'everything I have ever wanted'. William was in his fifties and when this teenage partner became pregnant, the couple moved to the city, where they gave up for adoption the baby he

The POW story

had fathered, 'due to the big differences in our ages'. Despite living in a cold, rented flat, with very few possessions, William described himself as 'contented' for the first time in years.

William's account of his peripatetic postwar life for the trust fund omitted some essential developments, especially his return to imprisonment. Details of the criminal trial for his offence reveal not only the difficulty in gauging to what extent wartime captivity could explain postwar dysfunction but also the ways in which contemporaries believed that it might. William's marriage had had its problems before the war, and it appears that Dorothy's tentative grip on respectability slipped once she had divorced William. For reasons that are unclear, within four years of their divorce, Dorothy was no longer in control of her daughters, who had become wards of the Children's Welfare Department. The youngest daughter, at least, continued to be in irregular contact with her father. One summer she visited him at a repatriation hospital while he was being treated for war neurosis. The events of the evening that followed resulted in William being convicted of carnal knowledge of his daughter and being sentenced to five years' jail.

In the company of his daughter William left his neurosis ward and went into town for a meal and a picture show. During the outing his daughter told him that she felt miserable, and he suggested that she spend the night at the YWCA. In response the daughter stated that she was so 'fed up' that if William left her alone she would commit suicide. William's solution was to book them into a hotel for the night. Perhaps the hotel keeper was suspicious; the following morning members of the vice squad burst in and demanded an explanation as to why this forty-year-old man had spent the night with a girl.

The court's interpretation of William's interaction with his daughter demonstrates how women and girls sometimes shouldered the blame for the shortcomings of men. At the trial, the daughter was painted as a 'temptress' who did not lead a chaste life. The issue of consent was blurry, at best. William's defence lawyer established that the daughter was not a virgin and that William had 'not exactly' forced himself on her: 'she went there willingly'. The daughter claimed that she had spent so little time with her father that she thought of him as 'just an ordinary man – not as a father'. Her response to the arrival of the vice squad, with its reference to a girls' home – 'This will mean Parramatta for me' – suggested a familiarity with the child welfare system rather than any kind of moral culpability for her father's behaviour. The judge considered that the girl's mother should 'bear her share of responsibility for the present tragedy', because she had 'associated with other men' while William was away at war.

William, who had a past record of heavy drinking, claimed events in the room were 'all a blank'. Yet it was he who had registered the couple as 'Mr and Mrs Curlewis' while claiming to have 'no thought of anything improper'. It might have been a coincidence, but Adrian Curlewis was a well-known ex-POW officer and judge and an eminently respectable public figure. This story also differed from William's response when the police had arrested him at the hotel. The arrest report stated that when faced with evidence of his crime (a used condom on the floor beside the bed), William had commented, 'I am only a mongrel and a heel for doing this to my own daughter'. Later at the police station William had said, 'It was all my fault from the start ... I cannot offer any explanation as to why I did this awful thing to my daughter'. Yet his counsel used his experiences as a POW as partial justification for his actions, arguing that his privations during that time were responsible for the 'sapping of his moral fibre'. Despite the efforts to shift blame onto a sexually precocious daughter and her equally deviant mother, the court found

William guilty of carnal knowledge. Sentencing him to five years, the judge nevertheless considered the incest the result of 'mental illness' and promised to release William on licence within six months if he had psychiatric treatment and appeared to be 'cured'.

William, as the girl's father, should not have crossed the boundary from affection to sexual interaction. Even if his daughter had been so damaged by her childhood that she struggled to differentiate between the two, as an adult man William bore the responsibility to hold the line. It is difficult to see how imprisonment in the war could have so sapped his 'moral fibre' that he could no longer make the distinction between daughter and sexual partner. His early marriage, to a sixteen-year-old girl, and his later partnering with a woman almost forty years his junior, would rather suggest that girls were his sexual preference. Captivity may not have caused that perversion, but in the eyes of William's defence counsel it went some way towards excusing it. The judge's assurance that William could prove himself 'cured' after psychiatric treatment suggests that he held at least some sympathy with this view.

William appears to have remained with the teenager he met at the RSL home for the rest of his life. He certainly married her and she is listed as the next of kin on his death certificate. Yet it seems unlikely that he found the happiness with her that he so craved. In February 1974 he wrote to the army records office, 'At present I don't think I have too much longer to go. I have too many complaints, and none that can be cured, easing of pain, yes, but curing me is not possible'. Within six months he was dead, the cause listed as 'wilfully self-administered barbiturate poisoning'. His wife had not been alarmed when he had stumbled into their home in the early evening in an alcoholic stupor and had gone to bed. She kept watching television and only discovered him dead some hours later. Whether William had been 'cured' of the problem that corrupted his relationship with his own child, or if he damaged any other children, is not clear.

Kenneth

Kenneth, an insurance salesman, was thirty years old when he enlisted. Recently married to Jean, he had been living a settled and semi-prosperous life before he went to war. The couple's wedding had been reported in minute detail in the newspaper of the bride's hometown, down to the shapes of necklines and floral bouquets. The groom's parents had not been present; his father was recorded as already dead and his mother was unable to attend. A little over two years later, now father to a toddler, Kenneth enlisted and in February 1942 sailed for Singapore. He saw a total of twenty-two days' action before being captured, when Singapore fell.

Kenneth was repatriated to Brisbane by the end of September 1945. He was unwell enough to spend the following four months at Repatriation General Hospital, Greenslopes. While a patient there, he put on some new boots – unfamiliar after years spent wearing worn-out shoes and cobbled-together replacements – and promptly lost his balance. This resulted in a skull fracture that the army deemed no fault of his own but sufficiently severe to impair his future capacity as a soldier and warrant his medical discharge. In January 1946 Kenneth rejoined his family.

Much had changed in the years Kenneth had been away. Like many other repatriates, he had to find a place in family dynamics that had moved on without him. Always wary of Jean's relationship with her overbearing parents – they had, he claimed, 'an inordinate influence' over her – he had pleaded with her to resist any overtures to go back and live with them. But alone with a young child, and soon to give birth to another, she could hardly resist. By the time Kenneth returned from captivity, he found that his mother-in-law had become firmly ensconced within his own family following his father-in-law's death during the war.

When he left Greenslopes Kenneth was already on a 30 per cent 'neurosis pension'. Even though he had enough money to purchase a house, the housing crisis meant that new homes were in short supply and Kenneth was forced to rent a half-house for his now-extended family. 'I could not escape from constant bickerings and interference', he later recalled, and he found his mother-in-law's assumption of control over his wife and children particularly galling. Long denied power over his own destiny in the prison camp, he had returned to find a domestic jailer from whom he could never escape. 'This condition was so ravaging to my mental equilibrium', he observed, 'that I began to retreat within the folds of alcohol oblivion'.

There were potentially several factors playing with Kenneth's 'mental equilibrium'. In April 1947 when making a statement to Australian war crimes investigators, he had revisited a shocking wartime incident to which he had been witness. Five years earlier, while still a prisoner, he had been assigned as a staff car driver to the *Kempeitai* in Burma. In May 1942 the *Kempeitai* arrested a Burmese man and Kenneth drove the party to a prison cell in Victoria Point, a town in the far south of Burma, on the Thai border. Kenneth later learned that the Burmese man had been a native policeman for the British administration and was suspected of burying papers for the British during their hurried evacuation. Each day for six days, Kenneth drove the *Kempeitai* to the cells and parked fifteen metres from the cell wall. There he heard 'screams of agony' and 'many sounds which sounded like heavy blows to a human body' that 'became feeble after a time'. A local man told him that the Burmese was being tortured 'by means of suspending him from a wooden rafter in the cell by the thumbs with pieces of cord so that his naked body was directly over a small fire on the concrete floor of the cell'. On the seventh day Kenneth was ordered to collect the Burmese man's wife and his daughter, whom he estimated was about five years old. Escorted into the cell, the woman and child started screaming and crying, sounds which intensified when the guards executed the man. After this episode concluded Kenneth drove the pair home; 'the woman was hysterical with grief and the child cried bitterly'. Kenneth did not mention these awful scenes in his correspondence with the Prisoners of War Trust Fund, but the detail in which he described them five years after the events suggests that his memory of such suffering remained acute.

The toll of a long captivity and of witnessing horrific events intersected with other elements in Kenneth's life and personality to shape his experience of homecoming. As he was suffering from an anxiety state as a result of his war experiences, living in close quarters with a mother-in-law he despised did not make for an auspicious return to civilian life. The situation also quite possibly triggered anxieties and psychic discomforts of an earlier period, given Kenneth's own rather mysterious past.

Kenneth had constructed an elaborate fiction about his family background. His mother had been only thirteen when she gave birth to him in South Australia in 1910. No father is named on his birth certificate. It is unclear where Kenneth spent his childhood, even though it is possible to trace his mother through newspapers, as she eventually married, blossomed into a teacher of some repute and joined the speakers circuit. There is no mention of this son, born when she was barely in her teens, in any accounts of her life, so we must presume he was raised by someone else, either a family member passing him off as a son or in a children's home or orphanage. In the early twentieth century, children born out of wedlock were often folded into families or institutions in this way. Kenneth did say his family was from South Australia, but exactly how he ended up in Queensland as a young adult is unclear. Communication was also rudimentary enough that his upstanding in-laws are unlikely to have been aware that he had been convicted of stealing in the mid-1930s. Still, he must have been a convincing salesman: a Salvation Army officer appearing at his trial had vouched that he deserved leniency because he was a superior type of person.

Kenneth's slide into alcoholism by the early 1950s eroded the modest material comfort that the family he created in Queensland had known before the war. He referred to his circumstances as a 'labyrinth of despair', which culminated in the family's five-year residence at Rocklea housing camp in Brisbane. The acute housing shortage in the city had led the Queensland Housing Commission to convert wartime service huts into temporary housing camps. By 1954 there were 8000 people living in five such camps across the metropolitan area. The camps became notorious in the press for their cramped conditions and crimes that occurred within them prompted fears of deviance and juvenile delinquency. In the Police Court a solicitor described the camps as 'one of the sores of our civilization'. The irony of his longed-for freedom being spent in a miserable former Royal Australian Air Force camp in overcrowded huts was not lost on Kenneth. He described the camp as 'squalor comparable with what was endured as a Japanese captive'. The drinking got worse when, while they were resident in Rocklea, Kenneth's two-year-old son died from diphtheria, a disease linked to overcrowded and unsanitary living conditions.

The camp environment and the dysfunction of Kenneth's relationships within the home did not help his rehabilitation. Jean had considered his initial decision to enlist a desertion of sorts and never forgave him for it. He claimed that she did not write for the entire period of his absence, but there were many men who received no letters. Despite the fractious and tense relationship between Kenneth and Jean, the children continued to arrive, in keeping with their Catholic faith. Kenneth's drinking also persisted and eventually led to criminal charges for driving under the influence of alcohol. His inclination was to escape; this began what he later described as 'three years of running'. His journey came to an end when he was admitted as a psychiatric patient at a repatriation hospital in Sydney, where he encountered Ted Fisher. Fisher's insistence on respectability, while not making him a man of deep empathy, in this case prompted Kenneth's return to his family. 'I was advised to stop running', Kenneth recalled, and he returned to serve out his three-month jail term in Brisbane for the driving offence, afterwards reuniting with his wife and children. He confessed that he could 'never attain a peaceful state', even when he was absent from his wife, as he 'felt oppressed by a sense of aggrieved injustice'.

Kenneth felt some hope had arrived when he made a successful application for a war service home, in a scheme providing modest houses built at concessional finance rates for veterans in recognition of their service. But it was still a fall from grace that he felt keenly. 'Had I not enlisted and become a P.O.W. I would have without doubt retained full control of my affairs', he insisted in 1954, 'with reasonable prospects of continuing my successful career and most certainly would not have degenerated to the appalling degree outlined in the forgoing'. The Prisoners of War Trust Fund helped him with the deposit, but the trustees were inclined to check with St Vincent de Paul (on whom his wife and children had depended during his absence) and the ex-POW association to see if he had indeed changed his ways. This level of surveillance, of his drinking, his familial relationships and his finances, all pointed to his reduced station in life.

The POW story

Throughout the late 1950s, Kenneth continued to attempt to rehabilitate himself and reach a compromise with his wife. 'There was always present an undercurrent of bitterness' from Jean, he felt, 'when many wounding remarks were made to the effect that I must have crawled to the Japanese to survive'. By then a mother of seven children, she resented the need to work part-time to contribute to the family's income when Kenneth's sales commissions failed. Kenneth felt that he might have tolerated such criticisms, but in combination with his mother-in-law's barbs he perceived 'a general ganging up' against him. 'I have found myself totally rejected.' By the early 1960s he had experienced a complete nervous breakdown and found himself back in Greenslopes.

The sales work at which Kenneth had excelled before the war was not suitable for a broken, alcoholic, neurotic and anxious person who seemed to take no joy in his life. In desperation, he sought vocational guidance and undertook a boot repair traineeship, but for a man in his fifties this was vain hope, and no work was found. By 1963 Repatriation had deemed him totally and permanently incapacitated, and the financial pressure eased somewhat. His absences from the family continued, however: in the late 1960s he resided for three years in a facility for the mentally ill at Wacol, in the western suburbs of Brisbane.

After 1968, having refused Kenneth any further assistance, after deeming him 'a chronic case' many years before, the trustees of the Prisoners of War Trust Fund heard no further word from him. He lived until 1982 and died at the age of seventy-two in a place that had become very familiar to him: Greenslopes hospital. Despite their travails – Jean's resentment and Kenneth's alcoholism and 'nerves' – the couple appear to have stayed together until the end. Jean still lived in the war service home Kenneth had fought so hard to secure in the 1950s. The upkeep on the house was a cause of great consternation for Kenneth as he struggled to make ends meet and educate their large family. Yet at one point it had been the haven that inspired him: 'You can well imagine my feelings when I observe this gleaming home which is so closely within reach, yet without help, so tragically remote'.

※

At the ends of their lives Ronald, William and Kenneth were three very different men: an unmarried loner, an aging sexual deviant and an anxious, alcoholic family man. Perhaps the only thing that united them was their experience of imprisonment during the war. We know little of Ronald's family background, and Kenneth's is equally elusive, although he appears to have had no contact with his father and to have been estranged from his mother. William witnessed violence in his childhood home, a pattern he continued with his own wife before going away to war. These men were not veterans who could be quietly folded back into families that had independent resources to support them or the ability to offer a period of solace and succour as they readjusted to freedom and civilian life. Perhaps William's membership of the British Commonwealth Occupation Force and Ronald's attempt to enlist for service in Korea suggest that the army had become a substitute form of security.

None of the three appears to have been highly educated or in professional employment before the war, but they had forged relatively stable working lives. Ronald had a thirteen-year career with the National Roads and Motorists' Association, William was a hairdresser with his own business and, after a slightly rocky start, Kenneth had married well and was an effective insurance salesman. Yet all three struggled to regain their standing in the world of work after the war. Employment in service and sales careers that presumably required a positive and cheerful disposition with the public militated against their successful resumption. Kenneth was explicit that such a high level of engagement was afterwards beyond him, Ronald could not stand up to the demands of the daily routine, and William never mentioned why he did not return to hairdressing. All three failed to rehabilitate to their prewar working level, spent long periods of time in repatriation hospitals and became increasingly reliant on the service pension to make ends meet. Kenneth at least owned his own, modest home; Ronald and William lived out their lives in boarding houses and hostels. These men were not well placed to ride the postwar economic boom, which ultimately saw full employment and rising living standards.

All three men spent periods on the road in a peripatetic and unsettled state. This most often coincided with intensive periods of alcoholism, another theme running through all three cases. Ronald and William were the most extreme in this regard, moving throughout Australia to more and more remote country towns, and William sometimes drying out in the local lock-up. They were engaged not so much in an effort to find a place to belong as in a relentless mode of escape from situations that did not work out. Kenneth described his own more modest geographical move from Brisbane to Sydney as 'running'. Ultimately, each man ended up back where he began – in a major city – with varying levels of connection to family.

Ronald died alone and did not have any children. We know that William's first marriage did not survive the war and that his second repeated a pattern of involvement with girls that, on the information available, appears to have been a form of sexual deviance. While it was extremely unlikely that there was any connection between wartime captivity and this type of offending, the case is instructive for what it reveals about the level of dysfunction in William's life and more particularly about the concessions given to servicemen in the court system. William avoided mention of his problems with the law to the trustees but was quite forthcoming about the difficulties of his first marriage and his love for his second wife. Kenneth was equally frank about the tensions and strains of his marriage.

The trustees left very few comments in the trust fund files on the level of intimacy with which former prisoners discussed their marriages, despite the astonishing frankness of some applicants. Entirely without intention, the trustees had designed an application form that encouraged former prisoners to offer what is now extremely rare testimony about men's views of marriage in the postwar period. It is worth considering in more detail what these views were.

6

POW marriages

> Are you experiencing material prejudice (from other than health causes) as a direct result of your captivity? If so, give full details.
>
> *Prisoners of War Trust Fund application form, 1952–77*[1]

In its twenty-five years of operation the Prisoners of War Trust Fund did not change its application form. This was despite the fact that one question, about 'material prejudice', caused an enormous amount of confusion. Since the First World War, Repatriation had used the phrase 'material prejudice' to describe financial and other forms of disadvantage.[2] For many veterans the meaning of this formal, legalistic phrase was unclear. Numerous applicants to the Prisoners of War Trust Fund could not understand the term. Some wrote a question mark in response to the query; others were more frank: 'Don't understand the question'.

There was a series of other responses to the question, however, that on first viewing seems curious. 'Yes. My married life was ruined.' 'Yes. Divorced my wife for adultery whilst in captivity.' 'Yes. My wife refuses to lie with me as a wife though I still support her. Told me her love for me had died whilst I was a POW.' One man replied that he had a 'lack of initiative to carry on normal marital relations'. Another was more blunt: 'Unable to have intercourse with a woman'. These applicants, it seems, thought that the trustees were asking them about their *marital* situation. The trustees could not have anticipated that their form would open a vein, and that out of it would pour returned POWs' stories of dysfunctional marriages, family breakdowns and impotence. Some men believed that their experience of captivity had been, quite literally, emasculating.

A broad range of matrimonial experiences appears in the fund papers, from acrimonious divorces and resentment about women who were unfaithful during the long years of captivity to songs of praise about stoic wives. The very few female POWs who applied to the fund did not discuss their relationships or reveal any particularly personal information. In contrast, some male applicants admitted to a fury that was barely quenched by alcohol and then temporarily sated by turning on the family. Less commonly, there were men prepared to expose their battle with impotence with surprising frankness for an era in which intimacy, sexuality and masculinity were most often handled with coy evasion. The most fortunate were men whose partners took up the battle when they no longer could, cared for them and fought for their entitlements from the government authorities.

The happily married formed the group least likely to correspond with a state bureaucrat about the nature of their relationships. A successful life, a supportive wife or husband, a functional family: these are memories former POWs have been willing to share in other contexts, as they are testimony to the strength of relationships that were essential to the hard work of rehabilitation.[3] We should not underestimate the happy or contented life that is less likely to leave its archival trace. However, here we are concerned with those for whom questions of sexuality, marriage and companionship were more, rather than less, fraught. It has been more difficult and uncomfortable for families and former POWs themselves to dwell on the legacy of living with a damaged man. 'We were never allowed to talk about what was troubling him', recalled Susan Moxham, daughter of Sandakan survivor Bill.[4] Susan's childhood and those of her siblings, and the married life of her mother Wilma were blighted by years of family violence and Bill's alcohol abuse. In 1956 her parents divorced: 'I'm sure he would have killed us if we'd stayed'. Susan's father committed suicide in 1961, and by the time of a 2007 interview her mother was suffering dementia. Some members of the second generation, like Susan, have been prepared to share their memories of living with returned prisoners, but evidence from the 1950s and 1960s, as former POWs and their wives renegotiated relationships, is still relatively rare.[5] The Trust Fund papers show that, while women prioritised captivity as an explanation for dysfunction, medical professionals were more likely to see work-shy, evasive or sexually neurotic men.

Libidinal impairment

Did captivity result in a condition that some Repatriation doctors referred to as 'libidinal impairment'? Former POWs used more colloquial and colourful terms, citing a loss of 'sexual power', 'will' and 'potency'. There were concerns during captivity that malnutrition might affect fertility and a deflection of fears about virility with the often-cited joke: 'The second thing I'll do when I get home is take my pack off'.[6] The causes of impotence can include emotional or psychological disturbance but also range from the side-effects of medication to cardiac conditions, endocrine diseases like diabetes and neurological and nerve disorders. While the incidence of impotence in a cohort of men might include any of these factors, particularly as they enter middle age, it is noteworthy that some former POWs linked their sexual troubles to the legacy of captivity. This was the compromised masculinity of captivity manifest in bodily form. In 1955 Harvey considered that life as a POW had rendered him 'absolutely a failure with women for intercourse'. For Arthur it was unclear whether the problem was impotence or sterility. He claimed that sterility caused him 'many mental upsets' but then qualified this by writing, 'This condition of mine is not a physical disability but the mental hardship of it cannot be stressed upon too much it has nearly caused a whole upset of my marriage and anyone who has the good position to be able to produce couldn't possibly know the feeling on one's mental state of mind'.

Returned POWs who suffered from impotence assumed that their wives were entitled to sexual satisfaction and were frustrated by their incapacity to provide it. By the 1950s experts, counsellors, therapists and, increasingly, women themselves insisted that a strong sexual connection and mutual enjoyment of sex were essential for a successful marriage.[7] The unhappiness of wives was a common refrain among men who complained about their failure to perform. Eugene thought that his impotence caused his wife to become 'indifferent' to him and that consequently their 'home life' was 'not what could be called happy'. Frank did not mention it on his application form but in 1952 wrote a separate letter to the trustees about his 'marital relations', which he had not mentioned previously, 'owing to personal embarrassment at the time … Sexual intercourse with my wife is in-frequent and unsatisfactory, & my wife is left in a state of frustration on almost every occasion. At times, as long as two months have lapsed between the times when we have attempted this very vital part of married life, & even then I have disappointed my wife'. To underscore the point, Frank noted that he was thirty-three and his wife twenty-seven years old. By 1960 they had separated. In 1952 Edward, who had been too nervous to drive a car since his release from captivity, was unable to 'indulge in sexual intercourse'. Almost ten years later he still complained about his 'inability to lead a normal married life' and the subsequent loss of affection from his wife.

Wives themselves were frequently baffled and distressed by this turn of events. One wife whose husband was hospitalised with extreme anxiety state in the early 1970s, told the trustees that after this episode there was 'a complete loss of desire for sex – absolute opposite to previous needs'. To her astonishment, the treating doctor asked if she was willing to 'live the rest of [her] life with a boy'.

Kissing blokes

Psychiatrists were suspicious of men who experienced impotence but appeared untroubled by it, particularly if they had other symptoms of psychological disturbance. Carl's impotence (which he said did not 'worry the wife') was the least of his problems in the early 1950s, which were years dominated by searing pain in his neck, chest and spine. 'I have been racked and racked and racked with pain', he told the psychiatrist. 'I have had feelings of things pumping in my head and chest and almost reached the blackout stage.' Despite the severity of Carl's discomfort, doctors could find no physical cause for his troubles. His brother-in-law insisted on speaking to the treating physicians and explained that up until the year before Carl had been a jovial type of fellow with a bright and active temperament. He was now completely changed: 'lethargic and couldn't care less'. Carl's wife, a 'pleasant, sensible, friendly woman', also reported him as an altered man in recent times. At a loss to account for Carl's symptoms, the doctors considered them to be hysterical and prescribed psychiatric medication, electroconvulsive therapy and residential accommodation at a Red Cross facility, Rockingham Home. Ultimately, a psychologist tested Carl in 1956 and concluded that he had a confused psychosexual identification – 'a lack of aggression and strong passive (oral) needs' – and that his marriage was likely to be an area of 'much (perhaps unrecognized) conflict'. Comments like these on the files of POWs reflect the growing influence of psychoanalysis, with its emphasis on unconscious mental processes and infantile sexuality, on the psychiatric profession in postwar Australia.[8] The predisposition theory that held sway with anxiety and neurosis cases in fact encouraged psychiatrists to explore the internal sources of marital dysfunction.

Suspicions of homosexual inclinations were never far from the minds of psychiatrists treating men who appeared indifferent to their wives, who married late in life or who seemed to pine for the companionship of the POW camp. One alcoholic man who did not marry until his early fifties, an only child who had previously relied on 'male companionships and gambling for his emotional outlets', was deemed 'weakly heterosexual' by his treating psychiatrist. The marriage appeared to be 'dictated largely by his sense of loneliness and loss of male companionship – particularly life long friends he lost as P.O.W.'. The intense drinking bouts occurred when he became despondent and nostalgic for his previously independent way of life. Yet the patient had also made a point of noting that while a prisoner he had worked on a mine-detailing party and saw 'four chaps blown to pieces ... [I] picked their remains up for burial, which did not improve my nerves any as I often think about it'. The devastating impact of witnessing such events was less important to the psychiatrists treating this man than their efforts to explore his sexual identifications.

It is difficult to determine the extent of homosexual activity in the prison camps; decreased libido of any sort is an observed phenomenon in situations of privation, and reticence prevailed in postwar POW literature.[9] In one often-cited instance, a POW who described himself as a 'normal male' when free confessed to feeling 'certain homosexual tendencies' during his years of male-only company in captivity.[10] In Changi, Warrant Officer Eric Bailey conducted nighttime patrols because 'certain couples were known to be going to particular spots and indulging in homosexuality'.[11] When undertaking research for his biography of author Russell Braddon, Nigel Starck elicited perhaps one of the most frank statements about homosexual practice in the prison camp, from former POW Jack Garrett. A heterosexual man, Garrett was asked if he had realised during their time together in Changi that Braddon was homosexual.

> JG: 'Yes. He had a boyfriend there [in Changi].'
>
> NS: 'That was apparent in Changi?'
>
> JG: 'Oh yes. Most of the concert party chaps, they had their own boyfriends.'
>
> NS: 'How could you tell he was gay, Jack?'
>
> JG: 'Because you saw him kissing blokes.'[12]

Although Braddon's sexual preference appears to have been well known in his POW camp, there was no mention of it in his memoir of his captivity, *The Naked Island*.

In the postwar period treating physicians often assumed that captivity had offered some men opportunities that they had difficulty relinquishing in civilian life. In an era when homosexuality was considered a mental illness and homosexual practice was illegal, former prisoners who admitted to same-sex desires were most frequently treated as psychiatric patients.[13] A case in point was a man who had been taken prisoner at the age of twenty, had married after the war and by the late 1950s had voluntarily admitted himself to a psychiatric ward: 'I am unable to state the real condition of my health due to my nervous condition. At times I think I am going mental'. The man was 'frigid', suspicious of his wife's conduct and prudish about her dress. Psychiatrists considered this attitude proof of the man's projection of his own 'unsatisfactory heterosexual adjustment'. The prison camp, in their estimation, had been the site of some 'equanimity' for him and he had accepted this withdrawal from the world of women. Yet once such men were released the enormous social pressure to comply with heterosexual norms, and the criminalisation of their sexual preference, meant that they sometimes found themselves as psychiatric patients, not because they were inherently unstable but because there was an unbearable tension between their sexuality and societal expectations. Although he admitted to his same-sex desires, this man entered a panic when he thought others on his ward knew he was homosexual. Psychiatrists prescribed the psychiatric drug chlorpromazine, in keeping with the increasing use of medication from the 1960s to treat mental illnesses, and eventually gave him insulin shock treatment and electroconvulsive therapy. By the early 1970s the patient was totally and permanently incapacitated and never worked again.

Psychiatrists had a professional interest in the sexual proclivities and neuroses of their patients, but the trustees remained silent in the face of evidence from Repatriation about sexual matters and were wary when it came to claims about impotence. When one applicant complained that his wife had left him 'throu sex resones', a trustee quipped, 'I think he is sorry for himself however $50 may buck him up'. There was no further discussion of the claim. Ted Fisher's response to another case was indicative of his attitude. A former prisoner complained of a 'nervous disorder causing upsets in sex relations in married life'. Noting that this man had two children born since his return from the camps, Fisher retorted that he had 'obviously established satisfactory sexual relations twice since return'. When another claimed that his disability consisted of 'sexual neurosis', which gave him an 'inferiority complex' and caused his wife to have a nervous breakdown, Arthur Blackburn was astonished: 'Queer type of major disability'. Fisher begged an entirely improbable naivety: 'I don't know what is implied by sexual neurosis'.

I'll never return to you

15 November 1945

My Darling Nell
    Please come back, life is so empty this way, the home is not complete and after all these years (*21*) you must feel a difference. I am so lonely surely you must think of the love & happiness which *was* ours, and for the darling Children's sake too, It means every thing to us both. & you know we are not getting younger, its just when we need one another. Please Darling I need you more than ever after those years of hell over there was bad enough, but to loose you too its too much. You know in your heart how I love you … we could be one happy little family, in our own little home its not asking much when I ask you to come back for me sake because I realy want and need you love. It is worring me sick I can't sleep don't let me go down, we can go away for a holiday how wonderful that would be you & I together

anywhere you like Darling, I miss your lovely meals, our company and your love. I often think of those happy times when we danced to your or our favourite tune three O'Clock in the morning and how thrilled we were with our first baby how careful we both nursed her.

Please come back I am anxiously waiting and long for you our home is still waiting for you to make it complete.

Your ever loving
Husband
Roy xxx[14]

Roy
I received your letter. I never have any intention of returning to you so this letter is definite. Please do not be writing to me any more as all your writing will not alter me as its definitely No I'll never return to you.

Yours Sincerely
Ellen[15]

Roy was excited to return home to Sydney after his release from Changi.[16] He and some other men jumped ship when it docked in Brisbane on its journey south in early October 1945 and roamed through the town eating ice cream in double cones and guzzling soft drinks. Roy was ebullient: 'We're the healthiest bunch of prisoners ever to come out of Singapore', he told reporters who had gathered to witness the antics.[17] Only two other ships had stopped in Brisbane with returned prisoners before then, and they had been hospital ships, their passengers not yet up to shimmying down the side of the ship on a rope. Already in his mid-forties, Roy was one of the older returning prisoners, but he was in remarkable shape. His delight turned to despair, however, when he reached his final destination in Sydney. His wife Ellen was no longer living in their family home.

The absence of a wife or sweetheart on the docks, at the aerodrome or at the showgrounds, where many families gathered to greet their returning POWs, came as a rude shock to men like Roy. Years of fantasising about reunion, the experience of being loved, eating home-cooked meals, dancing to favourite tunes and rolling over in bed to see a familiar face came to naught, and they became aware that while they had survived imprisonment their marriages had not. Returning POWs were not immune to a broader trend in Australia in the late 1940s which saw a sharp spike in the divorce rate.[18] Some attempted to compel their wives to return via a legal remedy known as the 'restitution of conjugal rights' to spouses abandoned or deserted without cause. The letters that passed between couples as part of this legal process, such as those exchanged between Ellen and Roy, revealed heartbreak and disappointment, even as applicants tried to fortify themselves against such emotions by recourse to the law.

Cedric shared Roy's experience of returning to an empty bed and fought hard to win back his wife. Soon after joining up in 1940 he had married Vera. They rented a property in a Sydney beachside suburb, but they hoped to build their own home after the war was over, so they decided to save as much money as they could. Vera continued to work and Cedric allotted all of his service pay to his wife, keeping only a shilling a day for his personal expenses. In early 1941 Cedric sailed for Malaya and kept the financial arrangement in place. Up to the point of Cedric's capture, he and Vera corresponded regularly and 'were always on affectionate terms', he later recalled. But during the entire three and a half years of his captivity, he received only one letter from Vera (not unusual, given the paucity of mail that reached POWs in Japanese captivity), which he described as a 'letter that kept within me the will to live, as it reconfirmed all our hopes and plans for the future'.

While Cedric spent his captivity contemplating the reunion with his wife, Vera underwent a change of heart in his absence. She lived in their beachside home for only a month. She was not at Mascot to meet Cedric's plane; nor was she at the showgrounds with the other families who assembled to greet returning prisoners. Cedric, still hopeful of a reunion, went and stayed with his in-laws in case his wife appeared there. Eventually, Vera made contact and told him that the marriage was over, but she refused to meet up or explain why. Cedric wrote to her in November 1945, 'Vera, I want you back. I am still very much in love with you and have a home for you to walk into tomorrow if you will only return ... Darling I have the money now to give you anything you want and a good job to go to as soon as I am discharged so together there is nothing we can not do. Think it over darling and write me soon'. Vera was resolute: 'I cannot see that I can ever be happy with you'.[19]

Ellen and Vera, in the brevity of their replies, revealed no clue as to their motivation for ending their marriages. Ellen and Roy's marriage was of long standing – they had two children, aged fourteen and eight – but Cedric and Vera were virtually newlyweds when he departed for Malaya. In other cases, prisoners' absences allowed women to move on from marriages that had been deeply troubled before the war, as was the case of William and Dorothy, discussed in the previous chapter. Some women assumed that their husbands were probably never coming home and, in the loneliness of waiting, formed attachments with other men that they were unable or unprepared to break when their Lazarus returned.

Hating the ones I love

Resuming a marriage after a long absence and in the wake of a difficult captivity sometimes proved more challenging than either party had expected. One man from Tasmania thought that his 'acute mental depressions' had prompted his wife to break up their home. 'I do not blame her but I do blame the four years I spent as a POW.' Complaints about psychiatric disturbance were common, the recourse to violence less so, but the incidence of family violence in the homes of former POWs is impossible to gauge on the evidence of fund applications alone. Historians have long noted the difficulties in establishing rates of domestic violence prior to the 1990s, and even then, problems of underreporting, underpolicing and muted tolerance have militated against a full appreciation of the extent and incidence of such harm inside the home.[20]

Former prisoners could not explain why they had trouble settling down or suddenly turned on their wives. The psychiatrists who treated them also struggled to understand such cases. They took detailed family histories that explored patients' attitudes to women and were attuned to any evidence of sexual neurosis, but were reluctant to attribute to captivity their patients' incapacity to stabilise mood or commit properly to family life. Men reported wanting a home but frequently feeling unable to achieve any kind of equilibrium in a space otherwise welcoming and comfortable. In the early 1950s a tailor from Adelaide who had been forced to give up his business and work in a factory because of his 'bad nerves and fatigue' would 'cause rows' with his wife and children, then go for long walks into the night, questioning why he had said 'such rotten and disgusting things to the ones I loved'. The tailor described this pattern as a form of 'nerve wracking punishment'. He was not alone in being perplexed by such self-destructive behaviour.

Clarence married three years after returning home, when he was in his mid-thirties, but within less than a decade the marriage was in trouble. The couple had one child, a son, whom Clarence described as giving him 'the will to live'. Clarence had a job with Trans Australia Airlines at Mascot and later felt that his war-caused disabilities meant he was not 'robust enough to stand up to the long hours'. By the mid-1950s, he was struggling to retain his job and had lost the ability to concentrate. Then, in late 1955, all at once he hated 'the ones I love and my place of abode'. Clarence would criticise his wife incessantly – about the way she was rearing their son, about her housework – but then would be 'very affectionate and annoy her because I ask her so many times does she love me'. He ended up in a state of nervous collapse and was admitted to a repatriation hospital. There, the psychiatrists reported that he looked thin and drawn and would continue talking 'without being stimulated to – especially over how efficient and popular he was' and about how he had 'faded' from that earlier self. They found him 'remorseful over his critical attitude to his wife'. The report continued, 'His eyes fill with tears when discussing this – admits to feeling depressed and remorseful one day – next day more critical and even sadistic to wife – next day more depressed'. Clarence claimed he 'couldn't be bothered' having sex with his wife after she had experienced some gynaecological problems.

Clarence wanted to reconcile with his wife but realised that his nasty and critical behaviour had permanently alienated her; he confessed to being 'mentally cruel' and that he had left a 'scar of bitterness on my wife's mind'. He continued with their plan of building a home with a war service loan, but his wife remained living with her relatives. Clarence turned one of the rooms into a workshop but was too scared to use it in case he ruined it. Worried about the integrity of this workshop, in the meantime he had utterly destroyed his marriage. The divorce papers lodged by his wife in 1956 make clear that his abuse of her was more than verbal: the court found that he had 'repeatedly assaulted and cruelly beaten' her for the best part of a year.

It seems, at least from the evidence of psychiatrists, doctors and Clarence himself, that he had developed a deeply ambivalent relationship to his wife and home, at once idealising and demonising them. The psychiatrist's observation that his behaviour towards his wife was 'sadistic' is telling: this was a word frequently used in postwar Australia to describe the behaviour of Japanese guards towards their prisoners. Elements of Clarence's case echoed the imprisonment experience: the psychological tug of war in which he attempted to control his wife, quite possibly transferring onto her his own experience of being dominated; the idealisation of home that had been a common fantasy in prison camps, but one which struggled to meet the reality of daily existence. Yet these possible explanations for Clarence's behaviour were not traversed in psychiatric reports on his neurotic state. Instead, there was a focus on his relationship with his 'placid' mother. He was quoted as saying 'I think wonderful women they seem to have a deep affection for their men'. A treating physician described Clarence's efforts at reconciliation as 'pathetic and sentimental'. No one commented on the physical abuse Clarence's wife had suffered at his hands, which was exactly coincident with his mental deterioration.

Without a large-scale statistical and demographic study, which is not possible owing to the privacy provisions governing archives containing personal information, it is difficult to determine the extent of domestic violence within the homes of former POWs. The first national survey data available about the incidence of domestic violence in Australia, from 1996, found that almost a quarter of women ever married or in a de facto relationship experienced some form of violence by a partner.[21] It seems unlikely that the rates would have been lower in the immediate postwar period, in the time before no-fault divorce, when the use of physical violence for disciplinary purposes remained culturally acceptable and a man's prerogative as the head of the household was firmly entrenched. Moreover, several studies have speculated that in the immediate aftermath of both of the world wars, the increased independence women had enjoyed in wartime and their subsequent assertiveness were in some cases reined in by a violent reassertion of male authority.[22]

The partners and children of returning POWs, men potentially emasculated by captivity, were perhaps even more vulnerable to the need or desire to reassert masculine power. Research into the most extreme form of male violence against children (paternal filicide) in this period suggests that its incidence was often related to men's failure to live up to expectations of themselves as fathers or to their disapproval of female family members' actions.[23] Given returned POWs' potentially compromised masculinity, their difficulties in re-establishing themselves in the labour market, their related incapacity to fulfil the socially sanctioned roles as breadwinners and providers for their families and their psychiatric disorders that could be linked to an experience of long captivity, they emerge as a group with a psychological profile marked by a propensity for violence.

Exactly where the impact of captivity sat in this mix, whether war itself encouraged male aggression, whether victims of brutality themselves became perpetrators or whether some of these men already carried a proclivity for violence before enlistment: these are difficult threads to disentangle.[24] Divorce records cross-checked with names derived from the Prisoners of War Trust Fund papers make clear that there were men who had a history of violence towards women before the war and who continued the pattern of offending thereafter. The extent to which the experience of imprisonment itself unleashed dysfunction is almost impossible to assess. One returned prisoner simply stated, 'Because of my captivity I find there are times when I am not responsible for my actions and either attack my wife or child'. The child was two years old. This man certainly believed that his experience of imprisonment exonerated him from blame for perpetrating violence.

Other men appear to have felt perfectly justified in terrorising their wives, as if that was their prerogative not because they were former prisoners but because they were men. Often such violence went hand in glove with the abuse of alcohol, the drunkenness itself unleashing tirades, abuse and humiliation. One former POW married to a woman who had served as a nurse during the war broke her nose on Anzac Day 1950. That event had been preceded by years of threats to kill her, calling her a 'filthy prostitute', belting her with a razor strap, tearing her clothes to shreds and playing the radio loudly all night so that she could not sleep. The wife repeatedly stated in conversations with her husband, 'I just want to be free'. The man applied to have his conjugal rights restored when she left the marital home to live with her sister. Ordering this woman to return to her husband, the judge cited the applicant's years as a prisoner as a mitigating factor in his behaviour: 'He is a returned soldier and was a prisoner in the hands of the Japanese for some years. Consequently, he may have suffered a great deal from that unfortunate position.' Despite the years of abuse detailed in the application, the judge declared, 'It would appear to me that he has been fond of her'.

Yet others could not understand why the shame of attacking a woman did not prevent them from doing so, or why their wives or partners remained with them despite years of domestic abuse. Lawrence was only seventeen years old when taken POW, and he married within six months of returning to Australia. His wife, Mary, was only nineteen. Within two years of marriage the couple had a daughter, and Mary filed for the first time for divorce on the grounds that Lawrence had 'repeatedly and cruelly beaten' her. He drank every day to excess and was bad tempered and aggressive. The papers lapsed three more times, over years when Lawrence was repeatedly brought before the courts of petty session for assaulting Mary. Finally, in 1955, Lawrence was imprisoned for three months following a violent attack on her. The marriage broke down irretrievably following the final attack, but Lawrence soon took up with another woman after his release from prison and repeated his violent behaviour. Describing Lawrence as fat, tense and chain smoking when admitted as a neurotic alcoholic to a repatriation hospital in 1958, the doctor said,

> [He] has been living with a 26 year old woman for 2½ years – during this time he has beaten her repeatedly, at first smacked and punched – now beating her at least once per week and ends up grabbing her by the throat she went unconscious on two occasions in the last 3/12. Under influence of beer two nights ago he broke her arm in region of elbow. She is now in St Vincent's Hospital. He has not the faintest idea why she remains with him.
>
> When an argument starts with her he gets the idea she is lying to him – he can stand anything but lies – then trembles all over and goes for her. He admits he tries to pick an argument and provoke her – that he feels real sorry seconds after his outburst.

The repatriation doctors concluded that Lawrence had a 'constitutional temperamental instability' and was an 'aggressive psychopath'. His first wife Mary finally obtained a divorce in 1961, but it has not been possible to trace the fate of the unnamed woman who so perplexed Lawrence by remaining with him.

Trustees' views

While Ted Fisher was dubious about the relationship between impotence and captivity, equally circumspect when it came to neurosis cases and mute when it came to evidence of violence perpetrated by former prisoners in their own homes, he evinced the greatest sympathy for men hurt by 'unfaithful wives', as he put it. In 1952 Fisher was prepared to give one man with a dependent teenage son the maximum grant of £250 on the grounds that his wife had left him and he needed the money to obtain a divorce and repair his home. Blackburn demurred. 'The fact that his wife walked out on him was not due to captivity but to absence.' There was support for Fisher's view among other trustees, who considered that had the applicant 'been able to correspond with his wife during captivity, the domestic upset might not have occurred'. The lack of correspondence with families was a particular problem for POWs of Japan, who were able to access very little post in the period of their imprisonment.

Fisher's sympathy had its limits, however, and he had no time for men who flouted convention. De facto relationships were beyond the pale, even when they were of long standing and of complex origin. In the early 1960s, Ernest had been living with a woman for fourteen years. When they met, she already had three children from a previous marriage to a much older man who did not believe in divorce. 'Mrs G', as she became known, had a further eight children with Ernest. Repatriation did not accept Ernest's de facto wife and children as dependants, so when he experienced periods of ill-health resulting from his years as a POW, his service pension entitlements did not cover them. The family spiralled into poverty. 'At the time I am on a pension they would starve if it weren't for people such as the Food for Babies & Red Cross also St Vincents' De Paul Society.' Their one hope was Mrs G's gaining a divorce, which her elderly first husband (an inmate of a state institution) finally agreed not to contest. Legal Aid had promised to assist Mrs G with the divorce for the cost of £30. Ernest wondered if the trustees would help him with this expense and in settling their bills with creditors. His 1962 letter concluded, 'BELIEVE ME SIR THINGS ARE GRIM HERE AT TIME OF WRITING'. The Red Cross wrote a strong letter of support on Ernest's behalf and reassured the trustees that this was an 'established family' and that Mrs G was 'a very good manager'. Fisher, unmoved, would only grant a small sum for Ernest's war-caused disabilities. 'As far as the difficulties inherent in his activities out of wedlock,' he concluded, 'they are not embraced by the terms of our deed of trust'.

Fully sharing the burden

Wives could be the biggest allies of former prisoners – in their home life, in their attempts to rehabilitate and find employment and in their battles with bureaucratic authorities. Many applicants evinced profound gratitude to the women who cared for them. 'Fortunately I have a good wife and she fully shares my burden', a Cabramatta man revealed in 1952. In contrast, Herbert's first marriage had broken down when he returned from captivity and experienced what he referred to as a 'loss of virility'. In 1952 he met another woman. He wrote, '[She] loves me for what I am, we have only just us two & without her great love for me I would surely die – should something or someone break us up … Even though I am completely useless with regards to personal joys of life, she loves me.' A Melbourne father of two felt that his own marriage had come close to divorce, but with the help of a psychologist in the early 1960s he began to 'feel more relieved from tension'. The intervention was crucial in saving his marriage. 'Fortunately I have a sensible wife who now realizes that my moods are due to P.O.W. days and we are both endeavoring to make it a happy marriage.' Another man, a former alcoholic, once sober, was eternally grateful for his wife's forbearance: 'Fortunately for me my wife stuck to me, she alone out of all my family, friends and relations realized that I was suffering from a sickness and her prayers and perseverance have been answered by seeing me starting to live a sober and more manageable life'.

Betty, a timber worker's wife, corresponded over many years with the trustees on behalf of her husband, Robert. 'I don't know how he finds the courage to keep going from day to day & suffer the way he does,' she wrote over twenty years after the war had ended, '& believe me from a silent man only a wife knows'. Robert was always a reluctant applicant, but Betty was determined to win some concessions from the trustees, because she felt his stamina had been compromised by the years spent as a prisoner. Diagnosed with a nervous condition, and in the mid-1950s still suffering the after-effects of beri-beri and malnutrition, Robert was forced to wear surgical boots. His situation was not helped when he broke a leg cutting timber, and he spent periods in and out of repatriation hospitals. The couple had twin sons and struggled to make ends meet in a series of homes in country Victoria and outer-suburban Melbourne. Betty described her husband as 'a different man to live with, still nasty and cutting when he is worried but he does work hard & give me all his money & believe me it doesn't go far'. In 1958 she insisted, 'It's fine to say be a man shake hands with the Japs the war is over[;] its not over in the homes of men who drag themselves to work & force themselves to stay on their feet then crawl into bed to[o] tired to enjoy their family no its not over in the homes & especially when men are to[o] proud to ask for help they would rather pray for release of suffering, please assist us'. When the trustees rejected Betty's application for further assistance in 1968, she confessed, '[I am] mad not because the application was refused but because when he comes home & I show him the letter he will drop his head in shame for having signed the application'. Betty considered her husband 'too proud' to ask for help, but pride and shame were often in awkward tension.

Betty was her husband's champion and did not shy away from the difficulties his condition posed to their domestic life. Her remark that the war was 'not over in the homes' was a view that resonated with other accounts of life with former POWs. Another wife's protectiveness of her husband and resentment about the invasiveness of the trust fund application form further reveals the juggling act a wife had to perform. When seeking to win assistance for war-caused disabilities, there was a precarious balance between remembering and forgetting, and sometimes the cost to a former POW's mental equilibrium was too great. As this woman pleaded to the trustees,

> Do you consider any person living in the hands of those brutal Japs to remain wholly sane, and don't you realise that the only way to fight mental disorder is to admit it and then force it into the backgrounds of one's mind. To dwell on it and be asked to write it on a cold form, for many to see, and to ask a J.P. to sign it. Well as I said I'm amazed and that is putting it mildly. I shall advise [my husband] not to fill it in of course, even if it means he will get no assistance, but

> I can tell you of his living over and over again in his dreams of his captivity and also his completely changed personality in fact at times I think he ceases to be quite human. Yes I think I might say the Japs almost destroyed his soul. Sorry if this letter shocks you but the form shocked me.

The focus here has been on marriage, but in more recent years the children of former POWs have also begun to speak about its impact on them. One has even described those whose fathers were on the Thai–Burma Railway as sharing a collective identity as 'children of the line'.[25] Sally Dingo's description of her childhood evokes the duality of absence and presence that permeates so many accounts of life with former POWs: 'We grew up knowing about the war from the day we were born. It lived in the curtains; under the carpet; in every room; in every glance from our parents, as innocently meant as those glances were. For we knew from the time our first cries were hushed, so as not to upset dad, that our father was wounded in his soul somehow. We could feel it. And we could sense that we could accidentally wound him even further. We grew up trying so hard not to do that'.[26]

Part III

Coming to terms with Asia

7
Reconciliation with Japan

As an ex-P.O.W., Malaya, I would like to enter a plea for mercy to the Japanese accused in Tokyo … Since my return I have realised that the wider Pacific war was bitter, racial, and merciless, and that the cruelties of which the enemy were guilty did not exceed those practised by us … Beside the mass cruelty of the white man in Europe, Japanese cruelties become relatively small in scope.

Charles Huxtable, 1948[1]

We who know them so well should have a little say in how to deal with the Peace Treaty, it is something we cannot believe can happen after such a short time and to think so many good British and Australian lives were thrown into such a Blood Bath as that … Japan should be made [to] suffer as she made us … our lives have been cut short by such treatment and we should be compensated in some way the same as if you are injured at your place of work. My thoughts are very clear on these things. I have buried with the help of others men who were murdered many of them too sick to work. No we don't forget these things.

John Geraty, 1951[2]

Government ministers, policy analysts and diplomats frequently laid anti-Japanese feeling in postwar Australia at the feet of former POWs, the families of those who died and a general public outraged on their behalf. Until the mid-1950s, POWs were nearly always mentioned when it came to the contemplation of future relations between Australia and Japan. In 1947 Norman Harper, an academic at the University of Melbourne, claimed that the 'brutal treatment of Australian prisoners of war' had produced 'bitterness' in the postwar relationship.[3] Australia's first Ambassador to Japan, the economist Dr E Ronald Walker, was prompted to mention the war in his opening public statement. Walker's aim was to improve the connection between the two nations. 'Even now', Dr Walker said in 1952, 'there is still a lot of bitter recollection of the war'.[4]

The case for reconciliation with Japan in the immediate postwar period is most often remembered as a convenient wish of politicians. Historians have argued that while the 'public mood' was punitive, politicians were realists.[5] The Liberal–Country Party coalition government, in office from 1949, initially followed the lead of the Labor government (1945–49) and prioritised attempts to prevent the rearmament of Japan as the surest path to security in the Pacific. The communist revolution in China in 1949 compounded a growing perception that communism was the biggest menace in Asia and that Australia's best interest lay in cultivating better relations with regional neighbours, including Japan.[6] Rather than being enfeebled, the Western wartime Allies agreed, Japan should become a bastion of capitalism. Reliant on defence relationships with Great Britain and the United States, which saw communism as the most serious threat to regional stability, and increasingly dependent on trade with Japan for its own prosperity, Australia could not shun this important neighbour.

Reconciliation with Japan

This characterisation of the Australia–Japan relationship, understood as swinging between the two poles of bitterness and pragmatism, does not allow space for a position that might fall between these two extremes. Yet there were Australian war veterans, POWs among them, who were keen to maintain peace and rebuild relationships in the postwar period. Some prominent former POWs were in the vanguard of normalising relations with Japan and promoting acceptance of contemporary political realities. For men like Wilfrid Kent Hughes, Albert Coates and Arthur Blackburn, reconciliation with Japan was at once a personal and a political act. All spoke frequently, even if sometimes admitting their own antipathy and reticence, about the need to forge a new relationship with Japan. Anti-communist political beliefs and a commitment to Japan as a sovereign capitalist state certainly influenced their views but did not entirely account for them. A Christian belief in forgiveness and a developing sense of relativity in regard to Japan's war crimes also helped to modify their views. The stereotype of the embittered POW has militated against recognition of the significant role played by POWs in promoting reconciliation in the immediate postwar period.

There was extensive discussion about Australia's relationship with Japan in the first twenty years after the war, both behind the closed doors of government bureaucracy and in the wider public sphere. A careful reading of this debate reveals greater complexity than that provided by the pathology of the prisoner or the expedience of the Cold War warrior. Exactly how Australia might negotiate the peacetime relationship with Japan was a compelling political and cultural question. It centred on three major issues: the punishment of Japanese war criminals; permission for Japanese nationals to enter Australia; and the re-establishment of political and diplomatic relations with Japan, specifically through peace (1951) and trade (1957) agreements. In all three issues, the 'feelings' of former prisoners or the families of those who had died became a leitmotif in discussions. Some of the most important voices to emerge in support of reconciliation were those of men who had themselves been prisoners of Japan. They set an important example for a community largely disinclined to forget the war.

The difficulty of forgiveness

It is possible to see in the figure of Wilfrid Kent Hughes just how hard won was the capacity for forgiveness. Kent Hughes, a Rhodes Scholar and Military Cross winner in the First World War, had enjoyed a career in Victorian politics in the 1930s. He had once described himself as 'a Fascist – without a shirt', an epitaph the Labor movement repeated with great glee for many years thereafter.[7] A Melbourne establishment figure with an American wife and father to three daughters, Kent Hughes again enlisted during the Second World War and went to Malaya in 1941 as a Colonel in the 8th Division of the 2nd AIF.[8] After the surrender to Japan he became a POW, first at Changi and later, like many senior officers, at Formosa and Manchuria. As an officer not required to undertake manual work, he used the empty days of captivity to write a long verse poem in classic style which he published with Oxford University Press as *Slaves of the Samurai* in 1946. After his return to Australia, he transferred his political ambitions from the state to the federal arena. In the 1949 federal election Kent Hughes was elected to the House of Representatives.

In the immediate postwar period, Kent Hughes retained the patois of the prison camp and evinced a physical reaction to his memories of captivity. In the preface to the first edition of *Slaves of the Samurai*, he still referred to his Japanese captors as 'Nips'.⁹ His response upon learning that an Australian parliamentary delegation visiting Japan in 1948 had an audience with the Emperor was to say that it made him want to vomit.¹⁰ 'Certain events in the life of a man can never be forgotten even to his dying day', he admitted once he had entered federal parliament. 'Only those who have had such experiences know how often we woke screaming after we returned home, and still are awakened by nightmares.' Bowing to the Speaker of the House each day made him relive the prison camp command ordering POWs to bend before each passing Japanese sentry and to bow to the Emperor every morning. He described the unnerving sensation as an echo that rang down the years.¹¹

International Military Tribunal for the Far East

Differences between POWs' attitudes to their former captors began to emerge during the Tokyo war crimes trials process. The major trial for Japan's 'class A' war criminals was held at the International Military Tribunal for the Far East in Tokyo between May 1946 and November 1948.¹² Numerous Australians travelled to Tokyo to act as witnesses, including Albert Coates, Arthur Blackburn and Vivian Bullwinkel.

Edward Dunlop refused a request from the government to attend because he considered that the trials were based on a desire for retribution.¹³ There was also a series of minor trials conducted by China, France, the Netherlands, Britain, the United States, the Philippines and Australia throughout the Pacific and Asian regions until 1956. They too attracted controversy. 'You won't change them by hanging a few war criminals from a tree in Darwin or Manus or anywhere else', declared one ex-POW.¹⁴ Bert Mudge, a journalist and former POW, considered the war crimes trials barbaric: 'Unless we adopt a less savage attitude in peace than we were obliged to pursue in war, there is little hope in realising world peace'.[15]

Others were motivated to oppose the trial process because they felt that the outcome produced what came to be known as 'victor's justice'.[16] Dr Charles Huxtable (1891–1980), who had spent the war in Changi (Bert Mudge had been one of his patients), was appalled that the trials did not admit evidence of Japanese compassion or acknowledge that the 'Pacific war was bitter, racial, and merciless, and that the cruelties of which the enemy were guilty did not exceed those practised by [the Allies]'.[17] The Allied policy in the Pacific appeared from his perspective to have been one of 'ruthless extermination' of the enemy, which meant a forfeit of the right to now sit in judgment of Japan.[18] 'The guilty amongst our own go unpunished', he insisted, arguing that victory had ensured that Allied crimes had not been subject to examination.[19] Others pointed to 'that hideous monstrosity', the atomic bomb, which had killed and injured thousands of innocent Japanese civilians, 'whose grotesque sufferings make the flesh creep'. One newspaper correspondent, discussing Australia's sentiment regarding the treatment of its POWs, conceded, 'Cruelty embitters, hate lingers'; he went on to remind his fellow citizens that 'as a whole' the nation's hands were 'not clean either'.[20]

Revulsion at the devastation caused by the atomic bombs at Hiroshima and Nagasaki and the fire-bombing of Tokyo had also inspired an attitude of compassion in others. Albert Coates returned from the tribunal preaching a message of peace and forgiveness: 'My friends, the debt has been paid in full'. He described 'the destruction and ruin of Japanese cities, the misery of the Japanese people'.[21] Coates' personal papers include an envelope of carefully preserved photographs of atomic bomb damage in Hiroshima.[22] Wilfrid Kent Hughes, who visited Japan some years later, acknowledged that two-thirds of Tokyo had been destroyed and up to 60 000 people had lost their lives, 'fried in the holocaust of fires'. 'In spite of the feelings I previously had towards the Japanese,' he confessed, 'one could, perhaps, believe that the Japanese had paid dearly for the atrocities which they committed and of which some of us have close knowledge'.[23] Tom Uren (1921–2015), a Labor member elected to federal parliament in 1958, became a committed anti-nuclear activist in the postwar years after witnessing the dropping of one of the atomic bombs while a POW in Japan. By 1960 he was well connected with Japanese socialists and gave the opening statement at the Sixth World Conference Against Atomic and Hydrogen Bombs and for Total Disarmament, in Tokyo:

> During the last war I was a prisoner of war for 3½ years. The first 2 years of my POW life were spent in Indonesia and on the Burma–Siam railway and I saw and experienced the brutalities inflicted by the Japanese militarists. I did not have any respect for the Japanese – in fact I had hate in my heart for them.
>
> But during the last years of the war, which I spent in Japan, still as a POW, I saw the great devastation created by the B29 allied bombers and I saw the great blast of the Nagasaki A-bomb.
>
> I found it was not the Japanese I hated, but the system under which they lived and those who created that system.
>
> I return today with great respect for the Japanese people who demonstrated against the Japan–US military pact. I believe Australia has nothing to fear from a peaceful Japan, but we would be greatly concerned about a re-armed Japan.
>
> I hope this conference is successful in its aim to bring us closer to total disarmament.[24]

While in Japan, Uren visited the manager of the mine in which he had laboured as a POW. He was shocked to find the man living in poverty after being 'purged' during the occupation. 'I considered him a fairly understanding man', Uren wrote to a friend and fellow former POW, 'and to be treated as a war criminal was an injustice'.[25]

Some former POWs argued that it was important to keep Japan's crimes against humanity in perspective, both during the Tokyo trials and in the years thereafter. Charles Huxtable noted that the Japanese were not unrivalled in their brutality to prisoners, pointing to Russian treatment of POWs in the First World War as resulting in death rates that exceeded those of the Thai–Burma Railway. Mention of Russian crimes quite possibly suited Huxtable's political agenda; he, like his frequent correspondent Wilfrid Kent Hughes, was a strident anti-communist. Massey Stanley, a prominent journalist and former editor of the army magazine *Salt*, drew on a more recent example, claiming that the Japanese 'did not achieve the fiendishness of white and Christian Germany' in the last war. Unusually for the time, he even mentioned the word 'genocide'. 'The destruction of the Jews in the Nazi gas ovens was on so unique and wholesale a scale that a new word, "genocide" had to be invented to comprehend its unprecedented horror.'[26] 'Beside the mass cruelty of the white man in Europe,' Huxtable concluded, 'Japanese cruelties become relatively small in scope'.[27]

Kent Hughes used another example. He was fond of pointing to Britain's concentration camps in the South African War (1899–1902), in which over 20 000 Boer people lost their lives. While fully cognisant that this did not reflect well on the British (and overlooked the fact that an equal, if not larger, number of black Africans had lost their lives in similar camps), Kent Hughes aimed to stress that positive Commonwealth relations in that case had relied upon South Africa and Britain being able to move on from this historical injustice. 'We have tried to make atonement since and have not been spurned.'[28] This explanation conveniently avoided the way in which memories of the concentration camps had fed Afrikaner nationalism in the interwar period, but it did contribute to the more general attempt to make relative the conduct of Japan in the Second World War.

These pleas to place Japanese war crimes in context and to consider the ramifications of 'victor's justice' formed only one element in a wide-ranging discussion of the enormity of Japan's war crimes. Most of the mainstream press was in full support of Australia's participation in the war crimes trials process and felt that the sentences handed down achieved some measure of justice for the many people who had suffered and died. And there were certainly ex-POWs who were vociferous in their support of the war crimes trials, Ted Fisher and Judge Adrian Curlewis among them.[29] But even as early as 1947 there were former prisoners prepared to offer an alternative view, to place Japan's war crimes in a longer historical perspective and to suggest the need for forgiveness.

Admitting Japanese to Australia

Almost contemporaneous with the war crimes trials, and for a long while thereafter, there was intense public debate about admitting Japanese nationals into Australia. Australia's Immigration Act, amended several times since its initial incarnation as the *Immigration Restriction Act 1901*, still contained provisions allowing for enforcement of the White Australia policy. In 1946 thousands of Australian residents of Japanese descent, who had been interned during the war, were 'repatriated', or deported back to Japan.[30] That same year Australia joined the British

Commonwealth Occupation Force. Between 1946 and 1952 almost 16 000 Australians served in Japan, and the inevitable mixing of Australian troops with Japanese women, and the marriages which followed, further stimulated the discussion. So too did the campaign of the pearling industry, which pushed for the entry of indentured labour from Japan. The debate was given added impetus after 1949 when Melbourne was announced as the host city of the 1956 Olympic Games. The vision of Japanese athletes running laps of the Melbourne Cricket Ground caused great consternation in some quarters.

Military metaphors abounded in commentary on the issue of Japan's attendance at the Melbourne Olympics. 'The only sport the Japs have is that of shooting nurses in the back, bashing defenceless prisoners and committing other atrocities', the President of the Ex-Prisoners of War Association of South Australia exclaimed.[31] Raising the spectre that war criminals might be among the sporting contestants, JR Lewis of the New South Wales RSL insisted that it was unreasonable to expect Australians to engage in 'fraternisation' with them.[32] 'If the Japs are permitted to land here,' the RSL claimed, 'all the bitterness and hatred in which they are held by ex-servicemen and their dependants will be re-awakened'.[33] Arthur Calwell, Labor's Minister for Immigration (1945–49), expressed the most strident views about refusing Japanese entry to Australia. In his reckoning, individuals stood for the nation, and the presence of Japanese would be a symbolic violation of Australia's borders and a slight on the sacrifice made by those who had perished in the war. The memory of Japan's atrocities was simply too recent, Calwell suggested, to allow such a visceral reminder of their occurrence. Relatives of Australians 'butchered fiendishly' by the Japanese were more worthy of consideration than any 'profits to be made from trade' or the benefits of sport.[34] In contrast, Charles Huxtable and Massey Stanley restated their views about the need to place Japan's wartime behaviour in context and made impassioned speeches in support of Japan's attendance at the Melbourne Olympic Games.[35]

The Melbourne Olympics also raised the question of how Australians might respond to their other former enemies the Germans and Italians. By 1949 the RSL considered reconciliation with them a realistic prospect, given the fact that both had behaved reasonably well towards their prisoners ('there were exceptions of course') and that it was possible to distinguish individuals from the belligerence of their nation during the war. The Japanese, however, were a different matter. They could not be approached as individuals. Returned service magazines were relentless: 'There is no place in this country for a single member of a barbarous people in whom there is so inbred the defects of treachery, double-dealing and animal ferocity'.[36] While trade and defence relationships would dictate some level of engagement with Japan in the future, it was too soon to welcome Japanese people to Australia's shores. According to the RSL, any decision on the entry of Japanese to Australia should only be made in consultation with former prisoners and the families of those who had died in Japanese POW camps.[37] In November 1949 the RSL Congress passed a resolution asking for sporting concessions to Japan to be deferred for five to ten years.[38]

A diverse range of groups agreed with a more conciliatory position, and Wilfrid Kent Hughes assumed a critical role in the resolution of the issue. He claimed that he was more justified in hating the Japanese than either Calwell or the President of the RSL. Yet, as a man who was devoted to 'British justice and British ideals', he believed in 'firmness and forgiveness', not 'eternal hate and heresy hunting'.[39] The representatives of Australian sporting associations generally supported the readmission of Japan to international competition. Why should Japanese youth 'be crucified for the sake of their fathers?' one asked.⁴⁰ Others wondered if Australia was afraid to compete and had lost its sense of sportsmanship.⁴¹ In the event, the International Olympic Committee readmitted Japan and the Federal Republic of Germany in 1950. Any attempt by the Australians to ban Japanese participation would have led to the loss of the invitation to host the 1956 games. In a move possibly designed to allay any sensitivities on the behalf of former POWs, Robert Menzies' government appointed Kent Hughes, who had represented Australia in the 400-metre hurdles at the 1920 Olympics, as Chairman of the Olympic Games Organising Committee.

Australia's participation in the British Commonwealth Occupation Force prompted further consideration of the admission of Japanese subjects. In 1948 the case of former POW John Henderson attracted a great deal of public attention to the Japanese partners of the occupation force's members and a series of requests to admit them to Australia. Henderson claimed there were other members of the occupation force, like himself, who lived with Japanese women in their family homes.⁴² Occupation force members had sometimes attracted opprobrium on their return to Australia for the very fact that they had spent time in Japan, and during the occupation they were the subjects of lurid press reports about their sexual misbehaviour.⁴³ Australian troops in Japan were subject to a strict but frequently breached non-fraternisation policy. The Department of Immigration did not allow wives of 'Asiatic' origin to enter Australia. In that climate, the idea that an ex-POW might actually marry a Japanese woman was particularly controversial. After revealing that he had married Mary Abe in a Shinto ceremony in 1946, Henderson was discharged from the army and sent back to Australia.⁴⁴ Henderson's daughter Shirley was born in Japan after his return. He said his wife, whom he had met when she was working as an interpreter at an army hospital near Kure, was a university graduate and excellent seamstress and cook.[45]

The Australian community's vilification of Henderson and his family was in keeping with the sentiments marshalled by Arthur Calwell in his efforts to prevent the migration of Japanese wives to Australia. No Australian wife or mother would have her feelings outraged by 'any Australian national flaunting a Japanese woman before her eyes', Calwell maintained.[46] Henderson's parents, in contrast, stood by his decision and supported his attempts to be reunited with his wife, even though the marriage had caused them 'a lot of worry'. 'We have always been highly thought of in this district,' Henderson's mother Jessie claimed, 'and now a few people are turning very nasty'. She had cried for three days and refused to leave the house after receiving an anonymous letter accusing her of betraying Australian womanhood. The Hendersons seemed bewildered by the attention but logical in their reasoning. Their son had been blind for a year after mistreatment on the Thai–Burma Railway, but his capacity for forgiveness had impressed them. 'He tells us there are lots of very nice Japanese people and one mustn't blame the whole race for war atrocities.'[47]

Despite the experiences of the Hendersons at a private level, the intemperate language to which Calwell resorted on occasion was becoming less acceptable in public life. In 1948 there was widespread coverage of his remark that Japanese wives would not be allowed to enter, and thereby 'pollute', Australia. All the newspapers that featured this headline placed the word 'pollute' in inverted commas. Even those who supported Calwell were sensitive to the awkward note struck by such coarse language. There was a small but growing section of the Australian population beginning to feel that a commitment to White Australia was unsustainable given the extremes to which racial thinking had been taken in the war and in light of Australia's position in a post-colonial world. While 'keeping out the Nips' was acceptable, one correspondent to a metropolitan daily insisted, Calwell should be careful not to borrow from 'the Nazi book of racial jargon'. White Australia might remain the policy aim, but regional sensitivities precluded such bold statements of its underlying principles.[48] Others thought that Calwell was in danger of replicating 'the racial purity rubbish that an erstwhile dictator foisted upon his people'.[49] The war had been fought against ideologies such as 'the superior race doctrine'.[50] Participation in international conferences at which Australia had argued for human rights also seemed to contradict the attitude of the government about the admission of the Japanese wives of servicemen.[51]

Christian duty to the vanquished

Wilfrid Kent Hughes believed that the Japanese had to be given a chance to redeem themselves – that, indeed, there was a 'Christian duty to the vanquished'.[52] The Australian section of the World Council of Churches certainly thought so and had issued a statement to that effect in 1947, declaring that the Japanese were 'children of God, capable of responding to forgiveness'.[53] This was a sentiment that struck a chord with Kent Hughes. 'Difficult as it may be,' he argued, 'perhaps we ought to remember that we are a Christian community – every sitting day in this chamber we say the Lord's Prayer'. He added that, although trust took a long time to be established, no good could be served by a continuation of hatred, which both 'breeds and feeds upon itself'.[54]

Connections between Australian and Japanese Christians and mission work were important vectors of reconciliation and models of forgiveness. The Reverend Father Lionel Marsden SM, an army chaplain, was a driving force in the late 1940s behind the establishment of the Marist Japanese Mission League, an organisation he formed along with other Catholic ex-POWs.[55] Returning to Japan as a missionary in 1949, Marsden established the Marist Mission Centre in Nara, Kyoto. The Catholic Church was keen to publicise Marsden – 'a priest who suffered privations as a prisoner of war' – and his willingness to work among the Japanese as proof that, to the church, 'all men, whatever their colour or nationality, have a common destiny'.[56] In the late 1950s, another priest linked to the Marist mission, Father Tony Glynn, organised the first large Japanese arts and crafts exhibition to tour Australia. Over 1000 items were displayed at department stores and exhibition halls across the country, in what was described as a 'spontaneous expression of the desire of the Japanese people for peace and friendship with Australia'.[57] The objects were also designed to offer an alternative vision of Japan in Australia, one that emphasised its refinement and culture. The relatively recent negotiation of a trade treaty with Japan in 1957 explained the willingness of Prime Minister Robert Menzies to open the exhibition, which was one of a number of cultural initiatives designed to soften Japan's image in Australia.

Christian connections were central to the resumption of Japanese travel to Australia, although such visits rarely escaped controversy. In 1950 Yashiro Hinsuke, Bishop of Kobe and presiding Bishop of Nippon Sei Ko Kai (the Anglican Communion in Japan), became the first Japanese visitor to postwar Australia. Sponsored by fundraising among British Commonwealth Occupation Force troops in Japan, Yashiro's visit was constructed as an exercise in Christian forgiveness and compassion. This did not stop some former POWs and their families from accusing the organisers of staging a 'whitewash' for 'the whole Japanese race'.[58] In 1953 another Japanese Christian, Hilary M Uyehara, was granted the first tourist visa issued to a Japanese national since the end of the war. In a symbolic gesture of reconciliation, Uyehara was photographed donating blood at the Red Cross blood transfusion centre in Hobart. The accompanying headline, 'Jap gives blood', presented readers with an unsubtle message about the spirit of Uyehara's visit.[59]

Wilfrid Kent Hughes was influenced by Christian arguments about forgiveness and reconciliation and, despite the missionary enthusiasms of a few, always remained conscious that it was his fellow former POWs who would take the most convincing of the need to reconcile with Japan. Albert Coates saw a similar challenge. In 1953 at a Shrine of Remembrance service commemorating the fall of Singapore, Coates called for an end to hatred. 'The grass has grown over the graves; the ulcers have healed', he reflected. 'Men of our race are not good haters. The welfare of this land is more important than the bitterness of a few, and we trust that Japan will be a friend to this country.' He then quoted a line, as he often did in public speeches, from Rudyard Kipling's 'Recessional': the injunction to avoid 'frantic boast and foolish word'.[60] 'Recessional' is most famously the source of 'Lest We Forget'. But the terms 'frantic boast and foolish word', which more directly reference the poem's main themes of the folly and danger of overbearing patriotism, rang true for men struggling to put aside their own experiences for the sake of the greater good.

Treaty of Peace with Japan

Former prisoners provided a strong voice in debates about a peace treaty with Japan, and Albert Coates and Wilfrid Kent Hughes played an essential role in attempting to make it palatable to the community. Given that the 1950 Owen Committee, which had denied former POWs the subsistence claim, had suggested that Japan was the appropriate source of any compensation payment,

Reconciliation with Japan

the ex-POW community watched the treaty negotiations with great care. The issues debated at the conference on what became the Treaty of Peace with Japan, in San Francisco in 1951, included compensation and reparations, the capacity for rearmament, the end of occupation and the restoration of Japan's sovereignty.[61] These concerns were closely followed in Australia, where fear of a resurgent Japan remained palpable.

In the late 1940s the desire for vengeance against Japan was still strong. It received its fullest expression from some Labor Members of Parliament and in ex-service magazines: 'No reason exists why a whole generation of Japs should not have to suffer throughout their lives for their misdeeds, as many of those they injured will have to suffer throughout theirs'.[62] Ex-POW organisations, in particular, were wary of suggestions that the peace treaty should not exact harsh reparations from the Japanese, who needed to rebuild their economy. 'Surely the concern should be for the men scarred in mind and body rather than for the country responsible', insisted Norman Cohen, Secretary of the NSW Ex-Prisoners of War Association.[63] Yet it was common knowledge that harsh reparations exacted against Germany in the 1919 Treaty of Versailles had destabilised that country and contributed towards its slide into Nazism.

Some former POWs made public pleas recalling the brutal behaviour of the Japanese during the war. In 1950 Captain Fred Stahl addressed radio station 5KA's Legacy Club in Adelaide and said that it was impossible for the Japanese to embrace reform. Recounting stories of horror and suffering in Japanese prison camps, Stahl told his audience, 'I have seen the Japanese drunk with power'. He pleaded with them to never allow Japan to grow strong again, if they 'would keep inviolate' their 'wives and daughters', and if they wanted to preserve the 'British way of life' for their sons. Anything less than a treaty which removed

Japan's capacity to rearm and extensive compensation for prisoners would be a travesty.[64]

The vehemence of statements such as Stahl's – and there were others who felt like him, both in the community and in the parliament – need to be calibrated by other opinions that also held sway in the public arena. Albert Coates attended the San Francisco conference as a representative of the RSL. The organisation was delighted. 'Only one name was considered' by the Executive, which felt that 'no finer' representative could be found.[65] If the RSL was looking for a hard-liner, they had chosen the wrong man. 'No one could have more bitter memories of their atrocities than I have,' Coates declared upon departure, 'but it's all over now'.[66] Once the treaty was signed, he urged his colleagues to 'bury the hatchet' and recognise that only goodwill and friendship would make both great nations of the Pacific prosper.[67] Most controversially, the peace treaty allowed for only minimal compensation for POWs and civilian internees (from existing seized Japanese assets) and for the creation of the National Police Reserve, a paramilitary force designated as essential to Japan's self-defence.

The Australian government had little choice but to ratify the terms of the peace treaty. The Department of External Affairs, led by Sir Percy Spender, had contemporaneously negotiated a three-way defence agreement between Australia, New Zealand and the United States (ANZUS). Australia was anxious to secure a US commitment to regional defence, so the government's willingness to agree to a relatively 'soft' peace treaty with Japan was an important context for negotiations. Yet the realpolitik of the situation did not prevent particular groups from greeting the need to ratify the treaty with howls of derision. The Combined Union Committee of the railway workshops in Newport, an inner-urban industrial area in Melbourne, described the treaty as 'an act of Treachery to the Australian people'.[68] The Federated Clerks' Union wrote to the Prime Minister and declared that 'vivid recollections' of the treatment of POWs meant that the treaty was 'an insult to the Australian people'.[69]

Former prisoners tried to temper the fury of some groups by pointing out the necessity to accept the terms of the treaty. The one who did so most reluctantly was Arthur Blackburn. Immediately upon his return from captivity Blackburn had declared publicly that he would always hate the Japanese 'for their utter untrustworthiness and sheer brutality'.[70] Two years later, in Tokyo for the war crimes trials, he had remained distrustful, arguing that it was impossible to tell if the Japanese appreciated the enormity of their crimes or were merely paying 'lip-service to their conquerors'.[71] Yet by 1951 Blackburn had seen the need to make peace with Japan in light of the regional threat posed by the Cold War. Blackburn justified his attitude towards the peace treaty as one of retribution. 'Someone has to be cannon fodder', he insisted. 'Let it be the Japs.'[72] Other officers also pointed to Japan as a buffer between Australia and China and to rearmament as necessary in the fight against communism.[73] Brigadier Cranston McEachern acknowledged how difficult it was to reconcile his experiences as a POW with support for Japan yet insisted to his fellow ex-POWs that they should support ratification of the peace treaty. 'Because of the present world situation', he insisted, 'we must submerge our hatred of the Japanese'.[74]

The Australian parliament's debate on ratification of the peace treaty in February 1952 brought matters to a head. In a canny political move, Prime Minister Robert Menzies nominated Wilfrid Kent Hughes to lead the debate in support of ratification. Kent Hughes was the ideal advocate: respectful of the pain of others but quietly insistent on the futility of revenge and the need for Australia to take heed of contemporary regional and political realities. The Australian Labor Party opposed the treaty but did not have the numbers to defeat it. Les Haylen, who had been so prominent in discussions about the subsistence allowance, described himself as 'almost completely disarmed' by Kent Hughes' emotional speech in support of ratification. Still, he remained staunch in his opposition: 'This treaty contains no reference to trade and no consideration is given in it to the Australian diggers who were incarcerated by the Japanese. That is completely disgusting. I reject it with contempt'.[75]

The strength of feeling stirred by the peace treaty was in evidence outside the parliament as well. During the final debate a delegation of 300 representatives from unions, churches and youth groups descended upon Canberra. They came from Sydney, Melbourne and Brisbane and carried a petition signed by 100 000 people opposing the treaty. One of the leaders of the delegation was an ex-POW of the Germans, Major Leo Probyn.[76] He had chaired a public meeting in Melbourne which passed a resolution declaring the treaty 'a deliberate and cold-blooded betrayal' of the Australian people and an insult to those who had died.[77] Calling for a plebiscite about the ratification, the delegation met with Prime Minister Menzies and urged him to make a separate peace for Australia with Japan. Menzies was resolute: with the United States and Britain bound to ratify, Australia alone could not prevent rearmament.

Opposition to the treaty was widespread and did not fall neatly into the political division of left or right. Unionists, politicians, academics, and writers like Mary Gilmore, Eleanor Dark and Clem Christesen wrote petitions, telegrams and letters and forwarded them to Canberra. The Union of Australian Women, 'the wives, mothers, sisters and daughters of the men who fought, and in many instances died, in the struggle to defeat the Japanese Army', opposed ratification on the grounds that it desecrated the memory of their loved ones.[78] Mrs G Shapper objected on behalf of her eight tennis companions, all of whom thought the treaty was a 'shockingly callous sneer at the people who have suffered so terribly at the hands of the Japanese'.[79] Correspondents to the Prime Minister complained about the capacity for Japan to rearm, the lack of compensation to POWs and the possibility of losing jobs to cheap Japanese imports. For most, the terms of the treaty were a tremendous insult to the suffering of POWs and paved the way for a possible return of armed Japanese aggression in the region.

The treaty also heralded the end of the British Commonwealth Occupation Force's role in Japan. In March 1952, a month before the treaty came into effect, the Minister for Immigration Harold Holt finally granted permission for the Japanese wives of Australian servicemen to enter the country. It was a relaxation of the White Australia policy – indeed, historians consider it a pivotal moment in the drawn-out dismantling of that policy – that came too late for the Henderson family.[80] Over 650 Japanese women subsequently migrated to Australia, but Mary Henderson was not one of them.[81] In 1954 John Henderson had still not been reunited with his Japanese wife and had applied to the Department of Immigration for custody of his daughter. At that time Immigration informed him that his wife no longer wished to come to Australia and, further, that she had an eleven-year-old son who was not interested in emigrating.[82] Henderson claimed to know nothing about the existence of Mary's son, whose father, a Japanese soldier, had been killed in China in 1944. Mary Henderson was adamant that her decision had been made with her son in mind: 'He would be made fun of by the other children'.[83] Given that she was initially prevented from following her husband to Australia by an immigration policy that considered her race the basis for exclusion, it is not difficult to see how a mother might feel reluctant for her Japanese son and mixed-race daughter to enter such a society.

Taking it like a man

While former prisoners' voices were prominent when it came to symbolic measures of reconciliation (such as placing Japan's war crimes in perspective, the entry of Japanese nationals to Australia and the peace treaty), economics and trade were not matters in which they sought to intervene. The peace treaty ratification was rent with controversy on a symbolic level, but the government had an even more delicate negotiation to pursue in its wake. Even though commentary on the peace treaty lamented that the floodgates would be thrown open to cheap Japanese imports, in fact, the trade relationship required a separate agreement of its own. The Department of Trade, overseen by Deputy Prime Minister Jack McEwen, was even more aggressive than External Affairs in its pursuit of normalisation of relations with Japan. Under pressure from its own trade officials and from the United States and Britain, which were overtly encouraging the Australian government to soften its approach to Japan, Robert Menzies' government made a conscious decision in 1954 to pursue closer relations. Menzies, aware of the stakes, played hard politics. In essence, he told former POWs and those who nursed a grudge on their behalf that it was time to take it 'like a man'.

Menzies' political skill in presenting the embrace of a former enemy in terms of political maturity and manhood helped to mute ongoing opposition to the normalisation of relations with Japan. In March 1954 Menzies broadcast a 'man to man' speech. Mindful of a recent US defensive agreement with Japan that allowed for limited rearmament, he appealed to his listeners for a mature reconsideration of their views. The domestic context of Menzies' speech, which he did not mention, was that from 1 April 1954 there would be relaxation of some Japanese import restrictions. He pointed to the trade imbalance: Australia exported goods worth sixteen times more than those it imported. This was not a situation that could be sustained into the future. Australia's standard of living was, in part, dependent on trade with Japan.

Almost a decade after its conclusion, the war was still a centrepiece of this crucial speech. Conceding that the Japanese were a 'cruel enemy', Menzies agreed that Australians had 'no reason to love them'. He pointed to the war service of members of his parliamentary supporters: of almost 100 men, 69 had served their country, almost half of them against the Japanese. Five, indeed, had been POWs. 'Are these members pro-Japanese', he asked, 'if they support trade with Japan, if they no longer wish to nurse the bitterness of the past?' In his most avuncular tones he insisted, 'The conduct of foreign affairs is not a job for children'. The United States, which had suffered too, was playing the role of the 'grown up nation', because 'the greatest stumbling-block to peace is the perpetuation of enmities'.[84]

Talk of manhood was a topic of particular sensitivity for former POWs, many of whom had struggled with their defeat and a war spent confined in a camp. There had been government decisions – about the subsistence allowance, for example – that had not fallen in their favour, owing to their status as defeated soldiers who were not to be encouraged. And there was a host of former POWs who reported experiencing an 'inferiority complex' when it came to mixing with people. If, for some, the psychological result of captivity was a desire to retreat from public interaction and discomfort with authority figures, it might seem that organised opposition to reconciliation with Japan would have been an unlikely prospect, especially when it was official policy of the government of the day. And indeed, the most virulent anti-Japanese statements tended to come from people who had not themselves been prisoners. Charles Huxtable claimed to have been surprised by the intensity of feeling against Japan when he had returned home in 1945, 'and by its uncompromising nature'.[85]

In public discussions of their attitudes towards former captors, POWs received a constant linguistic reminder – through the refrain of 'bitterness' – that any sense of injustice simultaneously carried the burden of their own failure as soldiers. 'Bitterness' conveys a meaning more complex than mere anger. There is a difference between bitterness and anger, psychologists suggest, because embitterment has 'the additional quality of self-blame and a feeling of injustice'.[86] The link between bitterness and a sense of iniquity has deep roots in Western cultures, stretching as far back as Aristotle.[87] This association echoed the shame of defeat and expressed again the ambivalent status of the POW.

Menzies, having prepared the ground by telling the electorate that it was a mark of manhood and maturity to re-embrace Japan, continued to insist on the necessity of reconciliation. In mid-1954 External Affairs began providing 'background material' to the Australian press in an effort to change public attitudes to Japan and the Japanese. It fostered a series of articles highlighting the growing communist menace in Asia and the dangers to Australia if Japan were to fall victim to it.[88] In the first months of 1955, Wilfrid Kent Hughes, in his capacity as Minister in Charge of the Anzac Agency of the Imperial War Graves Commission, was dispatched to East and South-East Asia to visit Australian war graves in British Commonwealth war cemeteries throughout the region, including the Yokohama War Cemetery. He also met with Emperor Hirohito. As an image of reconciliation, the photograph of the former POW laying a wreath at a site where Australian POWs were buried was hard to beat.

Reconciliation with Japan

The strategy appears to have worked. To almost no political effect, the Labor Party's Arthur Calwell and HV Evatt taunted Menzies that he was 'Jap Happy'.[89] By spring 1955 it was possible for almost 200 members of the crew of a Japanese merchant training ship, the *Taisei Maru*, to visit Sydney without incident. External Affairs was unsure if it should grant the vessel permission to enter. A ship's visit might prompt fear of a Japanese resurgence. After all, the last time a Japanese vessel had entered Sydney Harbour, it was a midget submarine. The Assistant-Secretary James Plimsoll, who was later appointed Australia's Ambassador to Japan, overruled this opinion. Here was an opportunity to make a gesture of goodwill that might leave a lasting impression. Plimsoll had only recently ghostwritten Richard Casey's book *Friends and Neighbors* (1954), which urged greater engagement with Asia. The visit proceeded without incident, even if one Australian officer did check to see if they should do anything 'to see that these little fellers don't get into any bother'.[90] After the ship left, one newspaper report marvelled that this was a sign of the times. Twelve years earlier, uniformed Japanese roaming the streets of Sydney would have produced a pitched battle; eight years earlier, it would have produced a lynching; but in 1955, 'Sydney practically ignored a Little Japan on its doorstep'.[91] In contrast to its judo-wrestling demonstrations and trips to the Blue Mountains and Taronga Zoo once in Australia, the *Taisei Maru* crew had been engaged in gruesome work prior to its arrival: collecting the remains of Japan's war dead from Papua New Guinea.

Recovery of Japanese war dead and confirming an agreement about the Commonwealth Yokohama War Cemetery, which contained the graves of Australian POWs, were two of several 'outstanding issues' from the war that needed to be finalised before trade talks could begin in earnest. Others included the release of

Japanese war criminals and compensation to POWs. By 1957 Australia had agreed to release all remaining war criminals, and Japan had finally honoured the terms of article 16 of the treaty of peace, which effectively released money to fund a further small compensation payment to POWs.[92] In April 1957 Menzies visited Japan. Editorials considered the visit as emerging 'from the fact, established by the Pacific war, that [Australia's] destiny, for better or worse, is irrevocably linked with events in Asia'.[93] Menzies' secret brief made clear that the purpose of the visit was to 'develop understanding' between Australia and Japan, for both government officials and 'the general public'.[94] Senior bureaucrats advised Menzies that he ought to point out that, unlike other Asian countries, Australia had not sought reparations from Japan. Indeed, Australia had actively worked to smooth Japan's path in the international arena. The examples to be cited could include Australia's support for Japan's entry into the United Nations and its sponsorship of Japan's admission to the list of Colombo Plan powers.[95]

The Agreement on Commerce between the Commonwealth of Australia and Japan, otherwise known as the Australia-Japan Agreement on Commerce, was signed in July 1957.[96] Australia became the first country after the war to grant Japan 'most favoured nation' status, which reduced tariffs and quotas on the importation of Japanese goods. In exchange, Japan became an important export market for Australia's resources. The agreement was a prescient move that contributed to unheralded economic prosperity for both countries by the 1960s. The peace treaty re-established diplomatic relations between Australia and Japan, but it was the trade agreement of 1957 that consolidated the postwar relationship. In its wake, Australia hosted the visit of Japan's Prime Minister Nobusuke Kishi.

Respect or insult?

Each step in the renegotiated relationship between Australia and Japan, particularly around treaties and agreements, required a diplomatic performance. That performance was most often played out in the theatre of the Australian War Memorial, in Canberra, with respect to the war dead as the central symbolic gesture. As individuals and the general public moved through their grief about the fate of POWs, a bargaining with loss and a deeply felt need to regain control of the process were projected onto these symbols of reconciliation. Consequently, ceremonial activities such as wreath-laying by visiting Japanese dignitaries became flashpoints for painful memories and contested attitudes about responsibility and forgiveness.

The appointment of the first Japanese Ambassador to Australia, Haruhiko Nishi, prompted intense consideration of protocols at the Australian War Memorial in 1953. According to tradition, every diplomatic mission in Canberra was invited to lay a wreath at the memorial's Anzac Day service. The Chairman of the memorial, CEW Bean, of Anzac legend fame, was nervous. Anticipating the arrival of the Japanese Ambassador, he ordered the removal of Japanese war relics – including swords, batons and the table on which Japan had signed its surrender at Singapore – from display. Bean replaced them with the more innocuous AIF colour patches. Ex-service organisations were outraged. 'Squeamishness', declared one state RSL President. They were further taxed by the idea that Nishi would lay a wreath during the Anzac Day service and threatened to withdraw their participation at the event.[97] Eventually a compromise was reached: the relics would be restored, but only Commonwealth missions were invited to place a wreath during the service. The Japanese Ambassador would be in attendance but would play no formal role.[98]

The changed dynamic of the Australia–Japan relationship was in evidence four years later, in 1957, when Prime Minister Nobusuke Kishi was due to visit, after the successful conclusion of the trade negotiations. There would be no polite displacement of Kishi; he would visit the Australian War Memorial, and he would lay a wreath. The one prominent ex-POW who had always resisted reconciliation with Japan, Ted Fisher, went on the offensive. He wrote a letter to the Prime Minister, which he released to the press. He argued that 7000 Australians had died of neglect while prisoners of Japan, a fact which embittered bereaved families and 14 000 survivors still 'living with their scars'. Allowing a Japanese national to lay a wreath at the war memorial was an insult to the memory and suffering of these people.[99] Wilfrid Kent Hughes was appalled. He told Fisher that releasing a letter of complaint about the wreath-laying was an error of judgment. 'No good can be served by a continuation of hatred which both breeds and feeds upon itself. After all, the "unspeakable" Turks of the First World War were recently our guests at Anzac Day parades.'[100] In the federal parliament, Kent Hughes made an impassioned speech in support of Kishi's activities: 'Who are we to pre-suppose and pre-judge such an action as the laying of a wreath as something that is either hypocritical or insulting? Who are we to refuse to accept as an apology this act of the Japanese Prime Minister and also probably as evidence of a fervent desire that in the future our two nations may live in amity and peace?'[101]

Despite Kent Hughes' criticism, there was some support for Fisher's position. Kishi's visit was, in one sense, unfortunately timed. It coincided with the publication of Lionel Wigmore's volume of the *Official History of Australia in the War of 1939–1945*, *The Japanese Thrust* (1957). The book contained an account of the campaigns in Malaya and the Dutch East Indies and three chapters on Japanese POWs, written by AJ Sweeting.

AE Field, a reviewer and a former POW of the Japanese, congratulated Sweeting for 'judiciously refraining from hysteria, but setting down in cold print authentic incidents of torture, brutality and sadism'.[102] A more dramatic account of the book's contents appeared in the *Sunday Telegraph* under the headline 'Allied prisoners wrote pages of glory: in the Jap horror camps' and included photographs of emaciated survivors. NSW RSL President Sir William Yeo clipped it from the paper and, in red pencil across the top of the article, wrote, 'LEST WE FORGET?????' and posted it to the league's national President in protest about the Executive's decision to support the Japanese wreath-laying ceremony.[103] Earlier, he had suggested that a guard of honour composed of the widows and children of men 'butchered during the war' should greet the Japanese Prime Minister.[104]

Perhaps the bellwether of reconciliation with Japan was the RSL. The reactionary nature of the league's position on the Australia–Japan relationship in the 1980s, personified in the views of the national President Alf Garland and Victoria's Bruce Ruxton, has obscured the organisation's more conciliatory attitude in the postwar years. After initial opposition to Japan's participation in the Melbourne Olympics, the RSL modified its position under the presidency of Sir George Holland (1950–60). Although Holland had his differences with some state Presidents, particularly William Yeo, in New South Wales, the tenor of the organisation shifted. Articles began to appear in its journal pointing to the damage wrought by 'an inflexible attitude of hatred and distrust' and to the importance of forgiveness for reform and calling for 'common sense' to reign in light of contemporary defence realties.[105] Encouraging closer ties with Japan became official RSL policy after 1957, in keeping with Australia's Cold War commitment to the containment of communism. The league welcomed Kishi's wreath-laying as a 'respectful salute' to Australia's war dead and as a 'sign of the growing awareness of the need for a strong mutual tie between our two countries'.[106] It too rapped Fisher over the knuckles for his troublemaking, telling him wreath-laying should be encouraged 'as a form of respect to Australian war dead'. Indeed, if the visiting Japanese Prime Minister had refrained from doing so, 'it would virtually constitute an insult to our war dead'.[107]

※

By 1960 the formal political work of Australia's postwar relationship with Japan had been completed. The war crimes trials process had concluded, the peace treaty had been ratified, immigration protocols had been established, and the trade agreement had been negotiated. The performance of reconciliation was a harder task; POWs, symbolically at least, were often a spectral presence, ghosts at the feast of forgiveness. Albert Coates and Wilfrid Kent Hughes, in particular, used their own experiences as prisoners to show that there was an attitude towards Japan that had virtues beyond political pragmatism. Their work in the ex-service community, at commemoration services and, in Kent Hughes' case, as a federal government Minister, insisted that hatred was not a salve to the wounds of war and that true peace, for the nation and themselves, lay in appreciating that war itself was the base cause of suffering.

8
Rewards and regional relationships

> REMEMBER – that exhausting march from Singapore to Changi of Feb. '42 – how the Chinese men, women and children plied us with food and drink.
> REMEMBER – the countless occasions on which they gave us shelter, 'Mukkan' and tobacco.
> REMEMBER – how they were abused for it – how they were tortured and how they died for it ...
> We have now come on better times in our own land, and we should, therefore, in all honour as men remember our obligations, personally and collectively, to these magnificent people.
> *AIF Malayan Nursing Scholarship, Fundraising flyer, c. 1945*[1]

POWs had first-hand experience of Asian countries during the war. Some emerged from their prison camps determined to honour local people who had helped them and to build stronger connections with the region. Policymakers and military strategists were also aware that POWs had interacted with people in areas that were increasingly prone to instability. They too sought to reward people who had shown compassion to Australian POWs, although their motives for doing so blended recognition with political expedience. Studies of politicians, intellectuals, bureaucrats and travellers have stressed that while Asia was a subject of growing interest and attention in the late 1940s, Australian responses to the decolonising region were ad hoc, personality driven and uncertain.[2] In the twentieth century, each generation of Australians, it seemed, 'discovered' Asia anew and called for greater engagement.[3] The postwar period was no exception. Reward and recognition initiatives that stemmed from the experiences of POWs in the Asian region encompassed the knowledge that it comprised diverse peoples and cultures. They also reflected tensions between the desires to acknowledge human kindness, to reassert Commonwealth bonds in the light of nationalist movements and communist insurgencies, and to manage perceptions of Australia as a racist country.

Compassion and covert operations

Australian POW Owen Campbell was one of only six survivors from among 2400 Allied POWs forced to march from Sandakan to Ranau, on the island of Borneo, in 1945. Campbell escaped from his Japanese captors and spent nineteen days in the jungle, living on fungi, crabs and scorpions. At one point, Campbell called out '*Abang*' (brother) to two local men, who witnessed the virtually naked white man faint as they approached. The men took Campbell back to a house at Kampong Maunad, and their female relatives dressed him in clean cotton and fed him for ten days. Campbell, who weighed little more than forty kilograms, was so weak that he had to be assisted to stand in the river while he bathed.[4] During this period Orang Tuan Kulang, the Dusun headman of Kampong Maunad, returned from his work as a guerrilla with the Australian Services Reconnaissance Department. The unit had dropped behind enemy lines as part of the

'Borneo project' to retake the island from the Japanese.⁵ 'When I approached the white man he was trembling and I was startled to see his condition', Kulang later recalled. 'He looked like an Orang-utan, he was thin and covered with hair and scabies.'⁶ In Kulang's perception, the white man had become simian and close to nature in his state of almost complete abjection.

Kulang's arrival in the village was the key to Campbell's survival. After giving Campbell a few more days to regain his strength, Kulang sailed with him back to the Services Reconnaissance Department camp. 'When the white men met I noticed that they were very emotional, they embraced each other and Hollingsworth [another Australian officer] embraced me. It was some time before we could speak, all three of us were crying.' After a few days at the secret camp, Kulang accompanied Campbell on the long walk to meet an Australian rescue crew. Eleven kilometres in, Campbell fainted, and Kulang tenderly massaged him with hot coconut oil until he regained consciousness. As the flying boat approached, Campbell shook Kulang's hand and thanked him for all he had done.⁷

Even though very few POWs escaped on Borneo, those who survived did so due to the compassion of people who had themselves endured a long occupation. Local people washed the escaped men's lice-infested bodies, dressed them in cotton sarongs, fed them boiled water, molasses and rice porridge in careful measure and placed them on sleeping mats. Furthermore, at Sandakan there was an extensive underground support network for civilian internees and POWs, which smuggled food, money, medicines and radio parts into the Japanese-run camps. In mid-1943 the Japanese uncovered the activities of this group, and over seventy people (including twenty-one members of the AIF) stood trial in Kuching. As a consequence the Japanese executed eight men from Borneo and Captain Lionel Matthews, an Australian intelligence officer central to the operation of the camp radio. Many others served long prison sentences for their parts in smuggling goods and information to Allied POWs.

When peace came, so too did an expectation that there might be some kind of reward for those who had supported the Allies at such risk to themselves. After Japan had been defeated and Australia's 9th Division occupied the island of Borneo, Australian war graves units moved in and began the task of recovering the bodies of deceased Australian POWs. Local people approached members of the war graves teams bearing grubby notes that Australian POWs had signed in pencil or crayon, promising reimbursement or compensation for assistance rendered during the war. Others had no hand-written promises but did possess compelling tales of helping the Allied POWs at much peril to themselves and their families. Members of the *Kempeitai* had beaten one of them, Pardi Bin Dulbar, so viciously for his role in providing material to Captain Matthews that they had knocked out his three front teeth and driven two other teeth back up into his gums.[8]

In 1946 the Australian Army sent to Borneo one of its most experienced investigators, Major Henry 'Harry' Jackson, to seek out and reward people for the help that they had given to Australian POWs. Jackson was the perfect choice: fastidious about documenting his task and sympathetic to those who had provided assistance. He set off with a thick folder containing the paybook photographs of all the Australian POWs incarcerated in Borneo, most of whom now lay buried in shallow graves or decomposing beside the trail of their forced march. Jackson carried a wad of cash: over $2000 in Straits currency (equivalent to £300 in Australia). He also took thirty-six pairs of shorts, safari jackets, singlets and six machetes as payment in kind to the 'natives of Borneo'. The reward mission circulated notices to the inhabitants in Malay, Chinese and English to publicise its purpose.

Rewards and regional relationships

En route to Borneo via Singapore, Jackson gathered a few more members for the Australian–British Reward Mission. Ex-POW Warrant Officer William Sticpewich (1909–77), one of the six survivors of the death marches, who had recently testified at the Tokyo trials, was one of them. Jackson also agreed to a request from the ABC to allow a writer, Colin Simpson, and radio technician, Bill MacFarlane, to accompany him. The ABC, in conjunction with the British Broadcasting Corporation, was interested in producing a documentary and planned to make 'actuality recordings'. Jackson was delighted. He was keen to document the mission and diligently collected the statements of people who had assisted POWs. His final report was brimful of rhetorical flushes: British North Borneo was rendered as 'the green cage' and the suffering of prisoners as 'one of the grimmest chapters of Jap frightfulness'. The more public ABC effort ultimately became *Six from Borneo*, a radio documentary written by Simpson and broadcast in 1947. It reconstructed the experiences of Australian and British POWs who had been transported to Sandakan to build an airstrip then force-marched to their deaths as the Allies threatened to reoccupy the island. Simpson interviewed the six survivors and they performed their own parts. Jackson introduced the documentary and stated that the story was 'of extreme importance to our people' and one of the 'most tragic chapters in the history of World War Two which should be known in every home of the Commonwealth'.[9]

The purpose of the Australian–British Reward Mission was more complex than handing out safari jackets or creating an audio memorial to the victims of the Sandakan–Ranau death marches. There were some complicated and politically sensitive matters to negotiate. Local indigenous people like Kulang had been drawn into guerrilla networks that the Allies had established and coordinated as part of the effort to liberate Borneo. The 20th and

24th brigades of the AIF's 9th Division had been entrusted with the task of recapturing the former British Borneo Territories (Sarawak, Brunei and North Borneo) from Japan. They could only do so with a preliminary infiltration of the area and recruitment of indigenous people in a series of covert operations against strategic enemy targets. In 1947 Jackson was in Borneo to reward not just members of the underground who had helped POWs but also the guerrillas like Kulang who had undertaken particularly outstanding service. It was more than coincidence that another late addition to his team was Major Roy K Dyce, formerly of the AIF but by 1946 on the British Army general list. Dyce had been in the Special Operations unit during the war and participated in covert actions himself.[10]

Ostensibly an exercise in gratitude, the Australian–British Reward Mission was enmeshed in the reassertion of British control in Borneo after the disruption to colonial rule that had occurred during Japan's occupation. Rewarding loyalty and making cash payments were also part of the effort to counter in South-East Asia the growing influence of communism, which had been an important factor in the resistance to Japanese occupation, especially among ethnic Chinese. British officials in North Borneo interpreted the reward mission as a positive way to rebuild relationships with local people in the immediate postwar period. Jackson met with Richard Evans, a British colonial officer known as a Resident, who was responsible for the West Coast of North Borneo. Evans considered it 'very gratifying to know that the Australian authorities had not forgotten the inhabitants of Borneo … the mission could achieve much and leave behind an impression that would last for many years'. The Acting Chief Secretary also 'expressed satisfaction that the Australian authorities were keeping faith with the natives'.[11] There was more divided opinion among the colonial old hands about whether or not some local applicants had conveniently manufactured a story about providing assistance to the Allies or POWs during the war in order to gain a reward. Jackson relented in many cases to allowing the British Resident to distribute money in small increments rather than giving the rewards in cash lump sums.

Jackson was not immune from engaging in colonialist behaviour himself. He gratefully accepted an offer from the British Resident of thirty-five local men to undertake 'bearer duties' for the mission. Each man carried between nine and thirteen kilograms in a woven basket. There were rations, the safari suits and radio equipment to be lugged about. Jackson was also prone to stereotyping the people he encountered. He described one resident of Borneo as 'a typical Dusan native[;] he is small in stature and could not be classed as a mental genius, his reasoning powers are definitely retarded'. Yet the statements Jackson collected, so explicit about the suffering that these people had endured during the war, did not fail to move him. He arranged for medical examinations and treatment of people who still had lingering injuries or wounds acquired as a consequence of the Japanese occupation.[12]

The Australian government, via mechanisms like the reward mission and individual grants, delivered both real and symbolic rewards to people it believed had demonstrated loyalty to the Allied cause. Over 100 people in North Borneo received cash grants, and the widows of men executed for their parts in helping Australian POWs were given pensions or grants for their children's education by the Australian government. Ultimately, the reward mission extended its remit to cover Sarawak and Malaya and by 1950 had distributed £7000 to men and women who had assisted the Allies.[13] Colin Simpson considered the mission a success. The people, he wrote, were 'tremendously gratified, indeed astonished that the Australian government should have sent men so far to say thank you to them in this fashion for the way they'd stuck their necks out'. He continued, 'And in terms of what we might call "public relations", I'm sure the mission paid off handsomely'.[14]

Ex-POW associations agitated for rewards to be paid also to people elsewhere who had provided assistance to POWs at huge risks to themselves and their families. Edward Dunlop was the Australian figurehead of a campaign, initiated by British ex-POWs based in Singapore, to assist Thai businessman Boonpong Sirivejjabhandu, most often referred to as Boon Pong. Boon Pong had used his canteen contract with the Japanese in Thailand as cover to smuggle food, cash and medicine to prisoners working on the Thai–Burma Railway. Dunlop estimated that these actions had saved almost 10 000 lives, and in 1951 the Australian government paid £500 to Boon Pong for the 'humanitarian and generous assistance' he had rendered to Australian POWs.[15]

Harry Jackson suggested another reward, more symbolic in nature. Having being approached by people who had requested a 'letter of good name', he thought letters of appreciation might be appropriate. He reassured the Australian government that 'anything in the form of a testimonial or certificate was highly treasured by the natives & assumed the proportion of a family heirloom'.[16] Whether or not such requests were caught up in postwar recriminations and tensions over collaboration he did not say. Subsequent to Jackson's request, a certificate was designed, issued by the Commonwealth of Australia, and approved and signed by the Minister for the Army. Printed in both English and Malay, it was testament to the new connections forged between Australia and its neighbours in the aftermath of the war. Although the British colonial connections remained strong, through ex-veteran networks and joint initiatives, such as the Australian–British Reward Mission, the Australian government was equally determined to create its own relationships with the region's people.

Regional friendships

One man whom Harry Jackson met on his travels through Borneo, and who had been tried alongside Captain Lionel Matthews at Kuching in 1943, was a local, Johnny Funk. During the war, Funk had helped to smuggle radio parts in to the POW camp at Sandakan. He had been sentenced to imprisonment and spent the rest of the war cutting timber and working on a road gang; the men in these gangs had been harnessed to each other like 'beasts of burden to a buffalo cart'.[17] In 1946 Funk was still 'a broken man', suffering ill-health as a result of his long imprisonment.[18] Jackson arranged for Funk to be transported to Singapore, where an Australian surgeon successfully treated him.[19]

Once he had made a full recovery from his war injuries, Funk sought to renew his association with Australia. He made a much-publicised trip to Australia in 1950, which was presented in the press as a thank-you gesture for his heroism from ex-POW associations. Funk was feted as a war hero and presented as an Asian person of the utmost reliability and integrity. He visited Perth, Adelaide and Melbourne; in the last of these he laid a wreath at the Shrine of Remembrance and stayed at the home of Harry Jackson. Several state ex-POW associations granted him life membership.[20] The newspapers were keen to claim that Funk was not a stereotypical small Asian and emphasised his height and good English. At 177 centimetres, 'with broad shoulders, a straight back and a firm handshake', he had an 'open face and a ready smile'.[21] 'Tall and bronzed, Johnny Funk spoke with just pride of "We Asiatic boys".'[22]

Migration, intermarriage and colonial presence had typified Borneo's history since the nineteenth century, and Funk's family was no exception. Funk told the papers that he was the grandson of a Tasmanian, leading one to conclude that he was 'Asiatic, but not quite pure blood'.[23] Funk's grandfather, New Zealand–born Ernest Pavitt, concluded his working life as Chief Surveyor of North Borneo and certainly retired to Tasmania, but not with Funk's maternal grandmother. Kwai, a Kadazan-Dusun woman, bore two children to Pavitt before their association ended. Funk's paternal heritage can be traced back to Chinese Hakkas who had emigrated from Hong Kong.[24] Funk and his brothers were educated at a Catholic mission school, were Christians and could speak English, Malay and Chinese.[25] Prior to the war, the Funk brothers had been members of the North Borneo Volunteer Force, a civil defence unit organised by the British colonial administration.

Funk therefore had much more complex associations with the British administration and with Australia than a story about being a compassionate war hero allowed. After his liberation by the Australian forces, he had joined them as a non-commissioned officer of the Field Security Team that assisted with the reoccupation of Borneo. While visiting Australia he stayed with Malcolm Armstrong, who had been a member of the British Borneo Civil Administration Unit, an interim military administration established by Australia in preparation for the return of British rule. Funk had escorted Japanese war criminals to trial and had shared a tent with Armstrong.[26]

After the war Funk put all of these connections with the Australian military and its intelligence arm to good use. Behind the scenes, Funk was on a personal mission to relocate his family to Australia. Legislative provisions about the entry of non-white people governed the entry of Funk himself and any family member. For all the accolades bestowed upon Funk during his visit, the fact remained that he was Asian. In Perth, he had discussions with Les Riches, the Secretary of the Ex-Prisoners of War and Relatives Association of Western Australia, about sponsoring his son Melvyn to complete his education in Australia. Melvyn required an exemption certificate. The application was also supported by Member of Parliament Frank Timson, who had worked in the intelligence corps during the war. Melvyn was ultimately granted permission to enter Australia for a period of three years and did so under the guardianship of Riches.[27] In late 1951 Funk's own application to become an Australian resident was successful, and he returned as a 'New Australian'.[28] He found work with the Australian Army in a civilian capacity. The following year he was joined by his wife and two children and the family reunited in Victoria. Melvyn, who had been studying in Perth, joined them.

Funk's entry to Australia did not go unnoticed in the broader Asian region, where the White Australia policy remained a controversial aspect of Australia's immigration regime. Newspapers in Singapore, for instance, pointed out that Funk was Eurasian, making clear that his mixed ancestry had contributed to the willingness to allow him into Australia.[29] In the immediate postwar period, Immigration Minister Arthur Calwell's ham-fisted efforts to enforce the White Australia policy by attempting to deport wartime refugees from Asia had been greeted with derision. A Singapore-based correspondent, Dennis Warner, highlighted Funk's case as receiving 'much favourable publicity', which formed a welcome contrast to the 'Calwell era outbursts of anti-Australianism'.[30]

The loyalty of Funk was ultimately remembered as not just to POWs and civilian internees suffering under Japanese control but to the broader British presence on Borneo. 'How do those who seek to make British Colonialism a dirty word explain this phenomenon?' one of Funk's supporters asked the Prime Minister in the late 1960s. The context for the communication was an effort to win repatriation benefits for Funk as he approached retirement, but the substance of the letter reveals the ways in which Funk's activities in the war and its immediate aftermath intersected with contemporary politics around postcolonial Asia. The underground to which Funk had belonged 'represented practically every race in Borneo', his supporter claimed. He added that, when with people like Funk, he had been 'always humbled by their common British loyalty'.[31]

A story centred on Funk was also capable of articulating a narrative about the friendship between Australia and the postwar state of Sabah (as North Borneo was renamed following its attainment of self-government in 1963). Second World War veterans were immensely proud that Sabah's coat of arms, from its inception until a redesign in 1982 depicted a ship with the symbol 'T' emblazoned on its sail, referencing the T-shaped colour patch of the AIF's 9th Division, which had liberated Borneo from Japanese rule.[32] When the division had arrived on Borneo, 'the only time an Australian force has liberated a people beyond Australian territories', Funk and his ilk had been humbled. In the eyes of the people of Borneo, 'the Australian soldier stood ten feet high … and won the hearts of these people'. The liberation of Borneo 'established for all time Australia's attitude towards its Asian neighbours as that of a free people being prepared to make a sacrifice to aid its friends'. In these ways, Funk also became symbolic of Australia's self-understanding as a friend to the region.[33]

By the 1960s, at the precise moment of Konfrontasi between Malaysia and Indonesia, Funk was again in the news as an individual who embodied the deep connections between the region's Commonwealth countries. The island of Borneo was the flashpoint of undeclared conflict between Indonesia, which controlled Kalimantan (in the south of the island), and Malaysia, which had incorporated Sabah and Sarawak (in the north) as two of its states. Indonesian President Sukarno viewed the Malaysian government, still part of the Commonwealth, as a colonial puppet. Unbeknown to the Australian public at the time, Australian troops supported the Malaysian government in its conflict with the Indonesians. Funk, born as a 'British subject' and now styled as a 'principal of the World War Two Borneo underground', personified the association between the nations. He was present in Singapore, courtesy of a flight chartered by the Australian Army, to renew his 'longstanding' connections there; his cousin Donald Stephens was a Minister in the Sabah government, and Funk's parents had been flown over for a reunion.[34] There appeared to be no purpose for the visit other than a display of the military and personal connections between Australia and its Asian regional neighbours.

Despite the heavy symbolic weight Funk carried in the postwar years, his work with the Australian occupation forces in Borneo was never recognised to be 'service' with the army. Indeed, Repatriation was most reluctant to grant him any entitlement, because to do so would open the floodgates to the 'large number of migrant servicemen now settled in Australia who were not members of an Australian military force'. Despite his trying to win benefits throughout the 1960s, Repatriation was resolute in its refusal.[35] Funk even enlisted his cousin Donald Stephens, by the 1970s the Malaysian High Commissioner in Canberra, to press Prime Minister Gough Whitlam to allow him access to repatriation benefits.[36] Funk's work did not accord with the strict legislative definitions of military service, but he performed a rather different function, as a symbol of the connections formed between Australia and its neighbours that flowed from the experiences of occupation and imprisonment.

Philanthropy and development

The AIF Malayan Nursing Scholarship was the official war memorial of the Australian Army's 8th Division. While waiting for their liberation from Changi, a group of Australian POWs devised a scheme to show their appreciation for the 'loyal and generous work and assistance given by sections of the Asiatic community in Malaya, especially the Chinese'.[37] Members of the division were deeply grateful for the support of the ethnic Chinese community during the battle against Japan and for the assistance its members gave to POWs during their captivity in Singapore. Men who became separated from their divisions in the chaos of war were sheltered, provisioned and assisted by the Chinese in Malaya. Chinese people also took outstanding risks to provide POWs with extra rations, cigarettes, medicines and other supplies.[38]

In keeping with the general trend in memorialisation following the Second World War, POWs were more interested in a utilitarian form of memorial, with broader benefits to the entire community, than a symbolic gesture or statue.[39] The memorial organising committee in Changi reached agreement that a nursing scholarship would be a fitting and useful tribute.[40] The scholarship, designed to 'improve the lot of all Chinese and other Asiatics in Malaya', would be limited to 'Chinese and Chinese-Eurasian nurses who could speak English, as the Chinese were the community to whom gratitude was felt'.[41]

The decision to limit the scholarship to Chinese applicants at once acknowledged the sacrifices made by the Chinese community for the Australians and attempted to reinscribe a previous racial hierarchy. The Chinese had suffered under Japanese occupation but 'had assisted so loyally in maintaining the British tradition'.[42] All former 8th Division members received a printed circular asking them to remember the Chinese men, women and children who had assisted them during captivity: 'Many of us would not have returned to our families had it not been for their sacrifice, service, and suffering. The Jap tried to reduce us to white coolies in the eyes of the Chinese. They failed. The more the Jap put on the screw, the more the Chinese men, women and children respected us and helped us'.[43]

The erosion of white prestige as a consequence of defeat and imprisonment by an Asian power was one of the many troubling aspects of the Pacific War for the Allies.[44] The circular's reference to the common designation of prisoners as 'white coolies' was itself acknowledgment that the racial order had been inverted in captivity. Former POWs were thereby exhorted to 'remember the Chinese' not just because they had provided much-needed food, drink and other resources but also since they had not lost respect for white men in a state of abjection. Loyalty to the 'British tradition' included refusing to accept Japanese inversion of the racial hierarchy.

From its earliest iterations the scholarship scheme contained a blend of assumptions about ethnicity, Commonwealth relations and philanthropy that were put to the test as Malaya made the transition from British colony to postcolonial nation-state.[45] By raising funds to sponsor the visit of Chinese nurses to Australia for a two-year study period, POWs hoped to assist poorer communities through the provision of expertise acquired in Australia. The scholarship was intended to be a 'novel form of War Memorial' and one capable of 'binding two parts of the British Commonwealth closely together'.[46] When seeking government support, the scholarship committee claimed that a federal donation would enable it to 'make an even larger contribution to Empire unity'.[47] The reference to 'Empire unity' demonstrated that a founding premise of the scholarship scheme was that

Malaya would remain a British colony. The scheme also assumed that it would be possible for a country like Australia to preference Chinese applicants over other ethnicities (Malays in particular) that populated Malaya and that existing training for nurses in Malaya was insufficient.

Early discussion of the scholarship demonstrated the political expedience that at times underpinned statements of empire loyalty and Commonwealth bonds. In 1945 Lieutenant Colonel Samuel Pond (1905–62), who had been a POW in Changi, told Prime Minister Ben Chifley that the nursing scholarship would 'be of great material value to Australia in promoting goodwill with Malaya and the East, and in extending Australian trade and commerce in consequence'.[48] The scholarship would also make Australia better known to the Chinese in Malaya. Scholarship supporters enlisted the Chinese Consul to announce that he could 'think of no likelier way of helping the friendship between our two countries'.[49] Acting Secretary of the Department of External Affairs John Burton (1915–2010), well known for his views promoting greater ties between Australia and Asia, was soon convinced of the scheme's utility. 'On political, social and commercial grounds', Burton concluded, there should be strong support for the scholarship scheme.[50]

Although the scholarship was a private initiative of former POWs, their extensive links with government and the military ensured high-level state support. The Commander-in-Chief of the Australian Military Forces General Sir Thomas Blamey granted his imprimatur, and subsequently the army printed 22 000 circulars calling for donations. The Department of Information gave publicity to the scheme on shortwave radio broadcasts. Former POWs subscribed £11 000, and the Red Cross donated £5000 from the unspent money it had raised within Australia for POWs during the war.[51] The Commonwealth government was ultimately persuaded to contribute and did so as part of its program for educational assistance to countries of South-East Asia under the United Nations Educational, Scientific and Cultural Organization's reconstruction schemes.[52] By March 1946 enough funds had been raised to constitute a board of trustees for the AIF Malayan Nursing Scholarship, and efforts to recruit the first nurses for the scheme began.

In order to capitalise on their regional connections and to ensure the choice of good candidates, the Melbourne-based board established a selection panel in Singapore. The Australian Commissioner for Malaya Claude Massey was in the chair. Prominent Singaporean-Chinese Sir Lim Han Hoe was a member; he had strong ties with Australia that had been forged during the war years. Lim's wife and children had been evacuated to Australia in 1942, and two of his children went on to study for and receive medical degrees from the University of Melbourne.[53] A Legislative Councillor in Singapore, Lim had remained behind. Sentenced to seven years' imprisonment by the Japanese for listening to the radio, he spent the war in the notorious Outram Road jail. He was very ill at the time of his liberation and joined his wife and children in Australia to recuperate. After returning to Singapore, Lim agreed to join the first Singapore selection panel, convened in 1946, but advised against referring to anyone as 'Eurasian-Chinese'.[54] The panel also included the Australian Dr Margaret Smallwood, a member of the Malayan Medical Service, who had spent the war interned in Singapore.[55]

The decision to limit the scheme to Chinese applicants betrayed ignorance of local political tensions that had escalated in the aftermath of the war. Australia's Commissioner Claude Massey was alert to the racial politics of his diplomatic post and advised caution to the scholarship board. The British reorganisation of the political structure of its Malay possessions in

1946 was made without consultation with the local population and ultimately formed a crucible for Malay nationalism. The new Malayan Union sought to terminate the special rights for Malays, which had been a tacit agreement for British rule, to put non-Malays such as the Chinese on an equal footing and to undermine the power and status of traditional Malay rulers. Malays began to organise in nationalist groups determined to protect what they perceived as the particular and innate rights of Malays as the historical and indigenous community.

In other words, 1946 was a time of heightened ethnic tensions between Chinese and Malays in Singapore and Malaya, and the nursing scholarship board waded in to waters it was ill equipped to navigate. Massey warned the board in July that he was concerned that if Malays were not allowed to apply and the scholarship was limited to only Chinese applicants this might be perceived as 'racial prejudice'. He had consulted with local medical directors who agreed that 'nurses should be selected on merit from any Asiatic races in Singapore and Malaya'.[56] The Australian-based board was resolute, however, advising Massey that he should point out that 'all races of Malaya' would benefit from the scheme and that it was no different from 'many others which are restricted to candidates of particular faith and race'.[57] Massey registered in the minutes that he 'still felt some uneasiness' about the restrictiveness and its capacity to arouse racial antagonisms. Margaret Smallwood further pointed out that it was best to avoid providing training in midwifery work and the treatment of diseases, which was already 'quite adequate in Malaya'.[58] This was another piece of locally sourced advice from Malaya and Singapore which the scholarship board in Melbourne chose to ignore.

Massey's concern about the capacity of the nursing scholarship's preference for Chinese nurses to be interpreted as racial prejudice at once referenced local tensions and Australia's reputation as a country with outdated attitudes to racial questions. Australian strategy towards the region more generally in the late 1940s was caught in the cleft stick of progressive foreign policy and ongoing commitment to White Australia.[59] Conscious that regional dynamics in the postwar world would be different from the imperial relationships that had preceded the war, the Labor government had been seeking a new approach in East Asia. Accordingly, the political scientist and government adviser William Macmahon Ball (1901–86) was dispatched on a goodwill mission in 1948 to assess communist influence and research new nationalist governments and political parties and offer them friendship, while also identifying opportunities to distribute Australian scholarships and other forms of relief. External Affairs was committed to educational assistance and in broad support of the AIF Malayan Nursing Scholarship but disturbed by its directive nature: it was 'going against the principle of the mission' to tell the governments visited what Australia could offer and 'then let them decide for themselves' what they required.[60] In order to overcome the perception of racial prejudice that dogged Australia's reputation, in 1948 the Australian government also supplemented the two scholarships available for Chinese nurses with a further government scholarship 'open to all races'. Massey described it as a 'gesture of goodwill from the Australian people to the people of Malaya' and as direct fulfilment of a promise made by Australia to the United Nations.[61]

The first recipients of the AIF Malayan Nursing Scholarship were two well-qualified nurses, Alice Chia of Singapore and Ooi Soh Im from Kuala Kangsar, in Malaya. Chia had been educated at the Convent of the Holy Infant Jesus in Singapore and trained as a nurse at Kandang Kerbau Hospital. Ooi was from Ipoh, where she had attended the Anglo-Chinese Girls School and trained at Ipoh Hospital before becoming a staff nurse at the Women's Hospital in Kuala Kangsar. When the nurses were appointed in 1947, Massey said that they would 'create another link in the chain of friendship which began in the difficult time of war'.[62] Designed as a living memorial, the scholarship was presented as ensuring that the memory of Australian sacrifice would live on in the region. 'Even if tall bamboos thrust through Malayan earth, which once held a rough-hewn cross', the *Australian Women's Weekly* declared in 1947, 'the memory of fallen members of the Eighth division will be evergreen in the hearts of the Malayan people'.[63] The rhetoric was admirable and was matched by a farewell reception for the nurses attended by the Governor of Singapore, but it soon became clear that the details of the scheme simply presumed the superiority of Australian training.

When the two women returned to Singapore after their two years in Australia, they gave a mixed report of their experiences. They had enjoyed the 'unity and friendliness' of Australian nurses. However, they were sorry to have had to complete a midwifery course, because the training had been 'not very much different from the training a nurse receives in Malaya'.[64] When Chia's sister Maisie received a scholarship in 1952 she made a similar complaint. 'Australian nursing standards are high', she said, 'but are not far in advance of those in Singapore and Federation hospitals'. She added that many Australians 'were amazed' to hear that there were big modern hospitals in Malaya.[65]

The standing of the extra qualifications the nurses gained in Australia and the benefits to which they were entitled as a result once they returned to Malaya or Singapore soon became a source of tension. There was little sense that the scholarship board had considered the implications of its intervention for the careers of the women concerned – it was more focused on the imagined subject of their ministrations, the 'poverty-stricken Chinese villager' – or their place in medical bureaucracies that were evolving from previous, colonial models.⁶⁶ In 1949 there was debate in the Singaporean press about the standing of the nurses who had participated in the scheme once they returned to Malaya and Singapore. What were 'the repercussions of these Australian qualifications superimposed on Malayan qualifications'? If the new qualifications were recognised and led to expedited promotion – contrary to the existing system, in which promotion was based on length of service – 'there would be natural resentment among other locally qualified nurses who ha[d] not had the luck to go to Australia'. The report continued, 'Some people think that if the Malayan Governments were really in earnest about Malayanisation of the public services they would not leave it to Australian ex-soldiers to give higher training to Malayan nurses'.⁶⁷

Uncertainty over the advantages derived by participants and the scholarship's susceptibility to a postcolonial critique meant that in less than a decade of operation it was seriously undersubscribed. By the 1950s, when Colombo Plan rhetoric was more commonplace, the scholarship was offered as being able to 'realise the noble aims of the English-speaking world for the under-privileged peoples of Asia'.⁶⁸

Once Malaya achieved independence in 1957, and after it united with Sabah, Sarawak and Singapore to become Malaysia in 1963, local health authorities were increasingly wary of participating in a scheme that still bore some colonial overtones. Apart from the racially restrictive nature of the scholarship, the selection of the nurses remained in the hands of expatriates rather than in those of Malaysians and Singaporeans themselves.

By the early 1960s the scheme was in abeyance, for want of cooperation of local authorities.⁶⁹ The Chairman of the nursing scholarship board, Wilfrid Kent Hughes, euphemistically referred to this as lacking the 'necessary moral administrative support'.[70] No longer were the heads of Malaysian and Singaporean medical services expatriate British and Australians; they were university-educated people from the region itself. In 1966 the Malaysian Red Cross wrote to the scholarship board and made clear that the Malaysian government would sooner not 'support any scheme whereby all benefits [were] to be conferred on a particular nationality', preferring instead 'that the offer be made to Malaysians irrespective of race'.[71] By 1967 the Australian High Commissioner was refusing to sit on the selection panel, in light of the sensitivity in Malaysia and Singapore to the restrictive nature of the scheme.

Determined to retain the scholarship as a sign of friendship between Australia and the region, the board was ultimately forced to alter its constitution to allow nurses of any ethnicity to apply for selection. Kent Hughes prepared the document outlining the need for constitutional amendment, pointing out that political circumstances in Malaysia and Singapore had changed since 1945. It was 'common knowledge' that the Malaysian and Singaporean governments had adopted the policy that their nations were 'multi-racial states', and a scheme devoted to Chinese nurses was unsustainable. The state-run health system did not provide separate nursing services for racial communities, so the stipulation that the nurses be employed within Chinese communities upon their return was also unworkable. There was a danger that the scholarship in its current formulation would have an 'adverse effect' on relations between Australia, Malaysia and Singapore. Change was necessary for the scholarship to continue 'the imaginative ideal of assisting people in South East Asia to whom the Australian soldiers who formerly served in these areas [felt] gratitude and goodwill'.[72]

In 1968 the scholarship board changed its constitution and handed over selection to the local authorities in order to keep its scheme alive. The Malaysian and Singaporean health ministries had firm views on appropriate candidates, training courses and postgraduate qualifications. With their cooperation, scholarship nurses were coming to Australia again by the 1970s. Survival of the scheme was given a further fillip in the late 1980s, when the board entered into an agreement with Curtin University of Technology and the Malaysian Ministry of Health.[73] The involvement of former prisoners remained an essential component of the scheme, with the chairmanship of the board held at that time by another former POW, and retired politician, Sir Reginald Swartz (1911–2006).

An image of the scholarship recipients taken at a graduation ceremony in Perth in 1998 shows these elements of continuity and change. The two nurses, Malaysian women, neither of whom was ethnic Chinese, were photographed with two famous ex-POWs: the former nurse Lieutenant Colonel Vivian Statham (née Bullwinkel), a board member in the 1970s and 1980s, and Reg Swartz. At the time of writing, in 2017, the AIF Malaya Memorial Nursing Scholarship continued, with nurses undertaking training at Curtin University, with the support of the scholarship fund, the Department of Foreign Affairs and Trade and the ministries of health in Malaysia and Singapore.[74]

One of the legacies that the war bequeathed to Australian society was the knowledge that 'Asia' was in fact a region of many peoples, with different political agendas and cultures. Just as pronounced as the idea that the Japanese had behaved with barbarity during the war but must afterwards be reformed, forgiven or retrained was the presumption that there were 'good' Asians, people who had been sympathetic to the Allies, who should not be forgotten in the postwar period. The Australian–British Reward Mission typified this approach, as did Edward Dunlop, who was a driving force behind the scheme to compensate Boonpong Sirivejjabhandu in the late 1940s. Likewise, the AIF Malayan Nursing Scholarship attests to the active involvement of war veterans in general, and former POWs in particular, in promoting connections and relationships between Australia and Asia in the postwar period. The ambition to create a 'novel form of war memorial', designed to train ethnic Chinese nurses, ultimately provided an education for the scheme's administrators about the contemporary realities of a postcolonial region.

Part IV

The battle resolved

9
Prisoners in the time of trauma

> All that brutalisation up there had left a weakness in him, a part of his mind that was open on one side to absolute darkness and the stench that came from that direction was so powerful at times that he gagged on it, not daring to turn his head, even in the clearest sunshine, for fear of having to face again the tattered columns of them, big-boned, filthy, with their muddy eyes and outsized hands and feet.
>
> David Malouf, 1990[1]

By the 1960s public interest in ex-POWs had diminished. POWs were now 'a forgotten race', one of them lamented. In the 1940s and 1950s a steady stream of popular memoirs and significant developments in the Australia–Japan relationship had kept the POW story prominent in the public mind. The muted response to the now-acclaimed trilogy by ex-POW Ray Parkin – *Out of the Smoke* (1960), *Into the Smother* (1963) and *The Sword and the Blossom* (1968) – demonstrated the extent to which interest in this facet of war experience had waned.[2]

War was in retreat as a defining element of Australian national identity. The veterans of the Second World War, now middle aged, and the elderly men who made up the thinning ranks of First World War soldiers appeared to be yesterday's people, men attached to a version of masculinity at odds with the values of youthful baby boomers. The sense of generational difference received its most famous expression in Alan Seymour's play *The One Day of the Year* (1958), in which a university student attacks the hollowness of Anzac Day and, by implication, the behaviour of his war veteran father. A former POW from Queensland articulated his personal experience of growing disillusion in 1972: 'Some of the present work staff are antagonistic towards war service in general & those affected by war service in particular'.

The movement opposing the Vietnam War further undermined the national mythology of Anzac and contributed to a growing construction of war as horror. Although there had been broad public support for Australia's intervention in Vietnam in the 1960s, by the 1970s controversy over national service had seen the war become a source of division and social tension. The peace movement and student groups presented the Vietnam War as an imperialist struggle in which Western countries such as Australia and the United States combined in an effort to quash the legitimate desire for independence of an Asian people.

Controversy over the Vietnam War compromised the capacity of Australia's military heritage to be a rallying cry for unity at exactly the moment that support for White Australia began to fracture, then break. Small numbers of non-white peoples had migrated to Australia since the late 1950s, including the Japanese wives of British Commonwealth Occupation Force servicemen, and incremental changes to immigration policy continued throughout the 1960s. White Australia was formally abandoned as official policy in the mid-1970s. The federal government promoted a new, multicultural identity that disavowed the emphasis on racial purity of earlier times. Yet this development coincided with the zenith of Japanese economic power and increasing Japanese tourism. White Australia was no longer government policy, but the fears about Australia's vulnerability to dominance by Asia that it had expressed did not entirely disappear from the public sphere.

In this confluence of events, POWs emerged as historical figures capable of expressing contemporary tensions about war, identity, race and region. By the 1970s the POW story could pull in many directions at once: as a metaphor to express ongoing anxiety about the potential for domination by Asia, as evidence that forgiveness and racial tolerance were possible, and as a reflection of outdated attitudes to racial difference. As a victim of war's terror, ultimately the POW was perfectly placed to revive interest, in a non-belligerent way, in the military history of a country that had, but for a short period, been particularly attached to war as an essential element of its national story.

From White Australia to multiculturalism

By the early 1970s older fears about military and population invasion had been replaced with new concerns about the potential for Japan to dominate Australia through capital, business and property acquisition.[3] John Romeril's stage play *The Floating World*, first performed in 1974, encapsulated both the ongoing qualms about Japan and the much more recent tendency to view POWs as embodying outdated views about race. *The Floating World* is set on a cruise ship sailing from Australia to Japan. Referred to with irony as 'Australia's invasion of Nippon', the journey is juxtaposed with a more telling 'invasion': the narrator's opening description of twelve Japanese businessmen exploring a potential development site near an Australian coral reef, and their 'white-fanged evasions' at a press conference.[4] There is no further reference to this opening scene, but concerns about Japanese interest in Australian land frame the play as a whole.[5]

Romeril's play explores questions of Australia–Japan relations, war and psychological suffering through the figure of its main character, Les Harding. Harding, a former POW of the Japanese, and his wife are passengers on the 1974 *Women's Weekly* Cherry Blossom Tour to Japan, a misguided present from their daughter and son-in-law. Harding is presented as an Australian male type, the 'ocker': a man who is gauche, sexist and racist. He and his wife are careless in their casual racism towards the non-white members of the ship's crew and its passengers. Yet as the cruise ship sails north to Japan and enters the Asian region, Harding's composure evaporates. The travel becomes temporal, as he descends into a psychotic state and relives the privations and physical torture of his period of imprisonment by the Japanese in the Second World War. In Harding's mental disarray, the crew and fellow passengers transmogrify into the cast of his prison camp days.

A new consciousness about race in Australia profoundly influenced responses to *The Floating World*. Criticisms of the White Australia policy, increasing Aboriginal activism and the influence of the new left in identifying ongoing forms of discrimination had heightened awareness of the role racism had played in Australia's history. When it was first performed, most reviewers interpreted *The Floating World* not primarily as a study of psychosis but rather as a commentary on Australia's racial attitudes and an inherent criticism of the war in Vietnam.[6] The published version of the play assures readers that its purpose is to critique, rather than endorse, the racist attitudes of its protagonists. The book includes a section entitled 'The yellow peril', which reproduces racist cartoons from the previous century and provides a potted history of the White Australia policy. An essay by theatre critic Katharine Brisbane frames the play as a brave exploration of Australia's 'shameful history of xenophobia'.[7] There was almost no public comment on Harding's traumatic war experiences or on the play as an examination of the personal legacy of captivity.

To employ the former POW as an exemplar of racist society was a relatively new development. This certainly turned on its head the older cultural logic surrounding POWs, which held that they were the unfortunate yet plucky victims of a 'brutal' and 'barbarous' enemy. The most popular memoirs of the immediate postwar period emphasised the stoicism, humour and inventiveness of Australian captives and the viciousness of their captors. A primary message of these books was that the Japanese were an inherently untrustworthy and callous race; POWs had been in the hands of a fanatical enemy who had persecuted them, in part, because they were white. By the 1960s, as Japan became Australia's most important trading partner and the number of independent and postcolonial states increased in the Asia-Pacific region, these older languages of civilisation and barbarism became muted. With growing criticism of Australia's restricted immigration policies, highly protected economy and controversial intervention in Vietnam, the country's own reputation in the region had been compromised. Whiteness was no longer the ace in the POW deck, capable of trumping the ambiguity of subjection. It had become the unpredictable, destabilising joker.

While *The Floating World* used the figure of the POW to explore Australia's xenophobic past, in many other cases reference to POWs acted as a metaphor for discomfort with Japan's economic power. Anxiety about the potential for a new 'Asian invasion' by stealth, in the guise of property investment and trade dominance, continued to erupt in the Australian public sphere. Two issues of particular prominence were Japanese real estate purchases (as *The Floating World* made clear) and a plan to encourage Japanese investment and technology development in Australia through a proposed futuristic settlement known as the Multifunction Polis.[8] Jill Shearer's play *Shimada*, first performed in 1987, uses the figure of the POW to examine the potential to conflate business drive with military aggression. The play centres on the attempted Japanese takeover of a Queensland bicycle company owned and operated by former POWs. 'It's a different war now – a trade war!' declares one character. 'We're a multicultural society, whether you like it or not.'[9] The new emphasis on ex-POWs' racism coexisted with, rather than displaced, older rhetoric that pointed to the fate of prisoners as the price once paid for Japan's ambition. Victorian RSL President Bruce Ruxton, a former member of the British Commonwealth Occupation Force, was one of the most vocal 'Japan-bashers' of the 1980s. Ruxton frequently invoked the memory of POWs' suffering to malign Japan's economic intentions.[10]

By the 1980s, however, there were limits on the extent to which ex-POWs, either symbolically or literally, might articulate opposition to Japan on the grounds of race alone. Ruxton, who had not himself been a POW, was frequently derided for his extreme views, even if they did have some traction in certain sections of the community. In 1983 when ex-POW Russell Braddon published *The Other Hundred Years War: Japan's Bid for Supremacy, 1941–2041*, the reception was at best subdued ('courageous'), at worst derisive ('it appeals directly to the old Yellow horde prejudice'). As this reviewer put it, Braddon's 'terrible obsession' with the Japanese, while understandable, was a legacy of the 1940s and prevented him from recognising the contemporary reality of Japanese society, which was both more plural and more international than ever before.[11] Self-fashioned as an oracle, Braddon was treated as an anachronism.

Just as former POWs could be represented as the unfortunate remnants of White Australia, so the more progressive among their number could be offered as evidence that Australia had the potential to become the multicultural society it now purported to be. In the early 1980s the response to the publication of Stan Arneil's war diaries anticipated this development. Arneil, like Labor politician Tom Uren, had taken the 'cooperative principle' as one of the primary legacies of his captivity and spent his postwar life putting it into practice. President of the ABC Staff Association in the 1960s and founder of the credit union movement in Australia, Arneil moved in cooperative circles. He was acquainted with the Director of the small, independent Alternative Publishing Co-operative, established in Sydney in 1975 and committed to an Australian list. At the company's behest, Arneil prepared his war diary for publication. *One Man's War* (1980) was an instant success and the first in a wave of prisoner diaries and memoirs published in the 1980s and 1990s. The book sold 5000 copies in its first year and ran to several editions.[12] It won the 1981 International PEN (Poets, Essayists and Novelists) Peter Stuyvesant International Cultural Foundation Award for a non-fiction book of literature that best dispelled racial, religious and class bigotry.

Left-wing intellectuals grasped the POW diary and memoir as evidence that Australia's military heritage was more complicated than the parade of jingoes and militarists whom they believed had come to dominate Anzac Day. Arneil's diary soon won praise from Manning Clark, Australia's most famous historian, who wrote a preface for the third edition. Clark praised the book as an *Everyman*, unusual for its time as being written by a 'rank and file' member of the army who had demonstrated 'what war does to human beings'. Only six years after the end of the Vietnam War and during a period of intense anti-nuclear activism, Clark declared that Arneil's work carried 'a lesson we need urgently and right now'.[13] Russel Ward, author of the classic *The Australian Legend* (1958), wrote the foreword. Ward claimed Arneil to be an exemplar of tolerance, declaring, 'Younger readers will learn too that not all of their ancestors forty years ago were racist'.[14] The diary offered considered portraits of Korean guards, Japanese officers, Indian fellow prisoners, and Malayan, Thai and Chinese civilians.

Post-traumatic stress disorder and empathy for the victim

Questions about Australians' racial attitudes, which fostered a new interpretation of the POW experience, coincided with withdrawal from Vietnam, completed in 1975. On the one hand, the divisiveness and unpopularity of the Vietnam War had led to a disengagement from Australia's military heritage. On the other, the conflict had also started – both within Australia and internationally – a new conversation about the impact of war on its participants. This focus on the damaging legacy of war ultimately contributed to renewed interest in POWs. The changes also helped to shift the ambivalence that had accompanied POW's defeat and subjection towards a more empathetic view of prisoners as victims and survivors of catastrophe.

The 1960s had witnessed a radical reformulation of trauma theory. After the First World War psychiatric orthodoxy had suggested that only those predisposed through existing illness or incapacity might become neurotic or anxious as a result of their war experiences. The suspicion that such malingering might be motivated by potential financial gain, in the form of compensation or a pension, compounded the stigma attached to war neurosis. In 1980 a newly defined condition, post-traumatic stress disorder, or PTSD, removed these a priori assumptions about weakness and insisted that there were events capable of causing traumatic responses in an otherwise healthy individual. A major revision to the US *Diagnostic and Statistical Manual of Mental Disorders* in 1980 declared that post-traumatic stress disorder could arise when a patient experienced 'a stressful event such as would lead to clear symptoms of distress in most people'.[15] No longer were traumatised individuals under a cloud of suspicion about their innate frailty or expedience. Post-traumatic stress disorder was a recognisable medical syndrome, and its sufferers were legitimate victims of a capricious twist of fate.[16] This model of trauma gained strength as the 1980s progressed, and it began to influence both the ways in which former POWs interpreted their experience and the public narratives surrounding it.

'Trauma', in the sense commonly used from the 1980s, was therefore historically specific; exposure to a violent or shocking event was potentially traumatising for an otherwise healthy person, and anyone thus affected should be recognised as a legitimate victim. A broader acceptance of trauma, of the centrality of the tragic event, ushered in new understandings of victimhood and to some extent influenced the idea of history itself. The past was reconfigured as a 'painful scar', the sociologists Didier Fassin and Richard Rechtman have suggested, and the trauma survivor was positioned as 'the witness to the horrors of our age', the author of its most authentic account.[17] Another historian, Annette Wieviorka, put it most succinctly in the English title of her 1998 book: the late-twentieth century became *The Era of the Witness*. These shifting perceptions of the meanings of trauma, its metaphorical dimensions in relation to victimhood and history, and the centrality of the individual survivor account drove the reinvigoration of public interest in the war experiences of former POWs.

Responses to *The Floating World*, which was restaged many times in the years following its first performance, prefigured broader shifts.[18] Les Harding was in many respects a most unlikeable character. Yet his mental anguish and suffering also held the potential to create empathy for the figure of the boorish, racist veteran so recently derided by radical students and intellectuals in Australia. By the 1980s critics had started to interpret *The Floating World* as a play about war damage rather than as a study of racism. In 1982 theatre critic Leonard Radic claimed that it was a 'compassionate study of an ocker ex-serviceman, whose mind snaps ... and not (as some have claimed) [about] the Australian's latent streak of racism'.[19] This was an interpretation of the play that gathered force as the 1980s progressed, the timing coincident with the creation of the psychiatric category of post-traumatic stress disorder. By 1986 the playwright himself claimed that his work was 'a solid look at ... the massive incidents of trauma in our lives'.[20]

The acknowledgment of psychological harm, now constructed as 'trauma', represented a significant shift from the ways in which imprisonment, particularly its impact on mental health, had been discussed prior to the 1980s. Given the prevailing views about war neurosis before that time, there was no sympathy or cultural cachet to be derived from constructing a narrative about imprisonment that emphasised its psychological effects. 'One of the striking things about POW life', Ted Fisher had insisted in 1949, 'was that men had no neurotic manifestations. They had no barbed-wire psychoses'.[21] Applicants to the Prisoners of War Trust Fund received no special understanding or sympathy if they suffered from anxiety or neurosis; indeed, such a diagnosis more often raised a flag of suspicion than a response of understanding. Albert Coates, the fund's trustees and other ex-POW doctors were also insistent that any discussion of war neurosis or psychological vulnerability could become a self-fulfilling prophecy. The memoirs published in the late 1940s and 1950s focused on bravado and humour rather than psychological disturbance. Russell Braddon did not mention that the completion of *The Naked Island* had been preceded by a suicide attempt and a period in a psychiatric ward after he returned to Australia from Changi.

The language of trauma entered the lexicon of war during the 1980s and gained a new respectability. The first mention of the word in *Barbed Wire and Bamboo*, the journal of the Ex-Prisoners of War Association of Australia, occurred in 1983. That year, Bill Hood, Secretary of the Western Australian branch, had cause to be reminded of a close friend's lingering and painful death from gangrene while working on the Thai–Burma Railway. 'It means reliving those days all over', he wrote, 'and Trauma is the only word which covers how it affects one'.[22] Trauma was also beginning to move into public discussion of the legacy of the POW experience. At the biennial conference of ex-POW associations held in 1983, the Governor of Queensland, Sir James Ramsay, congratulated the associations on their important work in bringing to the attention of governments the issues faced by former POWs. He praised the work of Dr Ian Duncan, who had recently surveyed 2000 POWs on behalf of the NSW Ex-Prisoners of War Association and had found significant evidence of mental health problems. Ramsay expressed his sympathy for 'the mental trauma' that the association's members had suffered.[23]

In the following years there was a plethora of medical research supporting the conclusion that POWs had been a group particularly susceptible to postwar psychiatric illnesses. One study, in 1986, found significant incidence of anxiety and depression but no cases that fulfilled the definition of post-traumatic stress disorder.[24] Despite mixed clinical results, the concept of trauma had taken hold. Perhaps its most telling resonance was the assumption that psychological suffering as a result of captivity was not a condition driven by weakness or malign intention.

Receptivity within the ex-POW community to the concept of trauma was matched by a renaissance of public interest in Australia's war history, most especially in the individual stories of veterans who could testify to the horror of war. A memory boom dominated by events deemed painful for individuals or the nation was also underway in other Western countries. One of its features was a 'politics of regret', which Jeffrey Olick defined as the practices through which 'many contemporary societies confront toxic legacies of the past'.[25] Historians, sociologists and cultural theorists have debated why such attention was now trained on difficult histories. They have considered factors ranging from the undermining of narratives of progress – such as the crisis in Western cultures occasioned by the Holocaust, total wars and genocides, the legacies of movements for social change in the 1960s and the subsequent turn to identity politics and histories of oppression and repression – to the impact of mass media and digital technologies.[26] The latter facilitated an explosion of interest in genealogy and family research into relatively well-documented military experiences, which allowed the interest in individual stories and painful events to coalesce.

In keeping with the privileging of survivor accounts that accompanied the interest in difficult histories, former POWs were soon the subjects of an extensive oral history project. Hank Nelson, an Australian National University historian who had worked in the late 1970s with the ABC's Tim Bowden on *Taim Bilong Masta*, a radio documentary series about Australian colonial experience in Papua New Guinea, suggested POWs as a project. 'Digger, we have to do Australian POWs of the Japanese', he told Bowden in 1982, as the fortieth anniversary of the fall of Singapore approached. 'They're in their 60s, they've never talked about it much, their mortality is starting to look at them, and their story has never been told.'[27] Over the course of two years, Nelson and Bowden recorded 350 hours of interviews with surviving POWs and ultimately produced a sixteen-episode Radio National documentary, *P.O.W.: Australians under Nippon*, first broadcast in 1984. It was an instant hit. Extracts from the interviews were published in a book, and the series was rebroadcast many times on the ABC in subsequent years.[28]

The series emphasises the authentic voice of the survivor and shows how beliefs about trauma had entered popular culture. Bowden later recalled that the POW story 'had never been told … because they felt, believe it or not, slightly ashamed … It was the most traumatic thing. And because we had an interest and a knowledge, these blokes started to talk.' He also confessed, 'What I didn't realise was the trail of sleepless nights I was leaving behind me'.[29] Advertisements for the series played on the tropes of survivor and trauma:

> *P.O.W. The story of Australians under Nippon*
> *(as it's never been told before)*

> Of the 22 000 Australian service men and women who were prisoners of war of the Japanese from 1942 to 1945, only 14 000 survived.
>
> This is their story, told by some of the survivors themselves. It's a poignant and powerful account of Australian bravery and resilience. And an extraordinary glimpse at the ingenuity of individuals and at the way the trauma of the time affected the people who lived through it. As a radio series, a book and cassette it's both a history lesson and a timeless lesson in courage.[30]

The last episode, 'Lost years and wounded minds', declared that 'the survivors of the intense trauma had to adjust to a changed Australia'.[31]

The success of the series and the renewed interest in POWs were developments that took some former prisoners by surprise. Others had been toiling for many years to keep the memory of their captivity alive and used the new interest in trauma to reacquaint the Australian public with their wartime experiences. The visual record of captivity, most particularly images of its harrowing physical toll, was well suited to illustrate the horrors of war. In 1984, when launching a collection of George Aspinall's secret photographs taken on the Thai–Burma Railway and at Changi, former POW Dr Lloyd Cahill commented that he had 'been intrigued by the resurgence of interest in the fate of P.O.W. in the Far East'.[32] Aspinall himself had encouraged interest in his work for much of the previous decade, following the conclusion of the Vietnam War. His photographs appeared in a special poster in the *Sun* newspaper for Anzac Day 1976, and at the Ballina RSL in 1979 he also screened films he had recorded in POW camps.[33] Fifty former POWs were in attendance at the Ballina screening, including Oscar 'Ossie' Jackson, depicted as the central figure in the famous *Fit for Work* photograph taken around 1943.[34] The image became central to the advertising for the Radio National documentary series.

The former POW network had remained strong throughout the 1970s and facilitated the renewal of interest in prisoners' experiences. Roy Whitecross, author of the memoir *Slaves of the Sons of Heaven* (1951), had spent the latter part of his career as an assistant university registrar and organised an exhibition of POW art, photographs and diaries at the University of Sydney's War Memorial Gallery in 1982. Senator John Carrick, leader of the government in the Senate and a former POW, launched the exhibition, which included the work of Aspinall and Wilfrid Kent Hughes' diaries.[35] At the 5th National Ex-POW Reunion, held in Melbourne in 1984, the Mural Hall in the Myer department store hosted a Historical Prisoner of War Display, which included material on loan from the Australian War Memorial and private memorabilia.[36] Veterans began to trawl through the war memorial's collections and discovered the dismantled chapel from Changi prison, carefully preserved by an Australian war graves unit at the end of the war, sitting in storage at the war memorial's warehouse. A public appeal for funds assisted in the reconstruction of the chapel at the Royal Military College, Duntroon, as a memorial to the 35 000 men and women taken prisoner in all wars. In 1988 Edward Dunlop and Vivian Statham (née Bullwinkel) were guests of honour at the dedication of Changi Chapel as a national memorial. While POWs were still not commemorated on Anzac Parade, the site of Australia's major military memorials, the army that had once regarded their imprisonment as a 'matter of dishonour' was now prepared to host a memorial to them in the grounds of its officer training college.[37]

The recasting of the Second World War as a potentially traumatic experience also began a process of reconciliation with their fathers for the generation that had been so alienated by the conflict in Vietnam. By the 1980s the baby boom generation was mid-life and mid-career and comprised many with influential voices in the media and cultural spheres. Their fathers had been shaped by war in different ways, most often by active service or, at the very least, through support for the war effort rather than opposition to it. Those who had suffered the misfortune to be taken prisoner by Japan in the Second World War had been fighting in Asia, the scene of Australia's most recent and most controversial war. In the 1960s and 1970s critics of the

Vietnam War had sometimes elided earlier wars into a confused mess of thinking about imperial wars in Asia. Novelist Peter Carey even claimed that his own 'anti-Vietnam' generation of writers 'completely ignored those Australian soldiers who fought and died' because of a perception that 'their really justifiable fear and hatred of the Japanese read to us like racism'.[38] While it is an overstatement to claim that writers 'completely ignored' POWs, Carey's observation of ambivalence towards them was well made. Indeed, when introducing Stan Arneil's war diaries, Russel Ward insisted that younger readers understand a 'basic difference between World War II and later Australian excursions into Asia'. During the Pacific War, 'the threat then was real and present; not one of the scarecrows that have since been agitated before ashen-faced voters at election times from Korea to Vietnam and Afghanistan'.[39]

The figure of the POW offered a point of connection between the two generations. Viewing war itself as traumatising created a path out of the fixation on the racism of veterans perceived to be anti-Japanese and fostered a rapprochement of sorts between baby boomers and their fathers. Stan Arneil's *One Man's War* provoked a telling response from Garrie Hutchinson, whose anti-Vietnam politics had led to a falling out with his father and a stint in the United Kingdom to avoid national service. 'I wish Sgt Arneil had published his diary sooner after the war, so that all the babies born in the 1940s might have read it earlier.' For Hutchinson, the book clarified the reasons 'our fathers fought in that war, and came back so taciturn. Little did we know how hard it was to express not only the horrors of the experiences of the men of the 2nd AIF but the moments of actual happiness as well.'[40] 'The World War II generation find it impossible to deal with their trauma,' reflected the scriptwriter for the 1990 film *Blood Oath*, about the Australian prosecution of Japanese war criminals on Ambon Island, 'and our generation has had to try and make sense of it'.⁴¹

This growing emphasis on psychological suffering tilted the axis of cultural response to former POWs away from the pole of race. In 1990 David Malouf published his prize-winning novel *The Great World*, a complex portrait of the friendship between Digger and Vic, two men who form an alliance in a POW camp. While Digger, in particular, reflects on a fellow prisoner's alarm that the Japanese want to treat them like 'coolies' ('the savage indignation of it, at the violation of all that was natural in the world, their unquestionable superiority as white men'), in the end, the lingering bitterness of captivity for these two men is not about race.⁴² The Japanese captors are barely mentioned in this novel, which at its heart is an extended meditation on the nature of shame, the lasting psychological impact of captivity and its two central characters' very different capacities for resilience and personal connection. As trauma became the dominant matrix through which former prisoners were viewed, their earlier, complex positioning in relation to questions of race and identity receded into the background. The decline of the Japanese tourist market from the mid-1990s, as Japan endured a recession, made its economic importance to Australia less visible and effectively ended intense public debates in which POWs featured as metaphors for Australia's attitude to questions of race in the region.

The most enduring development of the 1980s had been that of the perception of POWs as traumatised victims of war who bore witness to its horrors. By the time Malouf published his novel, POWs – and more particularly their travails in captivity – had become defining features of Australia's experience of the Second World War. Publicity surrounding the fortieth anniversary, in 1985, of the end of the Pacific War contained a stronger focus on POWs than had any previous commemorative activity.[43] The following year ex-POWs were top billing in stories about Anzac Day, with headlines focusing on their traumatic war: 'Anzac Day calls back memories of horror'.[44] Such a focus had been unthinkable for an Anzac Day story for most of the previous forty years. By the fiftieth anniversary of the fall of Singapore, in 1992, POWs were a strong presence in significant government-funded commemorative events. The 'residual fear and trauma from that POW experience' were now considered innate parts of Australia's experience of the Pacific War.[45] Australia Remembers, a well-funded federal government program to celebrate the fiftieth anniversary of the end of the Second World War, in 1995, chose the photograph of a returning POW (albeit one from Europe) as the central image on its logo. That year, Prime Minister Paul Keating addressed a POW commemoration at the Australian War Memorial that was attended by 1200 surviving prisoners and their families. The language of mental anguish was woven into such events. Keating insisted that it was important 'to imagine not just the physical suffering [POWs] endured, but the psychological suffering – the terrible loneliness and the sense of loss, the homesickness and the helplessness they had to live with'. 'Yet,' he concluded, 'as the life of Weary Dunlop tells us, we must allow the wounds to heal'.[46]

Edward Dunlop

Edward 'Weary' Dunlop died in 1993, one of the most feted men of his generation. The essence of his appeal, according to historian Graeme Davison, was his capacity to resolve the contradiction between competing values in Australian culture. Sporty yet intellectual, a pacifist who admitted to periods of incandescent rage against his captors, a patriot committed to the values of internationalism, Dunlop held these tensions in equilibrium.[47] These were contradictions of long standing in Australia, but it was only in the 1980s that Dunlop emerged in their symbolic resolution. The timing of his rise was certainly coincident with the reinvigoration of Anzac, but it was also implicitly linked to the rehabilitation of the POW in Australia. Moreover, as a doctor, Dunlop had been an intimate witness to the physical and mental traumas of the prison camps.

As the youngest of the former prisoners who had been so influential in the immediate postwar period, Dunlop outlived most of his contemporaries in that group. Even within veteran circles, his reputation was not unparalleled, and there were other ex-POW doctors who had been equally well regarded.[48] But the majority of prominent ex-POWs from the 1940s and 1950s had died by the time a new generation became fascinated by the POW story in the mid-1980s. Arthur Blackburn collapsed and died from an aneurism in 1960, aged sixty-seven; Ted Fisher was also in his mid-sixties when he died, from stomach cancer, in 1965. Wilfrid Kent Hughes, despite jogging around Lake Burley Griffin until he was in his mid-seventies, passed away in 1970. Frederick Galleghan followed him in 1971. Albert Coates was eighty-two years old when he died in 1977. Even Dunlop was almost eighty when he returned to public prominence in the mid-1980s.

Dunlop's rise was due to more than mere longevity, however. Although his was not a household name, as a member of the elite Melbourne Club he was extremely well connected, both professionally and politically. His alliances encompassed both sides of politics. Richard Casey, Minister for External Affairs in Robert Menzies' government and Governor-General from 1965 to 1969, was a lifelong friend. Dunlop also had the respect and affection of Tom Uren, with whom he had served on the Thai–Burma Railway. Uren's 32-year career as the Labor Member for Reid, with ministries in Gough Whitlam's and Bob Hawke's governments, positioned him well to agitate on behalf of former prisoners when their star rose. Along with Dunlop, he was a long-time advocate for ex-POWs seeking repatriation entitlements, often to the annoyance of members of the repatriation bureaucracy. In the 1960s and 1970s Dunlop had held a number of senior appointments on key advisory panels and boards. President of the Ex-Prisoners of War and Relatives Association of Victoria for many years, and Chairman of the Prisoners of War Trust Fund from 1968 to 1977, he also held the presidency of the Victorian Foundation on Alcoholism and Drug Dependence and was on the Executive of the Anti-Cancer Council.

Despite this continuous activity throughout the 1960s and 1970s, it was not until Dunlop participated in a well-publicised reunion tour to Java, Singapore and Thailand, in 1985, that he shot to broader fame again. Former POW Keith Flanagan, an actor and journalist from Western Australia, organised a Weary Dunlop Tour of Thailand to coincide with the fortieth anniversary of the end of the Second World War. Having sensed the groundswell of interest in POWs, Flanagan wanted to honour the 'courage, devotion and selflessness' that Dunlop had displayed on the railway, which he felt had never been adequately recognised by the Australian government or the Australian people.[49] 'If we don't tell his story, no one else will', Flanagan insisted, as he tried to muster popular and political support for his proposed tour.[50] He used his communication networks well, arranging for large pre-tour feature articles in the press and a film crew from *Nationwide* to accompany the group.

One of the journalists to join the tour was thirty-year-old Martin Flanagan (no relation to the organiser, Keith), whose own father, Arch, had been on 'the line' with Dunlop. Given his family connection, the trip was more than just another story, and his accounts of visiting the scenes of incarceration were infused with a sense of homage to Dunlop. Martin Flanagan's report of the trip for the Fairfax press explained carefully exactly whom Dunlop was and recounted his courage and ingenuity in the harsh conditions of the Thai–Burma Railway.[51] The tour was the beginning of a long association between Martin Flanagan's family and the revival of the POW story in Australian culture.[52] Thirty years later, Martin's brother Richard Flanagan won international acclaim for his POW novel, *The Narrow Road to the Deep North*.

The veneration of a soldier dedicated to saving rather than taking lives was not unique, as the earlier accolades for Gallipoli's stretcher-bearer John Simpson Kirkpatrick and his donkey attested.[53] However, it was a new twist for a prisoner to assume the mantle of hero and for the rank and file to accept a non-combatant as their main man.

Dunlop's status as a non-combatant was in fact crucial to his rejuvenated public profile in an era when the critique of militarism in Vietnam remained fresh. Dunlop had borne witness to miseries in the camps but had not succumbed to their horrors. Indeed, his role as a doctor had been to make them more bearable. Of all the tens of thousands of Australians taken prisoner in the Second World War, only doctors were able – albeit in circumscribed and difficult circumstances – to perform the work for which they had been trained. Soldiers had suffered the ignominy of defeat and were unable to continue fighting; doctors, on the other hand, continued to play valuable roles in their military units. Dunlop emerged from the camps with his masculinity intact, and indeed much was made of his tall stature (193 centimetres) and his willingness to stare down his Japanese captors. Ray Parkin recalled his height and considered him to be a 'profoundly altruistic man' whose 'gentle disarming smile' could command 'more from men than any army of officers waving a manual of Military Law'.[54]

Masculine yet compassionate, nurturing, brave and witness to unbearable suffering: Dunlop was an important antidote to the negative image of the Australian veteran that had emerged during the 1960s and 1970s. In 1984, as Keith Flanagan planned the Dunlop tour, he told Tom Uren that he had organised for a television documentary to be made about Dunlop as 'an Anzac Day answer to those who think we meet to glorify war, get drunk and justify rape'.[55] As if on cue, during the reunion tour, the print media grasped the story of Dunlop's selfless nurturing of his troops on the Thai–Burma Railway as a symbolic counterpoint to the feminist disruption of Anzac Day marches. 'The ones to remember are men like Weary' was the headline of a story printed directly below another about a clash between feminists and veterans during the Melbourne Anzac Day march in 1985.[56] Dunlop's elevation as a modern hero was a deliberate cultivation of an example of military service that might counter the claims of Anzac's critics.

Dunlop had one further asset that entrenched his appeal. At the end of a decade that had seen the arrival of approximately 90 000 refugees from Vietnam and a shift from White to multicultural Australia, Dunlop was the very model of a man committed to furthering Australia–Asia relations. His friendship with Richard Casey, a well-known exponent of building ties between Australia and Asia, had drawn him into the operation of the Colombo Plan. In 1957 Dunlop had made the first of many visits to Thailand, and he undertook further trips to Sri Lanka and India as part of medical and teaching exchanges. In 1963 he had assumed the presidency of the Australian Asian Association of

Victoria and oversaw activities designed to build connections and support for Asian students studying in Australia. Dunlop held the post until his death, in 1993. Far from being the embittered POW, he was the embodiment of the connections between Australia and Asia forged by war and, in his later life, of reconciliation with Japan.

Dunlop himself was astonished by the attention garnered by the reunion tour to Thailand in 1985. Upon his return he was overwhelmed with a spate of invitations to speaking engagements, which continued unabated until his death. *The War Diaries of Weary Dunlop: Java and the Burma–Thailand Railway 1942–45*, published to great acclaim in 1986, cemented his place in the canon. The Governor-General Sir Ninian Stephen launched the book, which was widely reviewed and ran to many editions. According to his biographer, Dunlop, who suddenly found himself in demand, pulled out his speeches from the 1940s and 1950s and reworked them with a modern sensibility. Previously focused on the individual themes of courage, service and sacrifice, his speeches of the 1980s and 1990s were more national in scope and tackled the issues of reconciliation and friendship in the region.[57]

Easing the trauma

Edward Dunlop knew, as well as anyone, that the Australian Army and the Australian government had a long history of ambivalence towards POWs. Despite the unwillingness of the government in the 1950s to countenance compensating or memorialising prisoners, this stance changed in the late 1980s. The dedication of the Changi Chapel had been an early sign. Prime Minister Bob Hawke further signalled the new receptivity to honouring POWs by visiting the Thai–Burma Railway and

The battle resolved

Kanchanaburi War Cemetery in 1989. With the ascension of Dunlop to iconic status, a new push began on behalf of POWs. Connections forged through ex-POW and battalion associations of long standing and the one remaining ex-POW in federal parliament, Tom Uren (Liberal Senator John Carrick having retired in 1987), contributed to the ultimate success of these campaigns. The prime ministership of Paul Keating (1991–96), marked by an effort to concentrate Australian attention on its Asian region, including the Pacific War, ensured greater visibility than ever before of the history of that conflict. Keating also had a personal connection: an uncle, William Keating, had died on the Sandakan–Ranau death marches in 1945.

Repatriation entitlements for former POWs improved somewhat in the 1970s, but the Department of Veterans' Affairs (renamed from Repatriation in 1976) retained its opposition to providing POWs with separate or special treatment until at least the 1990s. Gough Whitlam's government extended free medical and hospital treatment for any condition to all Australian POWs in 1974, a development which began to undermine the bureaucratic reluctance to treat prisoners as a 'class apart'. Still, in the late 1980s, Veterans' Affairs had poor recordkeeping in relation to former POWs and was unaware of their remaining numbers. It was only at Uren's insistence that statistics were finally produced about the number of POWs who were still alive. Uren was disappointed with the attitude of the 'upper echelons' of the department, whom he claimed were obfuscating and obstructionist.[58] Veterans' Affairs remained adamant in 1989 that to focus on a particular group would undermine the integrity of the repatriation system, because it would move away from the principle of 'demonstrated need'.[59]

Uren began to push hard in the federal parliament and within the Labor government for greater entitlements. In the week of Stan Arneil's funeral he wrote to Paul Keating, reminding him that only 5485 veterans who had been POWs of Japan were still alive. He hoped that Keating's 'personal commitment' to the plight of ex-POWs would prompt action. Medical research conducted in the 1980s had begun to reveal the extent of health problems among former prisoners: by 1960, they had been dying at four times the rate of other veterans, and they were still dying at a 20 per cent higher rate.[60] One of the researchers told a meeting of Veterans' Affairs officials and POW representatives, including Dunlop, that the extent of ignorance in the Department of Veterans' Affairs about the health challenges of former prisoners was 'scandalous'.[61] There were small victories: from 1989 certain medical conditions, including anxiety and depression, were automatically accepted as war-caused disabilities for POWs. As Australia entered economic recession, there was no support forthcoming to grant Uren's greatest wish – full service pensions for all former prisoners – despite a series of personal meetings with Keating once he became Prime Minister.

Outside parliament, the increasingly audible and personalised voices of ex-POWs fed into human rights campaigns, which further allowed old histories to be recast in new ways. In 1990 the Queensland Ex-POW Reparation Committee joined similar groups from Canada, the United States, the United Kingdom, the Netherlands and New Zealand when they made a claim for compensation from the Japanese government for human rights violations their members had endured while POWs.[62] In essence, recasting the maltreatment of POWs as human rights abuses reframed the discussion about them. No longer burdened by the ambivalence that had made part of the POW story awkward in the early postwar years, the applicants, now positioned as the victims of human rights violations, appealed to international bodies to advance their cases. The Australian submission, entitled *Nippon Very Sorry, Many Men Must Die* (coincidentally the title of episode 4 in the ABC radio documentary), included extensive survivor accounts.[63] In August, the United Nations Human Rights Commission advanced the suit, which included 10 000 Australian POWs asking for $250 million, or $25 000 each, to the Japanese government, with which it remained to the time of writing, in 2017.

Just over a decade later, the transition to understanding POWs as victims of human rights violations with a just right to compensation was complete. The Australian government had not supported the 1990 claim, citing the 1951 peace treaty as having settled the issue of compensation and the 'obvious changes to the relationship between Japan and Australia'.[64] Uninterested in troubling a major trading partner with unfinished business from the war and recognising that the compensation suit against Japan would not succeed, the government accepted moral, if not legal, responsibility for the payment of compensation. In the meantime, the governments of Canada, the United Kingdom and New Zealand had provided substantial one-off compensation payments to former POWs. In the following decade the Australian government passed the *Compensation (Japanese Internment) Act 2001*, which granted former POWs of the Japanese a $25 000 one-off payment.[65] In response, one newspaper declared, '$25 000 eases the trauma'.[66] The concerns of an earlier generation that compensating POWs might prove an incentive for later combatants to surrender had vanished. In 2004 the dedication of the Australian Ex-Prisoners of War Memorial in the Victorian regional town of Ballarat, presided over by the Governor-General Major General Michael Jeffery, gave physical form to the official embrace of POWs. Alongside a row of stone obelisks, the names of over 35 000 POWs from the Boer War, the First and Second World Wars and the Korean War are etched into a long, black granite wall.

By the twenty-first century, a willingness to compensate and commemorate not just POWs but any citizens traumatised by wartime experiences had become one of the hallmarks of a humane nation. Attempts to deny compensation in an earlier time, or to award it on a piecemeal, discretionary basis, revealed a great deal about Australia's attitude to its former prisoners. Such efforts also produced an archive of unparalleled richness, which documented the struggles of former prisoners in that much longer period of their lives, when they attempted to rehabilitate themselves, make a living and reintegrate into their families and civilian society.

While there had long been awareness that captivity might have a psychological impact, there was nothing like consensus in the 1950s and 1960s that this was the case and nowhere near the almost-universal sympathy that was so in evidence by the 1980s for those who had thus suffered. Rather than viewing this development only as growing enlightenment and overdue recognition, we need to see trauma as a historically specific way to comprehend and understand the experience of war. It certainly encouraged historians' interest in documenting imprisonment – as evidenced by the extensive oral history recordings made in the 1980s – and prompted a surge in memoir activity by former POWs. Unlike the memoirs of the 1940s and 1950s, some of these canvass the mental and psychological anguish of captivity, but others still replicate narratives that centre on mateship, humour and derring-do. The glossy publications and edited collections full of primary source material produced by the Department of Veterans' Affairs are testament to the huge variety of memoirs, video recordings and oral histories of POWs now available. Such testimony so proliferated by the 2000s, and its themes had become so familiar, that it had lost any radical potential to unsettle nationalist and celebratory narratives about war.[67] The POW, once viewed with ambivalence, has now become the exemplar of national traits in wartime.

Epilogue

The first locomotive to cross the completed Thai–Burma Railway now rests in the entrance hall of the Yushukan War Memorial Museum, in Tokyo. The museum is in the grounds of the Yasukuni Shrine, which commemorates the millions of people who died in service for the Empire of Japan between the mid-nineteenth century and the end of the Second World War. One of the great controversies that has attached to Yasukuni is that convicted war criminals are enshrined and therefore honoured in Shinto tradition in its grounds.

On my first trip to Japan, in 1993, I did not include Yasukuni on my itinerary. I had friends who were living in Nagoya as part of the Japan Exchange and Teaching Programme; they recommended Hiroshima as a priority. My mouth became dry as the *shinkansen* ('bullet train') pulled in to the station at Hiroshima. I felt self-conscious of my status as a *gaijin* ('foreigner') in this city, where so many people had suffered and died as the consequence of an Allied atomic bomb.

When I took my children to Hiroshima many years later, in January 2017, they felt the same way. 'Will people stare at us and be angry?' inquired my thirteen-year-old daughter. My daughters were willing to visit the Hiroshima Peace Memorial Museum, but I could not get any takers among them for Yushukan. When my husband and I set off to see it, on a cold winter's morning, the girls stayed behind in our rented apartment in suburban Tokyo.

The battle resolved

This choice marked them as more typical tourists; there were very few non-Japanese people at the shrine.

I knew about the war criminal issue before my visit to Yasukuni in 2017. Ascending the steps from the Kudanshita subway station, I was taken aback by the size of Daiichi Torii, the shrine's gate. I had seen photographs of the shrine itself, but not of this 25-metre-high structure that dominates the pathway and dwarfs its trees. Having researched, written and spoken about POWs for more than a decade, I felt anxious about entering these grounds – so hallowed for Japan, so fraught for the victims of its wartime aggression.

Locomotive number C5631 is installed in pride of place beside the escalator that takes visitors up to the museum entrance. A pair of crossed Japanese flags sits in front of the engine, framing its central headlight with two images of the rising sun. Children and a few adults were climbing up into the driver's seat and imagining themselves steaming through the jungles of Thailand and Burma.

I stayed on the ground and scoured the interpretive panels. The Thai–Burma Railway is presented as a feat of engineering, and the efforts of Japanese veterans to bring the locomotive back from Thailand in the 1970s win praise. My husband busied himself photographing everything for me, while my ears filled with the white noise of shock. 'Stand in front of the engine', he told me. I was photographed, looking nonplussed and awkward, with the black bulk of the steam engine looming behind me.

I am a scholar. I know that museums and commemorative sites the world over often present a very partial view of the past. Yet the fact that the tens of thousands of people who suffered and died during the construction of the railway in 1942 and 1943 receive no mention there completely floored me. I was close enough to the POW story to be moved to tears. What must it be like for those who have a personal connection? My first thought was that they must be angry.

※※

Visiting Yasukuni Shrine therefore gave me a new appreciation of the tremendous courage of the people in Japan who have tried to promote peace. In 2015 I participated in a conference at the University of Sydney entitled Wounds, Scars and Healing: Civil Society and Postwar Pacific Basin Reconciliation. The Australia-Japan Foundation funded a day-long 'grassroots workshop' to precede the main event. Speakers travelled from within Australia and from Japan to discuss how the hard work of reconciliation was continuing. An impressive array of Japanese people, all of whom were women, spoke about their activities. They included members of the POW Research Network, launched in 2002 to research the histories of POWs buried in the Yokohama War Cemetery but now involved in broader research initiatives and translation efforts. Mina Watanabe, from the Women's Active Museum on War and Peace, which is dedicated to documenting Japan's participation in military sexual slavery, was another.

Martin Flanagan, introduced as 'Richard's brother', was the keynote speaker. Richard Flanagan's novel about POWs had only recently won the Man Booker Prize; Martin has plugged away at this story since the 1980s, publishing journalism, memoir, biography and children's books. Martin and Richard Flanagan have created different artistic responses to a key part of their family's history. We chatted before the day's events got underway. Martin told me he grew up with two great silences: the silence about the original peoples of Tasmania, and a silent father.

Their father, Arch Flanagan, had died only two years previously, in 2013, at ninety-eight years of age. After listing the many members of his family, a death notice in *The Age* newspaper declared, 'North Hobart Football Club, TANFL and State Premiers, 1936 / Ex Japanese POW / One of Dunlop's Thousand'.[1] After family and football, being a POW had defined Arch Flanagan's life.

Martin Flanagan spoke about and showed excerpts from his documentary, *The Line* (2010), which includes interviews with his father.[2] He was in his mid-forties when his father started to tell him stories about the war; he could feel the story coming, he said, like a truck reverberating down the highway when you are hitchhiking. All six of Arch Flanagan's children have 'been back' to the Thai–Burma Railway, the grammatical quirk revealing the central role that a place very far from Tasmania assumed in their childhood. When Martin and Richard's brother Patrick extended his own quest for understanding to include a visit to the coalmine in Japan where their father had worked as a POW, he came into contact with the POW Research Network. In 2006, at the age of ninety-two, Arch agreed to receive into his home three Japanese women representing this group.[3] They recorded an oral history interview with him and continued to correspond until his death.

Fuyuko Nishisato, one of the women who visited the Flanagan home, was present at the workshop in Sydney. She witnessed Arch say in the documentary, 'Some people find it hard to forgive, not for themselves, but for the people who died up there. Those people would feel that you had let them down if you befriended the Japanese'.[4] In discussion after the screening, she asked Martin if there were people who had objected to their visit almost a decade earlier. Indeed there were, Martin confirmed, a situation he described as 'sad and unfortunate'. Nishisato reflected that perhaps her initial optimism when visiting Australia and meeting a POW survivor had been naive, but she did not regret the dignity of the occasion. When Arch died, Nishisato and her friends had written to the family, 'We know you are all proud of his noble mind and peaceful and objective attitude to his war time as a prisoner of the Japanese Army'.

Reconciliation between Japan and Australia is an ongoing process. There is less heat in the issue now than there was in the first thirty years after the end of the Second World War, and, as fewer and fewer of the generation who experienced that war remain alive, it is likely to decrease even further. Japan remains Australia's second-largest trading partner, after China, and the trilateral military relationship between Australia, Japan and the United States is critical to regional defence plans. Intensity and controversy about the conflict in Asia that began in the 1930s and ran until 1945 rest more squarely now in the Japan–China domain than ever before. If memories of Japan's war crimes have political purchase anywhere, it is primarily in China, closely followed by North and South Korea.

❖❖

A month before attending the workshop in Sydney, I spoke at a conference of The MHS Learning Network, which aims to improve mental health services in Australia and New Zealand. Along with staff from the Department of Veterans' Affairs, the Veterans and Veterans Families Counselling Service and a recent service veteran, I participated in a panel entitled 'The aftermath of military combat – the history, the personal consequences, the treatments and the recovery'. The conference was deliberately inclusive and designed to cater for practitioners in mental health services, communities of practice and mental health care consumers. As the audience gathered in the vast room we had been allocated at the National Convention Centre in Canberra, I wondered whether my historical paper would be of interest to combat and peacekeeping mission veterans, their families and the bureaucrats, psychologists and psychiatrists who worked with them. My paper was called 'A body of broken men', a reference to Albert Coates' frustration with the assumption that ex-POWs would be more prone to psychological difficulties than other returned service personnel. I used the papers of the Prisoners of War Trust Fund to describe the challenges faced by ex-POWs in their struggles to rehabilitate themselves; some of the examples I gave that day made their way into this book.[5]

When I resumed my place on the panel after speaking at the podium, the veteran – who had been to Somalia and East Timor – turned to me and said, 'Nothing's really changed'. During question time, people came to the microphone to express their frustration at how the issues of alcoholism, domestic violence, anxiety and thoughts of self-harm that I had described continued to plague some returned service personnel. They made clear that the support offered by the government to veterans and their families was inadequate to the task. In cases of family breakdown, former partners were no longer entitled to even the small amount of help they had received when still in a relationship with a veteran. There was anger in the room.

None of the people who spoke that day were ex-POWs; nor did any appear to be members of former POWs' families. The nature of modern warfare, which minimises troops on the ground and maximises the use of technology, means that it is unlikely that in a future conflict such large numbers of defence force personnel will be taken prisoner. With the receding possibility of large-scale capture, by the early 2000s the army had let go of its hard-line attitude towards compensating POWs, and all surviving POWs received increasingly generous benefits and entitlements.[6] In 2009 the esteem in which POWs were now held in the veteran community was made clear in almost absurd fashion when the President of the Ex-Prisoners of War Association of Australia was exposed as fabricating his entire service history in order to win the respect of his peers and family. 'I suppose it was just a sort of fantasy', he told reporters.[7]

While the public place of POWs has changed, the difficulties of rehabilitation that some of them have faced still manifest in subsequent generations of service personnel. The Australian Defence Force and the federal government face criticism for shortcomings in the provision of mental health services. The tremulous pleadings of heartbroken partners and families, and the frustrations of counsellors working on shoestring budgets, suggest that the issues are endemic. These problems are nothing new. Ex-POW associations, the RSL, veterans and their families have presented evidence about them for a very long time. In that sense, the battle within continues.

Coda

Australian Red Cross Society
(Queensland Branch)
Unofficial. For use of Patients in Hospital under Red Cross care.

31 August 1970

Dear Sir
    Please excuse writing. Sir can you please send me a p.o.w. grant form. I need help. I am in debt to the Bank also owe Rates on my *land*. I have been in hospital quite a lote this year. I am in hospital now by the time you send my p.o.w. *grant* form I may be out of hospital by the time you send the grant form. My health is not the best. I cant hold a job long. All I can do is country work as my health is bad. I have come to Brisbane I am 48 years old. I thing be a pow has court up with me. My wife left me because she say my nerves a bad, and all *POW* are mads. So long without women. And on drugs on doctor pre[scription]. I am not good to my Wife. I am going for a Divorce as I am no good to my Wife. Also get on my Wife nerves. I was so young when I was under the Japs. From 19 years until I was 22 years. I was a young farm lad.

    William

Acknowledgments

Mention POWs in casual conversation and inevitably one or two people make a personal connection. Baby boomers remember fathers, uncles and neighbours who were sometimes silent and broody men. I have no relations who were POWs, but I felt encouraged to persist with the work by people who listened to my public talks and showed such enthusiasm for them. Thank you to the people who approached me at conferences and who wrote me emails after public lectures and radio interviews, because your interest was inspiring.

I was privileged to receive the support of the Australian Research Council (DP 1094837) to complete the research for this book. The funding enabled me to deliver papers at international conferences and spend many hours at the National Archives of Australia and the Australian War Memorial, in Canberra, and I am grateful to the helpful archivists I encountered there. I also benefited from the expert research assistance of Lachlan Grant, Seamus Spark and Johnny Bell. The fabulous Jodie Boyd entered my life in 2014 and her finely honed skills of project management, research and editing have allowed me to manage multiple commitments without buckling under their weight.

At NewSouth Publishing I appreciated the early and sustained enthusiasm of Phillipa McGuinness, the eagle-eyed work and patience of Penny Mansley and the efficiency of Emma Hutchinson. Thanks also to Lisa White, who designed the brilliant cover.

As I worked through the research for this book, I published several book chapters and articles. Some sections of those publications are reproduced here. Chapter 1 draws upon 'Australian nurse POWs: gender, war and captivity', *Australian Historical Studies*, vol. 36, no. 124, October 2004, pp. 255–74 and 'Emaciation or emasculation: photographic images, white masculinity and captivity by the Japanese', *Journal of Men's Studies*, vol. 15, no. 3, autumn 2007, pp. 295–310. Chapters 3 and 4 contain some sections from 'Compensating prisoners of war of Japan in post-war Australia', in J Beaumont, L Grant & A Pegram (eds), *Beyond Surrender: Australian Prisoners of War in the Twentieth Century*, Melbourne University Press, Melbourne, 2015, pp. 254–75. Chapter 8 reproduces some sections of '"A novel form of war memorial": the AIF Malaya Nursing Scholarship and Australia-Asia relations', *History Australia*, vol. 14, no. 2, 2017, pp. 250–65. Chapter 9 draws upon some material in 'POWs: race and trauma in Australia, 1970–2005', *Journal of War and Culture Studies*, vol. 7, no. 3, August 2014, pp. 191–205. I thank the publishers for their permission to include the material here. Academic readers are encouraged to consult these publications for the historiographical, theoretical and conceptual discussions that were handled with a light touch in this book.

The trip I took to Thailand in 2012 to visit Kanchanaburi and Hellfire Pass provided a key turning point in this project. Tristan Moss and Kim McKenzie were excellent travel companions. The indefatigable Joan Beaumont also made that journey, one of many we have taken together to conferences, museums and sites of war memory. Joan did me the great favour of reading and commenting on the manuscript for this book, a time-consuming task she approached with her usual energy, good humour and generosity.

My colleagues at Monash University provided feedback on

Acknowledgments

sections at critical stages and engage me constantly in interesting debates about how to research and write history. Thanks in particular to Adam Clulow, Clare Corbould, Kat Ellinghaus, David Garrioch, Charlotte Greenhalgh, Michael Hau, Julie Kalman, Ernest Koh, Paula Michaels, Ruth Morgan, Lynette Russell, Agnieszka Sobocinska and Alistair Thomson. Barbara Caine and Clare Monagle have now left the Menzies Building, but I always value my conversations with them about work and life.

Other historians have also helped me think about the issues I cover in this book and provided much-valued research tips, advice and discussions. My thanks to Paula Hamilton, Kevin Blackburn, Yorick Smaal, Andy Kaladelfos, Stuart Ward, Daniel Botsman, Richard Waterhouse, Hank Nelson and Tim Bowden.

The Facebook world of historians who comment on 'hive mind' questions has been an unexpected and positive benefit of being on social media. Thank you to everyone who responded to my random queries. While it often feels like falling down a rabbit hole, being active on Twitter and Facebook has also generated an online community of historians that I value very much.

This book has taken me such a long time to write that it is almost possible to forget how much I relied on others to help care for my children during research trips and conferences. The kids, two of whom are now adults, were still going for holiday sleepovers at Granny and Grandad's when I began. I will always appreciate the assistance of my parents, Peter and Sandra Twomey, in caring for them.

My friends saw me through some tumultuous times during the decade and more that it took me to research and write this book, and I feel so fortunate to have their friendship and am grateful for their support. Cathy Coleborne, Cathy Farrell, Jane Finnis, Annalisa Giudici, Katie Holmes, Marina Henley, Elizabeth Knowles, Deborah Rechter, Sarah Tomasetti – thank you.

I also love my bookclub women, who remind me monthly why books and friendship are such a great mix.

I dedicate this book to my maternal grandmother, Alma Keir, and her brother, my great-uncle Norman Sherrington. The Second World War made a huge impact on them as young people in their twenties living in Townsville, and their stories about that time inspired my interest in the past. They are both gone now, and the family link to Queensland is almost broken. The memory of their tiny war service home in Beauvardia Street, its kitchen dominated by an octagonal red laminex table and a view of Mrs Bailey's mango tree, came to me often as I wrote this book.

Finally, to my sounding board, my first reader, my cheer squad of one, the maker of tea and Indian feasts, Andy May: despite his thinking that I use too many commas, this man is, quite simply, a treasure. He likes revisiting Queensland with me, and that is only one of the many things that we share.

Notes

Prologue
1   J Beaumont & A Witcomb, 'The Thai–Burma Railway: asymmetrical and transnational memories', in C Twomey & E Koh (eds), *The Pacific War: Aftermaths, Remembrance and Culture*, Routledge, Abingdon, 2015, pp. 67–87.
2   The Australian Broadcasting Commission became the Australian Broadcasting Corporation in 1983. The initialism ABC is used throughout this text to refer to both.
3   Research for this book concerning applications to the Prisoners of War Trust Fund was conducted under special access provisions from the National Archives of Australia (hereafter NAA). Hence, throughout this text, quotations of applicants and occasionally of public figures from documents within the Prisoners of War Trust Fund files are not individually referenced, and applicants are identified by pseudonymous first names. All documents from this archive can be found in NAA B503. Please contact the author if any further information is required.
4   The federal government established the Department of Repatriation in 1917. The Repatriation Commission, created in 1920, comprised a chairman and two other returned soldier members and was a body that sat within the department. Between 1928 and 1947, the Repatriation Commission undertook administration and the Repatriation Department was merely a ministerial portfolio. The Repatriation Department was reconstituted as an administrative entity in 1947, when the staff of the Repatriation Commission became public servants. Thenceforth, the Repatriation Department assumed a portion of the commission's administrative responsibilities. Its name changed to the Department of Veterans' Affairs on 5 October 1976. The archival records do not always distinguish clearly between the department and the commission, and it has therefore occasionally been impossible to do so here. In these cases I have simply referred to 'Repatriation'. NAA, 'Agency note', in 'Agency details for CA 16: Repatriation Department [I]', NAA, 2017, <www.naa.gov.au/go.aspx?a=CA+16>; NAA, 'Agency note', in 'Agency details for CA 225: Repatriation Commission [II]', NAA, 2017, <www.naa.gov.au/go.aspx?a=CA+225>.

Introduction
1   *Age*, 13 July 1993, p. 2.
2   J Howard, 'Commemorative address at Hellfire Pass, Thailand', 25 April 1998, PM Transcripts, <pmtranscripts.pmc.gov.au/release/transcript-22682>.

Notes to pages 1–4

3   G Davison, *The Use and Abuse of Australian History*, Allen & Unwin, Sydney, 2000, pp. 30–31.
4   P Stanley notes the relative lack of interest before 1980 in 'Remembering captivity: the prisoners experience as literature', in R Reid & P Stanley (eds), *Stolen Years: Australian Prisoners of War*, Department of Veterans' Affairs (hereafter DVA) & Australian War Memorial (hereafter AWM), Canberra, 2002, p. 101. See the critical interventions of J Beaumont, *Gull Force: Survival and Leadership in Captivity 1941–1945*, Allen & Unwin, Sydney, 1988; C Kenny, *Captives: Australian Army Nurses in Japanese Prison Camps*, University of Queensland Press (hereafter UQP), Brisbane, 1986; H Nelson, *P.O.W.: Prisoners of War; Australians under Nippon*, ABC Books, Sydney, 1985. For an early popular history see P Adam-Smith, *Prisoners of War: From Gallipoli to Korea*, Viking, Melbourne, 1992; S Garton, *The Cost of War: Australians Return*, Oxford University Press (hereafter OUP), Melbourne, 1996, pp. 209–210.
5   J Beaumont, 'Prisoners of war in Australian national memory', in B Moore & B Hately-Broad (eds), *Prisoners of War, Prisoners of Peace: Captivity, Homecoming, and Memory in World War Two*, Berg, New York, 2005, pp. 185–94; M Caulfield, *War behind the Wire: Australian Prisoners of War*, Hachette, Sydney, 2008; M Cunningham, *Defying the Odds: Surviving Sandakan and Kuching*, Lothian, Melbourne, 2006; M Cunningham, *Hell on Earth: Sandakan – Australia's Greatest War Tragedy*, Hachette, Sydney, 2013; P Ham, *Sandakan: The Untold Story of the Sandakan Death Marches*, William Heinemann, Sydney, 2012; L Reed, *Bigger than Gallipoli: War, History and Memory in Australia*, University of Western Australia Press, Perth, 2004; LR Silver, *Sandakan: A Conspiracy of Silence*, Sally Milner Publishing, Sydney, 1998; P Wright, *The Men of the Line: Stories of the Thai–Burma Railway Survivors*, Melbourne University Press (hereafter MUP), Melbourne, 2008.
6   Reid & Stanley, *Stolen Years*.
7   Anzac Portal, DVA, 2017, <anzacportal.dva.gov.au>; Australia, DVA, *Australian Prisoners of War*, DVA, Canberra, 2009; Australians at War Film Archive, UNSW Canberra at the Australian Defence Force Academy, 2017, <australiansatwarfilmarchive.unsw.edu.au>; R Reid, *Laden, Fevered, Starved: The POWs of Sandakan, North Borneo, 1945*, DVA, Canberra, 1999; R Reid, *Sandakan 1942–1945*, DVA, Canberra, 2008; M Tracey, *Australian Prisoners of War*, Department of Defence, Canberra, 1999.
8   H Grehan, 'Testimony and ambivalence in *Sandakan Threnody*', *Australasian Drama Studies*, no. 49, 2006, pp. 89–100.
9   Cunningham, *Hell on Earth*; Ham, *Sandakan*; Silver, *Sandakan*.
10 There has been a wave of research in recent years: K Ariotti, '"At present everything is making us most anxious": families of Australian prisoners in Turkey', in J Beaumont, L Grant & A Pegram (eds), *Beyond Surrender: Australian Prisoners of War in the Twentieth Century*, MUP, Melbourne, 2015, pp. 57–74; K Ariotti, 'Australian prisoners of the Turks: negotiating culture clash in captivity', in J Bürgschwentner, M Egger & G Barth-Scalmani (eds), *Other Fronts, Other Wars? First World War Studies on the Eve of the Centennial*, Brill, Leiden & Boston, 2014, pp. 146–66; J Lawless, *Kismet: The Story of the*

Gallipoli Prisoners of War, Australian Scholarly Publishing, Melbourne, 2015; P Monteath, 'Australian POW labour in Germany in World War II', *Labour History*, no. 103, 2012, pp. 83–102; P Monteath, 'Beyond the Colditz myth: Australian experiences of German captivity in World War Two', in Beaumont, Grant & Pegram, *Beyond Surrender*, pp. 116–34; P Monteath, *P.O.W.: Australian Prisoners of War in Hitler's Reich*, Macmillan, Sydney, 2011.

11 J Beaumont, 'Prisoners of war', in P Dennis (ed.), *The Oxford Companion to Australian Military History*, OUP, Melbourne, 1995, pp. 472–81.

12 J Beaumont, 'Officers and men: rank and survival on the Thai–Burma Railway', in Beaumont, Grant & Pegram, *Beyond Surrender*, pp. 175–76.

13 WG Turnbull, quoting Minister for the Army, *Commonwealth Parliamentary Debates* (hereafter *CPD*), House of Representatives (hereafter HR), vol. 188, 26 July 1946, p. 3230.

14 D Robson, E Welch, NJ Beeching & GV Gill, 'Consequences of captivity: health effects of Far East imprisonment in World War II', *QJM: An International Journal of Medicine*, vol. 102, no. 2, 2009, p. 90.

15 J Beaumont, 'Hellfire Pass Memorial Museum, Thai–Burma Railway', in M Gegner & B Ziino (eds), *The Heritage of War*, Routledge, New York, 2012, pp. 19–40; K Blackburn, 'Commemorating and commodifying the prisoner of war experience in South-East Asia: the creation of Changi Prison Museum', *Journal of the Australian War Memorial*, no. 133, 2000, <www.awm.gov.au/articles/journal/j33/blackburn.asp>; S Garton, 'Changi as television: myth, memory, narrative and history', *Journal of Australian Studies*, vol. 26, no. 73, 2002, pp. 79–88; L Grant, 'Monument and ceremony: the Australian Ex-POW Memorial and the Anzac legend', in K Hack & K Blackburn (eds), *Forgotten Captives in Japanese-Occupied Asia*, Routledge, London, 2008, pp. 41–56; L Grant, 'What makes a "national" war memorial? The case of the Australian Ex-Prisoners of War Memorial', *Public History Review*, vol. 12, 2006, pp. 92–102; P Hamilton, 'Contested memories of the Pacific War in Australia', in C Twomey & E Koh (eds), *The Pacific War: Aftermaths, Remembrance and Culture*, Routledge, Abingdon, 2015, pp. 50–66; P Hamilton, 'A long war: public memory and the popular media', in S Radstone & B Schwarz (eds), *Memory: Histories, Theories, Debates*, Fordham University Press, New York, 2010, pp. 299–311.

16 The return of Axis POWs, on the other hand, has prompted some excellent studies. See for example F Biess, *Homecomings: Returning POWs and the Legacies of Defeat in Postwar Germany*, Princeton University Press, Princeton, 2006.

17 Although see J Damousi, *The Labour of Loss: Mourning, Memory and Wartime Bereavement in Australia*, Cambridge University Press (hereafter CUP), Melbourne, 1999; Garton, *The Cost of War*; S Macintyre, *Australia's Boldest Experiment: War and Reconstruction in the 1940s*, NewSouth, Sydney, 2015. S Garton's work on the return of POWs is an essential background to this study and is especially insightful about the ambiguous position of POWs in the Australian military tradition.

18 A Faulkner, *Arthur Blackburn, VC: An Australian Hero, His Men, and Their Two World Wars*, Wakefield Press, Adelaide, 2008, p. 418.

19 *News*, 17 September 1945, p. 1.
20 The Returned and Services League of Australia (RSL) was initially called the Returned Sailors' and Soldiers' Imperial League of Australia (RSSILA, 1916–40); this was later changed to the Returned Sailors', Soldiers' and Airmen's Imperial League of Australia (RSSAILA or RSS & AILA, 1940–66) before its current name was adopted. For ease of reading, the current initialism, RSL, is used throughout the main text to refer to the organisation. In notes, however, the initialism in use at the time of creation is cited.
21 *News*, 22 September 1945, p. 1.
22 *Examiner*, 27 July 1949, p. 6.

1 A matter of dishonour?

1 D Malouf, *The Great World*, Chatto & Windus, London, 1990, p. 120.
2 Wilfrid Kent Hughes had represented Australia in the 400-metre hurdles at the 1920 Olympics, in Belgium. Rohan Rivett, although technically a civilian internee, because he was employed by the Malaysian Broadcasting Corporation at the time of his imprisonment, was sent to the Thai–Burma Railway with other POWs. Rivett was the grandson of Alfred Deakin. Sir Adrian Herbert Curlewis, a Sydney barrister and later judge, was Ethel Turner's son.
3 S Spark, 'Dishonourable men? The Australian Army, prisoners of war and Anglo-German POW repatriations in the Second World War', *Australian Historical Studies*, vol. 45, no. 2, 2014, p. 245.
4 J Beaumont, 'The long silence: Australian prisoners of the Japanese', in PJ Dean (ed.), *Australia, 1944–45: Victory in the Pacific*, CUP, Melbourne, 2016, pp. 79–97.
5 *P.O.W.: The Monthly Newsletter of the Prisoners of War Relatives Association*, nos 1–45, was published between January 1942 and January 1946.
6 *Age*, 19 June 1946, p. 3.
7 T Blamey to F Forde, c. November 1943, NAA MP742/1, 255/1/225, cited in Spark, 'Dishonourable men?', p. 250; M McKernan, *This War Never Ends: The Pain of Separation and Return*, UQP, Brisbane, 2001, p. 33.
8 R Reid, 'In captivity: Australian prisoners of war in the 20th century', in R Reid & P Stanley (eds), *Stolen Years: Australian Prisoners of War*, DVA & AWM, Canberra, 2002, pp. 12–19.
9 Before the Second World War, British Malaya consisted of the Straits Settlements (Malacca, Dinding, Penang and Singapore), the Federated Malay States (Selangor, Perak, Negeri Sembilan and Pahang) and the Unfederated Malay States (Johore, Kedah, Kelantan, Perlis and Terengganu).
10 AS Blackburn (Commander of Blackforce), Order, 10 March 1942, AWM 100923 (original emphasis).
11 M McKernan, 'War', in W Vamplew (ed.), *Australians: Historical Statistics*, Fairfax, Syme & Weldon Associates, Sydney, 1987, p. 415.
12 The number included 208 civilians and an estimated 845 members of Lark Force. H Nelson, 'The return to Rabaul 1945', *Journal of Pacific History*, vol. 30, no. 2, 1995, p. 146; NAA, '*Montevideo Maru*: list of prisoners of war and civilian internees on board', NAA, 2017, <montevideomaru.naa.gov.au>.

13 'The workers', Anzac Portal, DVA, 2017, <anzacportal.dva.gov.au/history/conflicts/thaiburma-railway-and-hellfire-pass/thaiburma-railway-and-hellfire-pass/workers>.
14 'Camps near Hellfire Pass', Anzac Portal, DVA, 2017, <anzacportal.dva.gov.au/history/conflicts/thaiburma-railway-and-hellfire-pass/locations/camps-near-hellfire-pass>; 'Camps of F Force', Anzac Portal, DVA, 2017, <anzacportal.dva.gov.au/history/conflicts/thaiburma-railway-and-hellfire-pass/locations/camps-f-force>.
15 McKernan, *This War Never Ends*, p. 2.
16 M Clisby, *Guilty or Innocent? The Gordon Bennett Case*, Allen & Unwin, Sydney, 1992; AB Lodge, *Deserter or Hero? The Gordon Bennett Royal Commission*, Sir Robert Menzies Centre for Australian Studies, Institute of Commonwealth Studies, London, 1989; AB Lodge, *The Fall of General Gordon Bennett*, Allen & Unwin, Sydney, 1986.
17 AE Coates & NH Rosenthal, *The Albert Coates Story: The Will That Found the Way*, Hyland House, Melbourne, 1977, p. 82.
18 D Griffin, 'Galleghan, Sir Frederick Gallagher (1897–1971)', Australian Dictionary of Biography, National Centre of Biography, Australian National University, 2017, <adb.anu.edu.au/biography/galleghan-sir-frederick-gallagher-10270>.
19 SF Arneil, supplement to *Makan*, no. 269, April–June 1983, p. 1, AWM PR00929, folder 1.
20 Spark, 'Dishonourable men?', pp. 251–52.
21 Adjutant-General to Minister for the Army, 16 July 1945, NAA MP742/1, 255/15/1735, cited in McKernan, *This War Never Ends*, p. 94.
22 SF Arneil, *One Man's War*, 3rd edn, Alternative Publishing Co-operative, Sydney, 1981, pp. 247, 64, 71.
23 ibid., p. 1.
24 J Beaumont, *Gull Force: Survival and Leadership in Captivity 1941–1945*, Allen & Unwin, Sydney, 1988, p. 3.
25 R Gerster, *Big-Noting: The Heroic Theme in Australian War Writing*, MUP, Melbourne, 1987, p. 272.
26 M Cooke, 'WO-man, retelling the war myth', in M Cooke & A Woollacott (eds), *Gendering War Talk*, Princeton University Press, Princeton, 1993, pp. 177–204; MR Higonnet, J Jenson, S Michel & MC Weitz, *Behind the Lines: Gender and the Two World Wars*, Yale University Press, New Haven, 1987; M Lake & J Damousi, 'Warfare, history and gender', in J Damousi & M Lake (eds), *Gender and War: Australians at War in the Twentieth Century*, CUP, Melbourne, 1995, pp. 1–20; P Summerfield, 'Gender and war in the twentieth century', *International History Review*, vol. 19, no. 1, 1997, pp. 3–15.
27 S Garton, *The Cost of War: Australians Return*, OUP, Melbourne, 1996, pp. 209–211; Gerster, *Big-Noting*, pp. 225–38.
28 P Adam-Smith, *Prisoners of War: From Gallipoli to Korea*, Viking, Melbourne, 1992, pp. 447–74; J Bassett, *Guns and Brooches: Australian Army Nursing from the Boer War to the Gulf War*, OUP, Melbourne, 1992, pp. 133–52; RD Goodman, *Our War Nurses: The History of the Royal Australian Army Nursing Corps 1902–*

1988, Boolarong Publications, Brisbane, 1988, pp. 145–63; C Kenny, *Captives: Australian Army Nurses in Japanese Prison Camps*, UQP, Brisbane, 1986; H Nelson, *P.O.W.: Prisoners of War; Australians under Nippon*, ABC Books, Sydney, 1985, pp. 69–83; AS Walker, *Medical Services of the R.A.N. and R.A.A.F.: With a Section on Women in the Army Medical Services*, Australia in the War of 1939–45, series 5, Medical, vol. 4, AWM, Canberra, 1961, pp. 441–55.

29 JE Simons, *While History Passed: The Story of the Australian Nurses Who Were Prisoners of the Japanese for Three and a Half Years*, William Heinemann, Melbourne, 1954, p. 119.
30 SF Arneil, *Black Jack: The Life and Times of Brigadier Sir Frederick Galleghan*, Macmillan, Melbourne, 1983, p. 122.
31 *Argus*, 19 September 1945, p. 3.
32 Convention Relative to the Treatment of Prisoners of War, signed 27 July 1929, 118 LNTS 343 (entered into force 19 June 1931), article 3.
33 C Twomey, 'Australian nurse POWs: gender, war and captivity', *Australian Historical Studies*, vol. 36, no. 124, 2004, pp. 255–74.
34 HM Windsor (Major, 2/14 AGH), Account of release of AANS, 19 September 1945, NAA MP742/1, 336/1/1389.
35 McKernan, *This War Never Ends*, p. 73.
36 *Cessnock Eagle and South Maitland Recorder*, 18 September 1945, p. 3; *Weekly Times*, 19 September 1945, p. 6.
37 *Bulletin*, 7 July 1954, p. 2.
38 McKernan, *This War Never Ends*, p. 7.
39 *Age*, 17 September 1945, p. 1.
40 E Cooper, *Fully Exposed: The Male Nude in Photography*, 2nd edn, Routledge, London, 1995.
41 A Sobocinska, '"The language of scars": Australian prisoners of war and the colonial order', *History Australia*, vol. 7, no. 3, 2010, pp. 58.1–58.19.
42 JW Dower, *War without Mercy: Race and Power in the Pacific War*, Pantheon Books, New York, 1986.
43 P Torney-Parlicki, *Somewhere in Asia: War, Journalism and Australia's Neighbours 1941–75*, UNSW Press, Sydney, 2000, pp. 74–75.
44 Arneil, *One Man's War*, pp. 54, 59, 125.
45 *Age*, 6 September 1945, p. 16.
46 R Mahoney to J Mahoney, 1945, in 'Mixed feelings as POW's waited to be released', Australians at War, DVA, 2001, available at Pandora, National Library of Australia (hereafter NLA), <pandora.nla.gov.au/pan/20401/20020911-0000/www.australiansatwar.gov.au/stories/stories9c3b.html?war=W2&id=121>.
47 Arneil, *Black Jack*, pp. 54–55.
48 *Argus*, 7 September 1945, p. 16.
49 ibid., 6 October 1945, p. 7.
50 AS Blackburn to EE Dunlop, 12 October 1945, AWM PR00926, 1/30.
51 EE Dunlop to H Ferguson, 23 September 1945, AWM PR00926, 1/30.
52 *Mufti*, September 1946, p. 8; October 1946, pp. 26–27; November 1946, pp. 26–27; December 1946, pp. 10–11.
53 *Ek dum*, according to the *Chambers Dictionary*, is a Hindi term meaning

'at once'. In the 1920s, Ellis drove from London to Delhi, suggesting that this phrase stems from his time there. The journey was later recalled in MH Ellis, *Express to Hindustan: An Account of a Motor-Car Journey from London to Delhi*, Bodley Head, London, 1929.
54 *Northern Standard*, 1 July 1949, p. 10.
55 *Reveille*, 1 October 1952, p. 9.
56 *Sydney Morning Herald*, 11 September 1946, p. 9.
57 During the war, POW relatives' associations in some states lobbied the government on behalf of their missing family members. In Western Australia and Victoria, these organisations embraced returning POWs and became ex-POW and relatives' associations, while in South Australia, Queensland and New South Wales, the POW relatives' associations folded, and new ex-POW associations (which did not include relatives) formed.

2 A bit queer

1 *Advertiser*, 25 September 1945, p. 4.
2 *Mail*, 29 September 1945, p. 1.
3 S Garton, *The Cost of War: Australians Return*, OUP, Melbourne, 1996, p. 209.
4 *Advertiser*, 25 September 1945, p. 4.
5 A Faulkner, *Arthur Blackburn, VC: An Australian Hero, His Men, and Their Two World Wars*, Wakefield Press, Adelaide, 2008, p. 417.
6 E Jones & S Wessely, 'British prisoners-of-war: from resilience to psychological vulnerability; reality or perception', *Twentieth Century British History*, vol. 21, no. 2, 2010, pp. 167–68.
7 P Panikos, *The Enemy in Our Midst: Germans in Britain during the First World War*, Bloomsbury, London, 1991, p. 126.
8 AL Vischer, *Barbed-Wire Disease: A Psychological Study of the Prisoner of War*, John Bales, Sons & Danielsson, London, 1919, p. 31.
9 *Times*, 1 January 1940, p. 5.
10 *Southern Argus*, 20 August 1941, p. 2; K Muir, '"Idiots, imbeciles and moral defectives": military and government treatment of mentally ill service personnel and veterans', *Journal of Australian Studies*, vol. 26, no. 73, 2002, p. 45.
11 *Times*, 1 January 1940, p. 5.
12 Jones & Wessely, 'British prisoners-of-war', pp. 167–68.
13 PH Newman, 'The prisoner of war mentality: its effects after repatriation', *British Medical Journal*, vol. 1, no. 4330, 1 January 1944, p. 9.
14 *Sun*, 10 July 1944, p. 4.
15 Medical procedure on demobilisation, 1945, AWM54, 838/3/12, cited in R Hearder, *Keep the Men Alive: Australian POW Doctors under the Japanese*, Allen & Unwin, Sydney, 2009, p. 185.
16 Resume of Red Cross services offered, given and being given to ex-prisoners of war through the Social Service Department, c. 1947, NLA MS 6609, box 177, file 2652c.
17 AJ Hill, 'Wootten, Sir George Frederick (1893–1970)', Australian Dictionary of Biography, National Centre of Biography, Australian National University, 2017, <adb.anu.edu.au/biography/wootten-sir-george-frederick-12073/text21659>.

18 RD Rivett, *Behind Bamboo: An Inside Story of the Japanese Prison Camps*, Seal Books, Rigby, Adelaide, 1973, p. 199.
19 CE Winston, 'Walter Edward Fisher', *Medical Journal of Australia*, vol. 2, 6 August 1966, p. 285. T Hamilton describes him as having a 'patrician bearing and a keen brain that did not suffer fools gladly' in *Soldier Surgeon in Malaya*, Angus & Robertson, Sydney, 1957, p. 30.
20 Australia, Repatriation Commission, *Some Aspects of Medical Investigation and Treatment*, Repatriation Commission, Melbourne, 1947, p. 2; C Lloyd & J Rees, *The Last Shilling: A History of Repatriation in Australia*, MUP, Melbourne, 1994, pp. 301–304.
21 Chairman, Repatriation Commission, to Official Secretary, High Commissioner for Australia in New Zealand, 16 August 1949, NAA A2421, G1084 Part 2.
22 AP Derham to EE Dunlop, 14 August 1950, AWM PR00926, 1/3 (original emphasis).
23 BM Cohen & MZ Cooper, *A Follow-Up Study of World War II Prisoners of War*, Veterans Administration Medical Monograph, US Government Printing Office, Washington, DC, 1955; AP Curtin, 'Imprisonment under the Japanese', *British Medical Journal*, vol. 2, no. 4476, 19 October 1946, pp. 585–86; WP Mallinson & W Warren, 'Repatriation: a psychiatric study of 100 naval ex-prisoners of war', *British Medical Journal*, vol. 2, no. 4331, 8 December 1945, pp. 798–801; E Roberts-Pedersen, 'A weak spot in the personality? Conceptualising "war neurosis" in British medical literature of the Second World War', *Australian Journal of Politics & History*, vol. 58, no. 3, 2012, pp. 409–410; WH Whiles, 'A study of neurosis among repatriated prisoners of war', *British Medical Journal*, vol. 2, no. 4428, 17 November 1945, pp. 697–98.
24 *Smith's Weekly*, 27 August 1949, p. 5.
25 *Sydney Morning Herald*, 12 October 1945, p. 2.
26 ibid., 18 September 1945, p. 2.
27 *Argus*, 8 October 1945, p. 5; M McKernan, *This War Never Ends: The Pain of Separation and Return*, UQP, Brisbane, 2001, pp. 81–83.
28 Muir, 'Idiots, imbeciles and moral defectives', p. 43.
29 J Bostock & E Jones, *The Nervous Soldier: A Handbook for the Prevention, Detection and Treatment of Nervous Invalidity in War*, AH Tucker, Government Printer, Brisbane, 1943, p. 26.
30 *Sydney Morning Herald*, 29 April 1947, p. 3.
31 HC Barnard, *CPD*, HR, vol. 201, 4 March 1949, pp. 1017–18.
32 WJ Cooper, *CPD*, Senate, vol. 208, 22 June 1950, p. 4706; Muir, 'Idiots, imbeciles and moral defectives', p. 46.
33 Australian Legion of Ex-Servicemen and Women to Minister for Repatriation, 23 June 1949, NAA A2421, G1084 Part 2.
34 M Oppenheimer, '"Our number one priority": the Australian Red Cross and prisoners of war in the world wars', in J Beaumont, L Grant & A Pegram (eds), *Beyond Surrender: Australian Prisoners of War in the Twentieth Century*, MUP, Melbourne, 2015, p. 91.
35 Resume of Red Cross services offered, given and being given to ex-prisoners of

war through the Social Service Department, c. 1947, NLA MS 6609, box 177, file 2652c.
36 Appendix, in Proceedings of Red Cross meeting about POWs, 1947, NLA MS 6609, box 177, file 2652c.
37 AE Coates, Statement at Red Cross Conference, 2 June 1947, NLA MS 6609, box 177, file 2652c.
38 Repatriation Committee on Repatriated Prisoners of War, Report, 4 July 1947, AWM PR89/186, item 9.
39 Chairman, Repatriation Commission, to Secretary, Commonwealth Public Service Board, Survey of Selected Groups of Those Who Served in the 1939–45 War, 2 October 1947, NAA A2421, G1846 Part 1.
40 Chairman, Repatriation Commission, to Deputy Commissioner, Department of Repatriation, 8 November 1948, NAA A2421, G1846 Part 1.
41 *Sydney Morning Herald*, 17 February 1950, p. 2.
42 Medical examination of ex-prisoners of war (J), c. 1949–50, NAA A2421, G1084 Part 2.
43 Chairman, Repatriation Commission, to Minister for Repatriation, 10 September 1947, NAA A2421, G1846 Part 1.
44 Australia, Repatriation Commission, *Some Aspects of Medical Investigation and Treatment*, pp. 2–3, 21.
45 Repatriation Committee on Repatriated Prisoners of War, Minutes of meeting, 24 October 1950, p. 4, NAA A2421, G1846 Part 3.
46 Medical examination of ex-prisoners of war (J), c. 1949–50, NAA A2421, G1084 Part 2.
47 *Smith's Weekly*, 27 August 1949, p. 5.
48 WE Fisher to Chairman, Repatriation Commission, 11 December 1948, NAA A2421, G1846 Part 2.
49 Australia, Repatriation Commission, *Some Aspects of Medical Investigation and Treatment*, p. 23.
50 Secretary, Katoomba Leura Repatriation Local Committee, to Minister for Repatriation, 6 October 1953, NAA A2421, G1846 Part 4.
51 *Argus*, 12 May 1952, p. 2.

3 Three bob a day

1 S Savige, Claim for special allowance to ex-prisoners of war, 1950, NAA SP186/1, SL57080 Part 4.
2 C Barrett includes details of early compensation campaigns but does not discuss the subsistence allowance claims in '"Matters still outstanding": Australian ex-POWs of the Japanese and claims for reparations', in M Crotty & M Larsson (eds), *Anzac Legacies: Australians and the Aftermath of War*, Australian Scholarly Publishing, Melbourne, 2010, pp. 187–210.
3 Blain was without voting rights, as the Member for the Northern Territory did not have full voting rights until 1968.
4 *Kalgoorlie Miner*, 27 September 1945, p. 2.
5 *Argus*, 12 January 1946, p. 12.
6 WG Turnbull, *CPD*, HR, vol. 186, 7 March 1946, p. 104.

Notes to pages 56–59

7   FM Forde, quoting Turnbull, *CPD*, HR, vol. 187, 12 July 1946, p. 2492.
8   WG Turnbull, *CPD*, HR, vol. 187, 12 July 1946, p. 2480.
9   Federal Executive, RSSAILA, Resolution no. 3, September 1946, in Assistant Secretary, RSSAILA, to Federal President, RSSAILA, 19 February 1947, NLA MS 6609, box 165, file 2387c Part 1.
10 RSSAILA, 33rd Annual Congress, Resolution no. 279, in General Secretary, RSSAILA, to Prime Minister, 17 November 1948, NLA MS 6609, box 165, file 2387c Part 2.
11 *Mufti*, February 1949, p. 30.
12 C Chambers, *CPD*, HR, vol. 190, 25 March 1947, p. 1098.
13 C Chambers (Minister for the Army), Prisoners of war: suggestion from Mr Turnbull MP that subsistence allowance be paid, 8 March 1947, NAA A816, 57/301/177.
14 FM Forde, *CPD*, HR, vol. 187, 12 July 1946, pp. 2488–89.
15 WG Turnbull, *CPD*, HR, vol. 187, 12 July 1946, p. 2489.
16 RSSAILA, 31st Annual Congress, Resolution no. 448, in General Secretary, RSSAILA, to Prime Minister, 20 November 1946, NLA MS 6609, box 165, file 2387c Part 1.
17 WG Turnbull, quoting Minister for the Army, *CPD*, HR, vol. 191, 14 March 1947, p. 692.
18 Convention Relative to the Treatment of Prisoners of War, signed 27 July 1929, 118 LNTS 343 (entered into force 19 June 1931), article 23.
19 In the European camps, the amount of convention pay officers received was roughly equivalent to their normal field allowance. By December 1944, the Australian government had decided to debit officers held in captivity by the Germans and Italians to a maximum of three shillings and four pence per day. Secretary, Prime Minister's Department, to Secretary, RSSAILA, n.d., NLA MS 6609, box 153, file 2110c.
20 Draft prepared by Treasury in response to question from Mr White in parliament, c. 1947, NAA A816, 57/301/177.
21 Federal Executive, RSSAILA, Resolution no. 153, September 1947, NLA MS 6609, box 165, file 2387c Part 1; RSSAILA, 32nd Annual Conference, Resolution no. 189, 1947, NLA MS 6609, box 165, file 2387c Part 1; RSSAILA, 33rd Annual Congress, Resolution no. 279, 1948, NLA MS 6609, box 165, file 2387c Part 2.
22 Council of the 8th Division to Prime Minister, 3 March 1949, NAA A2421, G1084 Part 2.
23 B Noonan to F Brennan (MHR), 28 January 1947, NAA A461, J350/1/16.
24 C Chambers (Minister for the Army), Prisoners of war: suggestion from Mr Turnbull MP that subsistence allowance be paid, 8 March 1947, NAA A816, 57/301/177.
25 FM Forde, *CPD*, HR, vol. 188, 9 August 1946, p. 4210.
26 *Sydney Morning Herald*, 28 November 1949, p. 2.
27 C Chambers (Minister for the Army), Prisoners of war: suggestion from Mr Turnbull MP that subsistence allowance be paid, 8 March 1947, NAA A816, 57/301/177.

28 This was mentioned regularly in later parliamentary debates. See LC Haylen, *CPD*, HR, vol. 220, 21 October 1952, p. 3464.
29 The Minister for the Army prepared a memo dated 6 March 1947, and Cabinet discussed Turnbull's suggestion; Minutes of meeting of full Cabinet, Agendum no. 1311, 11 March 1947, NAA A2703, 152. The item was also discussed the following month; Minutes of meeting of full Cabinet, 15 April 1947, NAA A2703, 154.
30 *Advertiser*, 28 March 1947, p. 1.
31 State Secretary, WA RSSAILA, to JC Neagle (General Secretary, RSSAILA), 18 April 1947, NLA MS 6609, box 165, file 2387c Part 1.
32 *Mufti*, April 1947, p. 18.
33 RT Pollard, *CPD*, HR, vol. 192, 25 March 1947, p. 1102; HE Holt, *CPD*, HR, vol. 192, 25 March 1947, p. 1102.
34 *Mufti*, September 1949, p. 7.
35 W Stones (President) & PC Smith (Honorary Secretary, NSW Ex-Prisoners of War Association) to RT Pollard (MHR), 26 May 1947, NLA MS 6609, box 165, file 2387c Part 1.
36 The War Claims Act (Public Law 896, 80th Congress) was passed in 1948 but did not come into operation until 14 September 1949, with the appointment of three commissioners. Major-General, Australian Military Mission, Washington, to AHQ, Melbourne, 3 February 1950, NAA SP186/1, SL57080 Part 9; General Secretary, RSSAILA, to Prime Minister, 5 July 1949, NLA MS 6609, box 165, file 2387c Part 1; GK Reynolds, *U.S. Prisoners of War and Civilian American Citizens Captured and Interned by Japan in World War II: The Issue of Compensation by Japan*, Congressional Research Service, Washington, DC, 2002, p. 6.
37 American Legion to RSSAILA, 20 May 1949, NLA MS 6609, box 165, file 2387c Part 2.
38 RG Menzies, *CPD*, HR, vol. 191, 25 March 1947, pp. 1100–101.
39 RG Menzies, *Joint Opposition Policy, 1949: Policy Speech of the Leader of the Opposition (Rt. Hon. R. G. Menzies), Delivered at Canterbury, Victoria, on November 10, 1949, Together with Supplementary Statements*, Liberal Party of Australia, Sydney, 1949, p. 39.
40 *Sun*, 2 December 1949, NLA MS 6609, box 165, file 2387c Part 2.
41 *Mercury*, 30 November 1949, p. 12; *Reveille*, 1 February 1950, p. 7.
42 *Herald*, 2 September 1949, NAA A2421, G1084 Part 2.
43 EE Dunlop (President, Ex-Prisoners of War and Relatives Association of Victoria), Distress patriotic fund 'P.O.W. appeal', 29 August 1949, NAA A2421, G1084 Part 2.
44 Secretary, Australasian Meat Industry Employees' Union, to Prime Minister, 8 September 1949, NAA A2421, G1084 Part 2.
45 *Herald*, 9 September 1950, NAA A2421, G1084 Part 2.
46 E Garney to Minister for the Army, 9 September 1949, NAA A2421, G1084 Part 2.
47 In 1949, Charles Anderson, Alexander Downer, Wilfrid Kent Hughes, Reginald Swartz, Winton Turnbull and Malcolm McColm were elected to the House of Representatives, and Justin O'Byrne was elected as a Labor Senator

for Tasmania. McColm and O'Byrne had been prisoners of the Germans; all the others were former prisoners of the Japanese.
48 WE Fisher to GW Holland (Acting Federal President, RSSAILA), 2 March 1950, NLA MS 6609, box 165, file 2387c Part 3.
49 HG Bennett to WS Kent Hughes, 10 February 1962, NLA MS 4856, series 2, file 10.
50 F Sinclair (Secretary, Department of Army), Subsistence allowance for prisoners of war, 7 February 1950, NAA A816, 57/301/177.
51 Views of Vice Chief of General Staff, cited in Minister for the Army to Prime Minister, 10 February 1950, NAA A816, 57/301/177.
52 J Francis (Minister for the Army), for Cabinet, Agendum no. 67, Prisoners of war subsistence allowance, 15 March 1950, NAA A816, 57/301/177.
53 GM Keating, 'Savige, Sir Stanley George (1890–1954)', Australian Dictionary of Biography, National Centre of Biography, Australian National University, 2017, <adb.anu.edu.au/biography/savige-sir-stanley-george-11617>.
54 Federal Executive, RSSAILA, Submission in relation to the subsistence allowance for Australian servicemen who became prisoners of war in enemy hands in the 1939–45 war, c. 1950, NLA MS 6609, box 165, file 2387c Part 4.
55 ibid. See also Submissions by the Federal Executive of the R.S.S. & A.I.L.A. in relation to the subsistence allowance, c. 1950, NAA SP186/1, SL57080 Part 9.
56 Submissions by the Federal Executive of the R.S.S. & A.I.L.A. in relation to the subsistence allowance, c. 1950, p. 3, NAA SP186/1, SL57080 Part 9.
57 W Yeo (State President, NSW RSSAILA) to GW Holland (Acting Federal President, RSSAILA), 14 June 1950, NLA MS 6609, box 166, file 2387c Part A.
58 *Daily News*, 30 June 1950, p. 14.
59 S Savige, Claim for special allowance to ex prisoners of war, c. 1950, p. 21, NAA SP186/1, SL57080 Part 4.
60 WG Turnbull, *CPD*, HR, vol. 220, 21 October 1952, p. 3441.
61 Australia, Prime Minister, *Report of Committee Appointed to Investigate Question of Payment of Special Subsistence Allowance to Australian Prisoners of War, 1939–45 War*, Government Printer, Canberra, 1950, p. 8.
62 WE Fisher to Prime Minister, 26 September 1950, in Australia, Prime Minister, *Report of Committee*, p. 10.
63 Australia, Prime Minister, *Report of Committee*, p. 6.
64 ibid., p. 7.
65 RE Northey, 'Haylen, Leslie Clement (Les) (1898–1977)', Australian Dictionary of Biography, National Centre of Biography, Australian National University, 2017, <adb.anu.edu.au/biography/haylen-leslie-clement-les-10466>.
66 LC Haylen, *CPD*, HR, vol. 211, 7 December 1950, p. 3980.
67 The 'Spender plan' was a reference to what ultimately became the Colombo Plan. LC Haylen, *CPD*, HR, vol. 211, 7 December 1950, pp. 3981–92.
68 *Mufti*, March 1951, p. 5.
69 *Reveille*, 1 November 1950, p. 7.
70 General Secretary, RSSAILA, to Prime Minister, 28 November 1951, NLA MS 6609, box 165, file 2387c Part 5.
71 *Mufti*, May 1951, pp. 5–7.

72 Treaty of Peace with Japan, signed 8 September 1951, 136 UNTS 45 (entered into force 28 April 1952), articles 14, 16.
73 P Yeend, *Compensation (Japanese Internment) Bill 2001*, Bills Digest no. 6, Information and Research Services, Department of the Parliamentary Library, 2001–02, <parlinfo.aph.gov.au/parlInfo/download/legislation/billsdgs/G1M46/upload_binary/g1m467.pdf;fileType=application/pdf>.
74 *Barbed Wire and Bamboo*, April 1952, pp. 8, 13.
75 LC Haylen, *CPD*, HR, vol. 220, 21 October 1952, p. 3434.
76 JH O'Byrne, *CPD*, Senate, vol. 220, 23 October 1952, p. 3632.
77 Reynolds, *U.S. Prisoners of War and Civilian American Citizens*, p. 3.
78 N O'Sullivan, *CPD*, Senate, vol. 4, 5 August 1954, p. 43; WH Spooner, *CPD*, Senate, vol. 11, 5 December 1957, p. 1741.
79 Yeend, *Compensation (Japanese Internment) Bill 2001*, p. 3.
80 General Secretary, Canadian Legion of the British Empire Service League, to Assistant Secretary, RSSAILA, 29 October 1952, NLA MS 6609, box 166, file 2387 Part 6 (a); R Joshua, *CPD*, HR, vol. 220, 21 October 1952, p. 3439.

4 The Prisoners of War Trust Fund

1 TW White, *CPD*, HR, vol. 192, 25 March 1947, p. 1107.
2 RG Menzies, *CPD*, HR, vol. 211, 12 October 1950, pp. 714–15.
3 Prisoners of War Trust Fund, Decision to phase out the fund, Trustees meeting no. 43, 16 April 1971, NAA B502. The move to decimal currency occurred in 1966.
4 *Argus*, 12 May 1952, p. 2.
5 E Harding, *Services Canteens Trust Fund: Steps Leading to the Establishment of the Fund by the Parliament of the Commonwealth of Australia with Effect from the 1st July, 1947*, Services Canteens Trust Fund, Melbourne, 1971.
6 Services Canteens Trust Fund, *39th and Final Annual Report, 1986*, Australian Government Publishing Service, Canberra, 1986.
7 Cabinet Committee on Prisoners of War Trust Fund, 14 March 1951, NAA A4933, POW/3; Secretary, Prime Minister, to RSSAILA, 24 October 1951, NLA MS 6609, box 324, file 3758c.
8 Prisoners of War Trust Fund, Circular letter, 4 April 1952, NLA MS 6609, box 324, file 3758c.
9 ibid.
10 Federal Executive, RSSAILA, Meeting, May 1952, NLA MS 6609, box 324, file 3758c.
11 Secretary, Vic. RSSAILA, to General Secretary, RSSAILA, 10 April 1952, NLA MS 6609, box 324, file 3758c; State Secretary, WA RSSAILA, to General Secretary, RSSAILA, 2 May 1952, NLA MS 6609, box 324, file 3758c.
12 *Mufti*, May 1952, p. 9.
13 LC Haylen, *CPD*, HR, vol. 211, 7 December 1950, p. 3982.
14 Prisoners of War Trust Fund, Trustees meeting no. 4, 19 June 1952, NAA B502.
15 Based on advertisements in *Canberra Times*, 18 June 1958.
16 Prisoners of War Trust Fund, Trustees meeting no. 12, 17–18 March 1953, NAA B502.

17 Chairman, Prisoners of War Trust Fund, to WK Hughes, 1 July 1953, NAA B503.
18 Prisoners of War Trust Fund, Decision to phase out the fund, Trustees meeting no. 43, 16 April 1971, NAA B502.

5 Rebuilding a life

1   In this chapter, information drawn from the archives of the Prisoners of War Trust Fund in NAA B503 (about which see Prologue, note 3) has been supplemented with that in service records available in NAA MT1486/1 and NAA B883; war crimes affidavits in AWM54; State Archives and Records NSW, NRS 13495; NSW Coroner's Court inquest records; NSW Quarter Sessions records; births, deaths and marriages records in Queensland, New South Wales and South Australia; and contemporary newspapers. Much of the supplementary material is available on public record, but, because of the sensitive nature of the material revealed in the fund files, pseudonyms are used here and all other references have been redacted.
2   C Tennant, K Goulston & O Dent, 'Clinical psychiatric illness in prisoners of war of the Japanese: forty years after release', *Psychological Medicine*, vol. 16, no. 4, 1986, pp. 837–38.

6 POW marriages

1   Prisoners of War Trust Fund, Application form, 1952–77, NAA B503.
2   *Argus*, 11 December 1918, p. 8.
3   J Bomford, '"A wife, a baby, a home and a new Holden car": family life after captivity', in M Crotty & M Larsson (eds), *Anzac Legacies: Australians and the Aftermath of War*, Australian Scholarly Publishing, Melbourne, 2010, pp. 107–125.
4   'A war widow's long fight', *Sydney Morning Herald*, 10 April 2007, <www.smh.com.au/news/national/a-war-widows-long-fight/2007/04/09/1175971023066.html>.
5   A Flanagan & M Flanagan, *The Line: A Man's Experience; A Son's Quest to Understand*, One Day Hill, Melbourne, 2005.
6   H Nelson, *P.O.W.: Prisoners of War; Australians under Nippon*, ABC Books, Sydney, 1985, pp. 32, 210.
7   M Lake, 'Female desires: the meaning of World War II', *Australian Historical Studies*, vol. 24, no. 95, 1990, p. 281; L Featherstone, '"The one single primary cause": divorce, the family, and heterosexual pleasure in postwar Australia', *Journal of Australian Studies*, vol. 37, no. 3, 2013, p. 350; F Bongiorno, *The Sex Lives of Australians: A History*, Black Inc., Melbourne, 2012, pp. 216–19.
8   J Damousi, *Freud in the Antipodes: A Cultural History of Psychoanalysis in Australia*, UNSW Press, Sydney, 2005.
9   AE Coates, 'Clinical lessons from prisoner of war hospitals in the Far East (Burma and Siam)', *Medical Journal of Australia*, vol. 1, 1 June 1946, p. 759; R Bourke, *Prisoners of the Japanese: Literary Imagination and the Prisoner-of-War Experience*, UQP, Brisbane, 2006, pp. 54–55; Bongiorno, *The Sex Lives of Australians*, p. 187.

10 K Harrison, *Road to Hiroshima*, rev. edn of *The Brave Japanese*, Rigby, Adelaide, 1983, cited in Y Smaal, *Sex, Soldiers and the South Pacific, 1939–45: Queer Identities in Australia in the Second World War*, Palgrave Macmillan, London, 2015, p. 73.
11 Nelson, *P.O.W.*, p. 25.
12 N Starck, *Proud Australian Boy: A Biography of Russell Braddon*, Australian Scholarly Publishing, Melbourne, 2011, p. 56.
13 On the history of responses to homosexuality in Australia see R Reynolds & S Robinson, *Gay & Lesbian, Then & Now: Australian Stories from a Social Revolution*, Black Inc., Melbourne, 2016; S Robinson (ed.), *Homophobia: An Australian History*, Federation Press, Sydney, 2008; G Willett, *Living Out Loud: A History of Gay and Lesbian Activism in Australia*, Allen & Unwin, Sydney, 2000; G Wotherspoon, *Gay Sydney: A History*, NewSouth, Sydney, 2016.
14 RWJ Fussell to E Fussell, 15 November 1945 (original emphasis), in RWJ Fussell – E Fussell, Divorce papers, 1946, State Archives and Records NSW, NRS 13495, 2195/1946.
15 E Fussell to RWJ Fussell, c. 1945, in RWJ Fussell – E Fussell, Divorce papers, 1946, State Archives and Records NSW, NRS 13495, 2195/1946.
16 Roy and Ellen Fussell's divorce papers are on the public record; their names have not been changed. The same applies to the subsequent case of Cedric and Vera Ewing.
17 *Courier-Mail*, 5 October 1945, p. 1.
18 GA Carmichael & PF McDonald, 'The rise and fall of divorce in Australia, 1968–1985', in *Proceedings of the Third Australian Population Association Conference 1986*, Flinders University, Adelaide, 1987, p. 19.
19 CJ Ewing to VJ Ewing, 20 November 1945; VJ Ewing to CJ Ewing, 14 December 1945, in CJ Ewing – VJ Ewing, Divorce papers, State Archives and Records NSW, NRS 13495, 193/1946.
20 J Allen, *Sex & Secrets: Crimes Involving Australian Women since 1880*, OUP, Melbourne, 1990, pp. 231–34.
21 Australian Bureau of Statistics, *Women's Safety Australia, 1996*, cat. no. 4128.0, Australian Bureau of Statistics, 1996, <www.abs.gov.au/ausstats/abs@.nsf/cat/4128.0>.
22 E Nelson, *Homefront Hostilities: The First World War and Domestic Violence*, Australian Scholarly Publishing, Melbourne, 2014, pp. xi–xii.
23 A Kaladelfos, 'The dark side of the family: paternal child homicide in Australia', *Journal of Australian Studies*, vol. 37, no. 3, 2013, pp. 344–45.
24 S Garton, *The Cost of War: Australians Return*, OUP, Melbourne, 1996, pp. 198–201.
25 Flanagan & Flanagan, *The Line*.
26 S Dingo, *Unsung Ordinary Men: A Generation Like No Other*, Hachette Australia, Sydney, 2010, p. 300.

7 Reconciliation with Japan
1 *Sydney Morning Herald*, 31 May 1948, p. 2.
2 J Geraty to Prime Minister, 12 June 1951, NAA A462, 619/1/3.

3   ND Harper, 'Australian policy towards Japan', *Australian Outlook*, vol. 1, no. 4, 1947, p. 14.
4   'Feeling towards Japan still not good', *Mainichi* (newspaper), 25 June 1952, translated extract, NAA A1838, 3103/10/1 Part 1.
5   Gerster, 'Six inch rule: revisiting the Australian occupation of Japan 1946–1952', *History Australia*, vol. 4, no. 2, 2007, p. 42.3. See also C de Matos, 'Diplomacy interrupted? Macmahon Ball, Evatt and Labor's policies in occupied Japan', *Australian Journal of Politics & History*, vol. 52, no. 2, 2006, pp. 194, 200; C de Matos, *Encouraging 'Democracy' in a Cold War Climate: The Dual-Platform Policy Approach of Evatt and Labor toward the Allied Occupation of Japan 1945–1949*, Australia-Japan Research Centre, Canberra, 2001; C Waters, 'War, decolonization and postwar security', in D Goldsworthy & PG Edwards (eds), *Facing North: A Century of Australian Engagement with Asia*, MUP, Melbourne, 2001, pp. 97–133.
6   RN Rosecrance, *Australian Diplomacy and Japan, 1945–1951*, MUP, Melbourne, 1962; A Watt, *The Evolution of Australian Foreign Policy, 1938–1965*, CUP, London, 1968.
7   P Strangio, *Neither Power Nor Glory: 100 Years of Political Labor in Victoria, 1856–1956*, MUP, Melbourne, 2012, p. 214.
8   F Howard, *Kent Hughes: A Biography of Colonel the Hon. Sir Wilfrid Kent Hughes*, Macmillan, Melbourne, 1972.
9   WS Kent Hughes, *Slaves of the Samurai: An Australian Odyssey, Which Gives an Account of the Life and Thoughts of a Slave of the Samurai, during His Three Years and Seven Months as a Prisoner of War in the Hands of the Japanese*, OUP, Melbourne, 1946, p. ix.
10 *Canberra Times*, 23 July 1948, p. 4.
11 WS Kent Hughes, *CPD*, HR, vol. 216, 21 February 1952, p. 238.
12 N Boister & R Cryer, *The Tokyo International Military Tribunal: A Reappraisal*, OUP, Oxford, 2008; TP Maga, *Judgment at Tokyo: The Japanese War Crimes Trials*, University Press of Kentucky, Lexington, 2000; PR Piccigallo, *The Japanese on Trial: Allied War Crimes Operations in the East, 1945–1951*, University of Texas Press, Austin, 1979; RJ Pritchard (ed.), *The Tokyo Major War Crimes Trial: The Records of the International Military Tribunal for the Far East; With an Authoritative Commentary and Comprehensive Guide*, 124 vols, E Mellen Press, New York, 1998–2006; Y Totani, *The Tokyo War Crimes Trial: The Pursuit of Justice in the Wake of World War II*, Harvard University Asia Center & Harvard University Press, Cambridge, MA, 2008.
13 *Age*, 9 July 1993, p. 3.
14 *Sunday Sun and Guardian*, 11 December 1949, p. 3.
15 *Sydney Morning Herald*, 11 June 1948, p. 2.
16 RH Minear, *Victors' Justice: The Tokyo War Crimes Trial*, Princeton University Press, Princeton, 1971.
17 *Sydney Morning Herald*, 31 May 1948, p. 2. Huxtable later wrote a memoir of his experiences, *From the Somme to Singapore: A Medical Officer in Two World Wars*, Kangaroo Press, Sydney, 1987.
18 *Sydney Morning Herald*, 8 June 1948, p. 2.
19 *Nation's Forum of the Air*, April 1950, p. 3.

Notes to pages 162–171

20   *Examiner*, 14 July 1950, p. 2.
21   *Barrier Miner*, 2 May 1947, p. 6.
22   Atomic bomb, Hiroshima, envelope containing photographs, AWM PR89/186, item 6.
23   WS Kent Hughes, *CPD*, HR, vol. 6, 28 April 1955, p. 293.
24   T Uren, Opening statement at the first plenary session, 2 August 1960, NLA MS 6055, box 28, series 5, file 9.
25   T Uren to B Bedford, 16 August 1960, NLA MS 6055, box 28, series 5, file 9.
26   *Nation's Forum of the Air*, April 1950, p. 3.
27   *Sydney Morning Herald*, 31 May 1948, p. 2.
28   WS Kent Hughes, Draft of adjournment speech, 28 November 1957, NLA MS 4856, series 22, file 23.
29   *Sydney Morning Herald*, 2 June 1948, p. 2; 10 June 1948, p. 2; 13 November 1948, p. 3.
30   G Nicholls, *Deported: A History of Forced Departures from Australia*, UNSW Press, Sydney, 2007, pp. 76–79.
31   *Daily News*, 16 November 1949, p. 8.
32   *Reveille*, 1 June 1950, p. 8.
33   ibid., 1 February 1950, p. 7.
34   *Argus*, 14 December 1948, p. 6; *Sydney Morning Herald*, 16 November 1949, p. 3. The Ex-Prisoners of War Association of South Australia supported Calwell's stance; *Advertiser*, 13 March 1948, p. 1.
35   *Nation's Forum of the Air*, April 1950, p. 3.
36   *Mufti*, September 1949, p. 20.
37   ibid.
38   *Reveille*, 1 February 1950, p. 7.
39   *Sydney Morning Herald*, 24 November 1949, p. 1.
40   *Courier-Mail*, 14 November 1949, p. 1.
41   *Mercury*, 5 December 1949, p. 3.
42   *Barrier Miner*, 9 March 1948, p. 7.
43   Gerster, 'Six inch rule', p. 42.4.
44   JW Henderson, born 26 May 1920, discharged 27 February 1948. See NAA B883, NX50679, file OWE.
45   *Newcastle Sun*, 22 July 1954, p. 6.
46   *Advertiser*, 10 March 1948, p. 1.
47   *Mail*, 13 March 1948, p. 3.
48   *Advertiser*, 1 March 1948, p. 2.
49   *West Australian*, 11 March 1948, p. 9.
50   *Sydney Morning Herald*, 12 March 1948, p. 2.
51   *Advertiser*, 11 March 1948, p. 3.
52   *Canberra Times*, 23 February 1954, p. 2.
53   *Sydney Morning Herald*, 28 August 1947, p. 2.
54   WS Kent Hughes, *CPD*, HR, vol. 13, 28 November 1957, p. 2728.
55   B Hills, 'God's man in Japan in Japan: the Catholic priest who inspired Australia's post-war reconciliation with Japan', Ben Hills, 2014, <benhills.com/articles/japan-unlimited/gods-man-in-japan-in-japan/>.

56 *Catholic Weekly*, 3 March 1949, p. 25.
57 *Canberra Times*, 22 April 1959, p. 2.
58 *Mercury*, 30 June 1950, p. 3.
59 ibid., 7 July 1953, p. 12.
60 *Mufti*, April 1953, p. 28.
61 Treaty of Peace with Japan, signed 8 September 1951, 136 UNTS 45 (entered into force 28 April 1952).
62 *Mufti*, April 1947, p. 19.
63 *Herald*, c. May 1949, NLA MS 6609, box 165, file 2387c Part 2.
64 *Barrier Miner*, 5 April 1950, p. 4.
65 *Sunday Herald*, 9 September 1951, p. 2; *Reveille*, 1 January 1957, p. 42.
66 *Sunday Herald*, 9 September 1951, p. 2.
67 *Barrier Miner*, 13 September 1951, p. 3.
68 Combined Union Committee, Railway Workshops, Newport, to Prime Minister, 4 March 1952, NAA A462, 619/1/3.
69 Secretary, Federated Clerks' Union of Australia, to Prime Minister, 3 March 1952, NAA A462, 619/1/3.
70 *Daily News*, 13 September 1945, p. 6.
71 *Mail*, 22 February 1947, p. 3.
72 *Sunday Herald*, 15 July 1951, p. 3.
73 *Sunday Mail*, 18 February 1951, p. 4.
74 *Cairns Post*, 18 February 1952, p. 1.
75 LC Haylen, *CPD*, HR, vol. 216, 21 February 1952, p. 246.
76 Society Opposed to the Ratification of the Peace Treaty, Citizens declaration for peace, c. 1952, NAA A462, 619/1/3.
77 LK Probyn to Prime Minister, 4 February 1952, NAA A462, 619/1/3.
78 J Appleton (Union of Australian Women) to Prime Minister, 21 February 1952, NAA A462, 619/1/3.
79 G Shapper (Mrs) to Prime Minister, 22 February 1952, NAA A462, 619/1/3.
80 G Tavan, *The Long, Slow Death of White Australia*, Scribe, Melbourne, 2005.
81 Gerster, 'Six inch rule', p. 42.11. See also K Tamura, *Michi's Memories: The Story of a Japanese War Bride*, Pandanus Books, Canberra, 2001.
82 *Canberra Times*, 23 July 1954, p. 3.
83 *Newcastle Sun*, 14 September 1954, p. 1.
84 RG Menzies, *Man to Man – Australia Today*, broadcast, 17th March 1954, transcript, NAA A1838, 3103/10/1 Part 1.
85 *Nation's Forum of the Air*, April 1950, p. 9.
86 M Linden, M Rotter, K Baumann & B Lieberei, *Posttraumatic Embitterment Disorder: Definition, Evidence, Diagnosis, Treatment*, Hogrefe, Cambridge, MA, 2007, p. 22.
87 Aristotle, *Nicomachean Ethics*, trans. R Crisp, CUP, New York, 2014, book 4, part 5.
88 Newspaper article on Japan, 30 August 1954, NAA A1838, 3103/10/1 Part 2.
89 *Canberra Times*, 25 January 1955, p. 1.
90 TW Eckersley, Minute, 7 July 1955, NAA A1838, 480/2/8/2.
91 *Sun-Herald*, 14 August 1955, NAA A1838, 480/2/8/2.

92 D Aszkielowicz, 'Repatriation and the limits of resolve: Japanese war criminals in Australian custody', *Japanese Studies*, vol. 31, no. 2, 2011, pp. 224–25.
93 Newsclipping, c. April 1957, NAA A1838, 3103/10/11/2 Part 1.
94 Secret, Prime Minister's brief, Japan, c. April 1957, NAA A1838, 3103/10/11/2 Part 1.
95 The Colombo Plan, initiated in 1949, was designed to provide education to Asian students in order to strengthen the social and economic fabric of Asian countries and make them less vulnerable to communist influence. A Kobayashi, 'Australia and Japan's admission into the Colombo Plan', *Australian Journal of Politics & History*, vol. 60, no. 4, 2014, pp. 518–19.
96 Agreement on Commerce between the Commonwealth of Australia and Japan, signed 6 July 1957, ATS 1957 no. 15 (entered into force 4 December 1957).
97 *Sunday Herald*, 29 March 1953, p. 3; *Sydney Morning Herald*, 17 April 1953, p. 1.
98 Forty-fourth meeting of Board of Management of the Australian War Memorial, 16 April 1953, AWM315 235/002/009.
99 WE Fisher to Prime Minister, 26 November 1957, NLA MS 6609, box 292, file 4578c.
100 WS Kent Hughes to WE Fisher (President, Council of the 8th Division), 27 November 1957, NLA MS 4856, series 2, file 23.
101 WS Kent Hughes, *CPD*, HR, vol. 13, 28 November 1957, p. 2727.
102 *Canberra Times*, 15 November 1957, p. 2.
103 W Yeo (State President, NSW RSSAILA) to G Holland (National President, RSSAILA), 6 January 1958, NLA MS 6609, box 292, file 4578c.
104 *Canberra Times*, 31 October 1957, p. 18.
105 *Mufti*, September 1954, p. 6; May 1953, pp. 11–12; January 1950, p. 18.
106 RSSAILA National Headquarters, Press statement, Canberra, 1 December 1957, NLA MS 6609, box 292, file 4579c.
107 National Secretary, RSSAILA, to WE Fisher, 28 November 1957, NLA MS 6609, box 292, file 4579c.

8 Rewards and regional relationships

1 AIF Malayan Nursing Scholarship, Fundraising flyer, AIF Nursing Scholarship – Malayan Chinese, c. 1945, University of Melbourne Archives (hereafter UMA) NO39, unit 6, 2016.0061.
2 A Broinowski, *The Yellow Lady: Australian Impressions of Asia*, OUP, Melbourne, 1992; N Brown, 'Australian intellectuals and the image of Asia, 1920–60', *Australian Cultural History*, no. 9, 1990, pp. 80–92; D Fettling, 'An Australian response to Asian decolonisation: Jawaharlal Nehru, John Burton and the New Delhi Conference of Non-Western Nations', *Australian Historical Studies*, vol. 45, no. 2, 2014, pp. 202–219; L Grant, *Australian Soldiers in the Asia-Pacific in WWII*, NewSouth, Sydney, 2014; A Sobocinska, *Visiting the Neighbours: Australians in Asia*, NewSouth, Sydney, 2014; D Walker, *Anxious Nation: Australia and the Rise of Asia, 1850–1939*, UQP, Brisbane, 1999; C Waters, 'The Macmahon Ball mission to East Asia 1948', *Australian Journal of Politics & History*, vol. 40, no. 3, 1994, pp. 351–63.

3   D Walker & A Sobocinska, 'Introduction: Australia's Asia', in D Walker & A Sobocinska (eds), *Australia's Asia: From Yellow Peril to Asian Century*, UWA Publishing, Perth, 2012, pp. 1–23.
4   Campbell, Owen Colin, NAA B883, QX14380.
5   Ooi KG, 'Prelude to invasion: covert operations before the re-occupation of northwest Borneo, 1944–45', *Journal of the Australian War Memorial*, no. 37, 2002, <www.awm.gov.au/journal/j37/borneo.asp>.
6   Orang Kya [*sic*] Kulang of Kampong Mannad [*sic*], Beluran District, Statement made to VX48544 Major HW Jackson at Beluran, concerning assistance rendered to escaped POW, 11 January 1947, NAA MP742/1, 66/1/578A. For other accounts of Campbell and Kulang's interaction see M Cunningham, *Hell on Earth: Sandakan – Australia's Greatest War Tragedy*, Hachette, Sydney, 2013; P Ham, *Sandakan: The Untold Story of the Sandakan Death Marches*, William Heinemann, Sydney, 2012; LR Silver, *Blood Brothers: Sabah and Australia, 1942–45*, Opus Publications, Kota Kinabalu, Malaysia, 2010; LR Silver, *Sandakan: A Conspiracy of Silence*, Sally Milner Publishing, Sydney, 1998.
7   Orang Kya Kulang of Kampong Mannad, Beluran District, Statement made to VX48544 Major HW Jackson at Beluran, concerning assistance rendered to escaped POW, 11 January 1947, NAA MP742/1, 66/1/578A.
8   Pardi Bin Dulbar, now employed as cook at Mile 8, 31 Aust. War Graves, 9 February 1947, NAA MP742/1, 66/1/578A.
9   H Jackson, 'Foreword', in C Simpson, *Six from Borneo: Documentary Drama of the Death Marches*, transcript, ABC, Sydney, [194–].
10 RK Dyce, VX108017, born 13 March 1900, died 9 May 1954 at 113th AGH, Concord. See National Archives, London, HS 9/464/2. Dyce was in the Special Operations Executive during the war.
11 HWS Jackson, Report by VX48544 Major H.W.S. Jackson, c. August 1947, p. 74, NAA MP742/1, 328/1/32.
12 ibid., p. 89.
13 *Sydney Morning Herald*, 2 October 1953, p. 3.
14 C Simpson, Colin Simpson: author and radio documentary feature writer, recorded January 1973, typescript, NLA MS 5253, box 88, file 254.
15 EE Dunlop to Secretary of Army, 6 October 1950, NAA MP742/1, 66/1/1080; Minister for the Army to Boon Pong, 18 September 1951, NAA MP742/1, 66/1/1080.
16 HWS Jackson, Report by VX48544 Major H.W.S. Jackson, c. August 1947, p. 89, NAA MP742/1, 328/1/32.
17 Secretary, Department of Army, to Housing Commission, Victoria, n.d., NAA A463, 1968/4056.
18 *Argus*, 4 November 1950, p. 1.
19 ibid., 6 November 1950, p. 3.
20 ibid., 15 November 1950, p. 1.
21 ibid., 6 November 1950, p. 3.
22 *Advertiser*, 22 November 1950, p. 1.
23 *Advocate*, 23 November 1951, p. 1; *Argus*, 4 November 1950, p. 1.
24 'Pavitt family, U.K., New Zealand, Australia & North Borneo', Australian Postal

History & Social Philately, 2017, <www.auspostalhistory.com/articles/1891.php>.
25 F Sinclair (Secretary, Department of Army) to Secretary, Housing Commission, n.d., NAA A463, 1968/4056.
26 *Albany Advertiser*, 30 November 1950, p. 12; Ooi KG, *Post-War Borneo, 1945–1950: Nationalism, Empire, and State-Building*, Routledge, New York, 2013.
27 Secretary, Department of Immigration, to Commonwealth Migration Officer, 8 December 1950, NAA PP9/1, 1951/61/4548; Commonwealth of Australia, Certificate of exemption: Melvyn Francis Funk, 20 April 1951, NAA PP9/1, 1951/61/4548.
28 *Advocate*, 23 November 1951, p. 1.
29 *Straits Times*, 23 November 1951, p. 1.
30 S Brawley, *The White Peril: Foreign Relations and Asian Immigration to Australasia and North America, 1918–1978*, UNSW Press, Sydney, 1995; K Neumann, 'Guarding the flood gates: the removal of non-Europeans 1945–9', in M Crotty & DA Roberts (eds), *The Great Mistakes of Australian History*, UNSW Press, Sydney, 2006, pp. 186–202.
31 W Henderson to Prime Minister, 22 August 1968, NAA A463, 1968/4056.
32 RJ Brooks, *Under Five Flags*, Pentland Press, Edinburgh, 1995, p. 253; RA Lind, *My Sabah: Reminiscences of a Former State Secretary*, Natural History Publications, Kota Kinabalu, Malaysia, 2003, p. 12. Henderson's letter to the Prime Minister of 22 August 1968 (NAA A463, 1968/4056) claimed that the 'T' symbol demonstrated that 'the feeling of the people of Borneo remain[ed] the same towards us'.
33 W Henderson to Prime Minister, 22 August 1968, NAA A463, 1968/4056.
34 *Canberra Times*, 13 December 1963, p. 11.
35 D Gilfedder, Representations concerning Messrs Alec and John Funk, 14 October 1968, NAA A463, 1968/4056.
36 D Stephens (Malaysian High Commissioner) to Prime Minister, 28 June 1973, NAA A463, 1968/4056.
37 AIF Malayan Nursing Scholarship, First annual report and financial statement, c. 1948, NAA A1068, PI47/13/2/3.
38 SF Arneil, *One Man's War*, 3rd edn, Alternative Publishing Co-operative, Sydney, 1981.
39 KS Inglis, *Sacred Places: War Memorials in the Australian Landscape*, 3rd edn, MUP, Melbourne, 2008, pp. 334–40.
40 Australian Red Cross Society, *History of the A.I.F. Malayan Nursing Scholarship: Official War Memorial of the 8th Australian Division and A.I.F. Malaya*, Australian Red Cross Society, Melbourne, 1990.
41 AIF Malayan Nursing Scholarship, History of establishment of AIF Nursing Scholarship, in Minute book, Appendix after 2 March 1946, p. 5, UMA NO39, unit 6, 2016.0061.
42 AIF Malayan Nursing Scholarship, First annual report and financial statement, c. 1948, NAA A1068, PI47/13/2/3; *Advocate*, 20 November 1945, p. 2.
43 *Army News*, 8 November 1945, p. 2.
44 G Horne, *Race War: White Supremacy and the Japanese Attack on the British*

Empire, New York University Press, New York, 2004; C Thorne, *Racial Aspects of the Far Eastern War of 1941–1945*, OUP, London, 1982.
45 In an attempt to simplify administration of British Malaya, the federated and unfederated Malay states, Penang and Malacca became the Malayan Union in 1946 and the Federation of Malaya in 1948. The federation was granted independence within the British Commonwealth in 1957. When Penang and Malacca left the Straits Settlements in 1946, Singapore became a Crown colony and was granted self-governance in 1959 and independence in 1963. Upon independence, Singapore merged with North Borneo, Sarawak and Malaya to become Malaysia but was expelled by Malaysia in 1965. The constitutional privileges granted to Malays were a point of particular tension in Singapore, where ethnic Chinese formed the majority of the population.
46 AIF Malayan Nursing Scholarship, First annual report and financial statement, c. 1948, NAA A1068, PI47/13/2/3.
47 Secretary, AIF Nursing Scholarship, to Secretary, Department of External Affairs, 13 September 1946, NAA A1068, PI47/13/2/3.
48 S Pond to Prime Minister, 10 December 1945, NAA A1068, PI47/13/2/3.
49 *Army News*, 8 November 1945, p. 2.
50 JW Burton, *The Alternative: A Dynamic Approach to Our Relations with Asia*, Morgans Publications, Sydney, 1954; JW Burton (Acting Secretary, Department of External Affairs) to Secretary, Department of Treasury, 3 December 1945, NAA A1068, PI47/13/2/3; Secretary, Department of External Affairs, to Secretary, Prime Minister's Department, 2 January 1946, NAA A1068, PI47/13/2/3.
51 AIF Malayan Nursing Scholarship, First annual report and financial statement, c. 1948, NAA A1068, PI47/13/2/3; *Advocate*, 4 March 1947, p. 5.
52 Secretary, Department of External Affairs, to Honorary Secretary, AIF Malayan Nursing Scholarship, 31 August 1948, NAA A1068, PI47/13/2/3.
53 *Straits Times*, 1 April 1950, p. 4; 22 December 1951, p. 9.
54 AIF Malayan Nursing Scholarship, History of establishment of AIF Nursing Scholarship, in Minute book, Appendix after 2 March 1946, p. 6, UMA NO39, unit 6, 2016.0061.
55 *Straits Times*, 18 July 1946, p. 5; *Age*, 21 October 1947, p. 5.
56 C Massey (Australian Commissioner, Singapore) to Department of External Affairs, 6 July 1946, NAA A1068, PI47/13/2/3.
57 S Pond to Australian Commissioner, Singapore, 12 July 1946, NAA A1068, PI47/13/2/3.
58 Malayan Committee, AIF Malayan Scholarship Scheme, Minutes of the first meeting, 14 July 1946, NAA A1068, PI47/13/2/3.
59 Waters, 'The Macmahon Ball mission to East Asia 1948', p. 351. See also G Woodard, 'Macmahon Ball's Goodwill Mission to Asia 1948', *Australian Journal of International Affairs*, vol. 49, no. 1, 1995, pp. 129–34.
60 Department of External Affairs, Note on file, 22 July 1948, NAA A1068, PI47/13/2/3; Department of External Affairs to Mr Shann, 6 August 1948, NAA A1068, PI47/13/2/3.
61 *Straits Times*, 1 November 1948, p. 1. For an advertisement where the

Australian Government Scholarship appears alongside the AIF Malayan Nursing Scholarships see *Straits Times*, 14 December 1948, p. 12.
62 *Straits Times*, 9 February 1947, p. 7.
63 *Australian Women's Weekly*, 29 March 1947, p. 13.
64 *Straits Times*, 27 June 1949, p. 5.
65 *Straits Times*, 15 June 1954, p. 5.
66 S Pond to Prime Minister, 10 December 1945, NAA A1068, PI47/13/2/3.
67 *Straits Times*, 17 December 1951, p. 7.
68 *West Australian*, 25 February 1952, p. 2.
69 AIF Malayan Nursing Scholarship, Minute book, 18 April 1966, p. 58, UMA NO39, unit 6, 2016.0061.
70 Supreme Court of Victoria, In the matter of a deed of trust establishing the AIF Malayan Nursing Scholarship Fund, affidavit, no. 3145, 1968, UMA NO39, unit 6, 2016.0061.
71 DKK Lee (Malaysian Red Cross) to S Pond, 12 September 1966, UMA NO39, unit 6, 2016.0061.
72 Supreme Court of Victoria, In the matter of a deed of trust establishing the AIF Malayan Nursing Scholarship Fund, affidavit, no. 3145, 1968, UMA NO39, unit 6, 2016.0061.
73 DW Watts (Vice Chancellor, Curtin University) to R Swartz (Chairman, AIF Nursing Scholarship Board), 10 June 1987, UMA NO39, unit 6, 2016.0061.
74 See AIF Malaya Nursing Scholarship Trust, *AIF Malaya Nursing Scholarship: A Living Memorial*, Australian Red Cross, 2017, <www.redcross.org.au/files/AIF_Brochure.pdf>.

9 Prisoners in the time of trauma
1 David Malouf, *The Great World*, Chatto & Windus, London, 1990, p. 193.
2 R Gerster, 'The old man and the sea', *Age*, 27 October 2012, <www.theage.com.au/entertainment/books/the-old-man-and-the-sea-20121026-28arf.html>.
3 D Walker, *Anxious Nation: Australia and the Rise of Asia, 1850–1939*, UQP, Brisbane, 1999.
4 J Romeril, *The Floating World: With Notes on the Yellow Peril and Comment from Allan Ashbolt, Katharine Brisbane and the Official History of Australia in the Second World War*, Currency Press, Sydney, 1975, p. 5.
5 JG Hajdu, *Samurai in the Surf: The Arrival of the Japanese on the Gold Coast in the 1980s*, Pandanus Books, Canberra, 2005.
6 H Gilbert & J Lo, *Performance and Cosmopolitics: Cross-Cultural Transactions in Australasia*, Palgrave Macmillan, New York, 2007, pp. 142–54; L Jacobs, 'About face: Asian-Australians at home', *Australian Literary Studies*, vol. 20, no. 3, 2002, p. 201; D Varney, 'Political lessons of the "new wave": Romeril's *The Floating World*', *Double Dialogues*, no. 11, 2009, pp. 1–11.
7 K Brisbane, 'The play in the theatre', in Romeril, *The Floating World*, p. xxiv.
8 P Parker, *The Multi-Function Polis 1987–97: An International Failure or Innovative Local Project?*, Pacific Economic Paper no. 283, Australia-Japan Research Centre, Canberra, 1998.
9 J Shearer, *Shimada*, Currency Press, Sydney, 1989, p. 11.

10 N Morris, *Japan-Bashing: Anti-Japanism since the 1980s*, Routledge, New York, 2011.
11 *Canberra Times*, 3 September 1983, p. 14.
12 *Canberra Times*, 22 April 1982, p. 9.
13 CMH Clark, 'Preface', in SF Arneil, *One Man's War*, 3rd edn, Alternative Publishing Co-operative, Sydney, 1981, [p. v].
14 R Ward, 'Foreword', in Arneil, *One Man's War*, [p. vi].
15 D Fassin & R Rechtman, *The Empire of Trauma: An Inquiry into the Condition of Victimhood*, Princeton University Press, Princeton, 2009, p. 77. See also American Psychiatric Association, Taskforce on Nomenclature and Statistics, *Diagnostic and Statistical Manual of Mental Disorders*, 3rd edn, American Psychiatric Association, Washington, DC, 1980.
16 R Leys, *Trauma: A Genealogy*, University of Chicago Press, Chicago, 2000; A Young, *The Harmony of Illusions: Inventing Post-Traumatic Stress Disorder*, Princeton University Press, Princeton, 1995.
17 Fassin & Rechtman, *The Empire of Trauma*, p. 22.
18 Gilbert & Lo, *Performance and Cosmopolitics*, pp. 142–54.
19 *Age*, 29 April 1982, p. 10.
20 *Sydney Morning Herald*, 23 July 1986, p. 16.
21 *Smith's Weekly*, 27 August 1949, p. 5.
22 *Barbed Wire and Bamboo*, April 1983, p. 15.
23 *Barbed Wire and Bamboo*, December 1983, p. 9.
24 C Tennant, K Goulston & O Dent, 'Clinical psychiatric illness in prisoners of war of the Japanese: forty years after release', *Psychological Medicine*, vol. 16, no. 4, 1986, pp. 833–39.
25 JK Olick, *The Politics of Regret: On Collective Memory and Historical Responsibility*, Routledge, New York, 2007, p. 122.
26 TG Ashplant, G Dawson & R Michael (eds), *Commemorating War: The Politics of Memory*, Transaction, New Jersey, 2006; D Bell & J Hollows, *Historicizing Lifestyle: Mediating Taste, Consumption and Identity from the 1900s to 1970s*, Ashgate, Aldershot, 2006; JK Olick, V Vinitzky-Seroussi & D Levy, *The Collective Memory Reader*, OUP, New York, 2011; JM Winter, *Remembering War: The Great War between Memory and History in the Twentieth Century*, Yale University Press, New Haven, 2006.
27 A Ramsey, 'How the POW voices were immortalised', *Sydney Morning Herald*, 9 August 2008, <www.smh.com.au/news/alan-ramsey/how-the-pow-voices-were-immortalised/2008/08/08/1218139074481.html>.
28 T Bowden, *P.O.W.: Australians under Nippon*, sound recording, ABC Audio, Sydney, 1985, available at Radio National, ABC, <www.abc.net.au/radionational/programs/australians-under-nippon/>; H Nelson, *P.O.W.: Prisoners of War; Australians under Nippon*, ABC Books, Sydney, 1985.
29 Ramsey, 'How the POW voices were immortalised'.
30 *Age*, Saturday Extra, 2 June 1984, p. 4.
31 T Bowden, 'Lost years and wounded minds', episode 16, *P.O.W.: Australians under Nippon*, sound recording, ABC Audio, Sydney, 1985, available at Radio National, ABC, <www.abc.net.au/radionational/programs/australians-under-

nippon/lost-years-and-wounded-minds/8248660>.
32 L Cahill, Speech at the launching of *Changi Photographer*, POW Rooms, Sydney, 21 May 1984, transcript, AWM PR00929, folder 2.
33 *Northern Star*, 29 December 1979, p. 3; *Sun*, 23 April 1976, AWM PR00929, folder 1.
34 G Aspinall, *Fit for Work*, photograph, c. 1943, AWM P02560.192.
35 *University of Sydney News*, 2 November 1982, p. 237.
36 Ex P.O.W. National Reunion, Melbourne, Australia, 2nd–7th October 1984, pamphlet, c. 1984, AWM PR01216, series 2, folder 10.
37 *Canberra Times*, 16 August 1988, p. 3.
38 P Carey, 'Man Booker prize: Peter Carey criticises decision to include US writers', *Guardian*, 14 October 2014, <www.theguardian.com/books/2014/oct/13/-sp-man-booker-prize-peter-carey-criticises-decision-us-writers>.
39 R Ward, 'Foreword', in Arneil, *One Man's War*, p. [vi].
40 *Age*, Saturday Extra, 24 April 1982, p. 13.
41 *Sydney Morning Herald*, 19 May 1990, p. 76.
42 Malouf, *The Great World*, p. 152.
43 See for example *Sydney Morning Herald*, 12 August 1985, pp. 10–11.
44 *Age*, 25 April 1986, p. 3.
45 *Age*, 25 April 1986, p. 3; 8 February 1992, p. 36.
46 PJ Keating, 'Speech by the Prime Minister, the Hon P.J. Keating, MP POW ceremony, Australian War Memorial, 14 February 1995', PM Transcripts, <pmtranscripts.dpmc.gov.au/sites/default/files/original/00009476.pdf>.
47 G Davison, *The Use and Abuse of Australian History*, Allen & Unwin, Sydney, 2000, p. 22.
48 R Hearder, *Keep the Men Alive: Australian POW Doctors under the Japanese*, Allen & Unwin, Sydney, 2009.
49 *Age*, 15 April 1985, p. 3.
50 Weary Dunlop Tour, Newsletter, c. 1984, NLA MS 6055, box 19, series 4, file 6.
51 *Age*, 19 April 1983, p. 3; 20 April 1983, p. 3; 15 April 1985, p. 3; 24 April 1985, p. 5.
52 A Flanagan & M Flanagan, *The Line: A Man's Experience; A Son's Quest to Understand*, One Day Hill, Melbourne, 2005; M Flanagan, *Archie's Letter: An Anzac Day Story*, One Day Hill, Melbourne, 2011; M Flanagan & T Uren, *The Fight*, One Day Hill, Melbourne, 2006.
53 P Cochrane, *Simpson and His Donkey: The Making of a Legend*, MUP, Melbourne, 1992.
54 Weary Dunlop Tour, Itinerary, c. 1984, NLA MS 6055, box 19, series 4, file 6.
55 K Flanagan to T Uren, 9 March 1984, NLA MS 6055, box 19, series 4, file 6.
56 *Age*, 26 April 1985, p. 1; C Twomey, 'Trauma and the reinvigoration of Anzac: an argument', *History Australia*, vol. 10, no. 3, 2013, p. 104.
57 S Ebury, *Weary: The Life of Sir Edward Dunlop*, Viking, Melbourne, 1994, p. 630.
58 T Uren to PJ Keating (Treasurer), 30 October 1989, NLA MS 6055, box 205, series 25, file 29.
59 Department of Veterans' Affairs, Paper submitted to Caucus Community Services and Welfare Committee, 29 May 1989, cited in T Uren to PJ Keating

(Treasurer), 30 October 1989, NLA MS 6055, box 205, series 25, file 29.
60 OF Dent, B Richardson, S Wilson, KJ Goulston & CW Murdoch, 'Postwar mortality among Australian World War II prisoners of the Japanese', *Medical Journal of Australia*, vol. 150, 3 April 1989, pp. 378–82; KJ Goulston, OF Dent, PH Chapuis, G Chapman, CI Smith, AD Tait & CC Tennant, 'Gastrointestinal morbidity among World War II prisoners of war: 40 years on', *Medical Journal of Australia*, vol. 143, 1 July 1985, pp. 6–8.
61 Conference on the Health Needs of Ex-Prisoners of War Held in Grace Building, Sydney, 9 February 1989, Minutes, NLA MS 6055, box 205, series 25, file 29.
62 G McCormack & H Nelson, 'Introduction', in G McCormack & H Nelson (eds), *The Burma–Thailand Railway: Memory and History*, Allen & Unwin, Sydney, 1993, p. 7.
63 Queensland Ex-Prisoners of War Association, Queensland Ex-POW Reparation Committee, *Nippon Very Sorry, Many Men Must Die: Submission to the United Nations Commission of Human Rights (ECOSOC Resolution 1503)*, Boolarong, Brisbane, 1990.
64 *Sydney Morning Herald*, 27 February 1991, p. 6.
65 For the background to the Act see P Yeend, *Compensation (Japanese Internment) Bill 2001*, Bill Digest no. 6, Information and Research Services, Department of the Parliamentary Library, 2001–02, <parlinfo.aph.gov.au/parlInfo/download/legislation/billsdgs/G1M46/upload_binary/g1m467.pdf;fileType=application/pdf>.
66 *Australian*, 26 September 2001, p. 2.
67 A Goldberg, 'The victim's voice and melodramatic aesthetics in history', *History and Theory*, vol. 48, no. 3, 2009, pp. 220–37.

Epilogue
1 'Archibald Henry "Arch" Flanagan', obituary, *Age*, 24 April 2013, <tributes.theage.com.au/obituaries/theage-au/obituary.aspx?pid=164413318>.
2 A Flanagan & M Flanagan, *The Line*, documentary, 31 January 2010, <www.youtube.com/watch?v=9wZDwJozNDU>.
3 M Flanagan, 'Tea and sympathy in the quest for the truth', *Age*, 2 September 2006, <www.theage.com.au/articles/2008/05/27/1211653997962.html>.
4 Flanagan & Flanagan, *The Line*.
5 C Twomey, '"A body of broken men": POWs in post-war Australia', in C Twomey, S Hodson, N Hill & A O'Kane (panellists), 'The aftermath of military combat – the history, the personal consequences, the treatment and the recovery', Featured Symposium, moderated by S Brand, TheMHS Conference, Canberra, 25–28 August 2015.
6 Australia, DVA, 'Factsheet POW01: benefits available to Australian prisoners of war and their dependants', DVA, 23 February 2017, <www.dva.gov.au/factsheet-pow01-benefits-available-australian-prisoners-war-and-their-dependants>.
7 L Bessar, 'POW chief a prisoner of his own lies', *Sydney Morning Herald*, 3 October 2009, <www.smh.com.au/national/pow-chief-a-prisoner-of-his-own-lies-20091002-ggid.html>.

Bibliography

Primary sources

Unpublished works
Australian War Memorial
AWM54. Written records, 1939–45 war.
PR00926. Papers of Sir Edward 'Weary' Dunlop.
PR00929. Papers of George Aspinall.
PR01216. Papers of Vivian Bullwinkel.
PR89/186. Papers of Lieutenant Colonel Sir Albert Coates.

National Archives, London
HS 9/464/2. Roy Keith Dyce – born 13.03.1900.

National Archives of Australia
A461–A463. Prime Minister's Department. Correspondence files.
A518. Department of Territories. Correspondence files.
A649. Defence Division, Department of the Treasury. Correspondence files.
A816. Department of Defence. Correspondence files.
A1068. Department of External Affairs. Correspondence files.
A1501. Australian News and Information Bureau. Photographic negatives.
A1671. Australian News and Information Bureau. Photographic negatives.
A1838. Department of External Affairs. Correspondence files.
A2421. Repatriation Commission. Correspondence files.
A2700. Secretary to Cabinet/Cabinet Secretariat. Curtin, Forde and Chifley ministries – folders of Cabinet minutes and agenda.
A2703. Secretary to Cabinet/Cabinet Secretariat. Curtin, Forde and Chifley ministries – folders of Cabinet minutes.
A2998. Department of Immigration. Correspondence files [restricted immigration].
A4933. Secretary to Cabinet/Cabinet Secretariat. Fourth and fifth Menzies ministries – folders of Cabinet committee papers.
B501. [Prisoners of War Trust Fund]. Registration cards for application forms for grants and associated documents.
B502. [Prisoners of War Trust Fund]. Prisoners of War Trust Fund trustees – Secretary. Minute book for trustees' meetings.
B503. [Prisoners of War Trust Fund]. Application forms for grants and associated documents.

B883. Department of Defence. Second Australian Imperial Force personnel dossiers.
MP742/1. Department of the Army. General and Civil Staff correspondence files and army personnel files.
MP927/1. Department of the Army. General and Civil Staff correspondence files and army personnel files.
MT1486/1. Applications to enlist in the Australian Imperial Force.
PP9/1. Department of Immigration, Western Australian branch. Correspondence [client] files.
SP186/1. Crown Solicitor's Office, New South Wales branch. Correspondence on common law matters.

National Library of Australia
MS 4856. Papers of Sir WS Kent Hughes, 1914–86.
MS 5253. Papers of Colin Simpson, 1931–82.
MS 6055. Papers of Tom Uren, 1941–94.
MS 6609. Records of the Returned Services League of Australia, 1916–97.

State Archives and Records NSW
NRS 13495. Divorce and matrimonial cause case papers.

University of Melbourne Archives
NO39. Red Cross archives, 1940–2015. 2016.0061: AIF Malayan Nursing Scholarship. Unit 6: Australian Red Cross, National Office, board minutes and annual reports (and associated correspondence, 1947–2000).

Published works
Australian parliament
Commonwealth Parliamentary Debates, House of Representatives, March 1946 – November 1957.
Commonwealth Parliamentary Debates, Senate, August 1954 – December 1957.
Prime Minister, *Report of Committee Appointed to Investigate Question of Payment of Special Subsistence Allowance to Australian Prisoners of War, 1939–45 War*, Government Printer, Canberra, 1950.

Contemporary books, articles and pamphlets
Australia, Repatriation Commission, *Some Aspects of Medical Investigation and Treatment*, Repatriation Commission, Melbourne, 1947.
Bostock, John & Evan Jones, *The Nervous Soldier: A Handbook for the Prevention, Detection and Treatment of Nervous Invalidity in War*, AH Tucker, Government Printer, Brisbane, 1943.
Burton, John W, *The Alternative: A Dynamic Approach to Our Relations with Asia*, Morgans Publications, Sydney, 1954.
Coates, Albert Ernest, 'Clinical lessons from prisoner of war hospitals in the Far East (Burma and Siam)', *Medical Journal of Australia*, vol. 1, 1 June 1946, pp. 761–66.
Cohen, BM & MZ Cooper, *A Follow-Up Study of World War II Prisoners of War*, Veterans Administration Medical Monograph, US Government Printing Office, Washington, DC, 1955.

Bibliography

Curtin, AP, 'Imprisonment under the Japanese', *British Medical Journal*, vol. 2, no. 4476, 19 October 1946, pp. 585–86.
Harper, ND, 'Australian policy towards Japan', *Australian Outlook*, vol. 1, no. 4, 1947, pp. 14–24.
Mallinson, WP & W Warren, 'Repatriation: a psychiatric study of 100 naval ex-prisoners of war', *British Medical Journal*, vol. 2, no. 4331, 8 December 1945, pp. 798–801.
Menzies, Robert G, *Joint Opposition Policy, 1949: Policy Speech of the Leader of the Opposition (Rt. Hon. R. G. Menzies), Delivered at Canterbury, Victoria, on November 10, 1949, Together with Supplementary Statements*, Liberal Party of Australia, Sydney, 1949.
'The nervous disorders of service personnel: an urgent problem', *Medical Journal of Australia*, vol. 1, 3 June 1944, pp. 515–16.
Newman, PH, 'The prisoner of war mentality: its effects after repatriation', *British Medical Journal*, vol. 1, no. 4330, 1 January 1944, pp. 8–10.
Vischer, AL, *Barbed-Wire Disease: A Psychological Study of the Prisoner of War*, John Bales, Sons & Danielsson, London, 1919.
Whiles, WH, 'A study of neurosis among repatriated prisoners of war', *British Medical Journal*, vol. 2, no. 4428, 17 November 1945, pp. 697–98.

Memoirs
Arneil, Stan, *One Man's War*, 3rd edn, Alternative Publishing Co-operative, Sydney, 1981.
Bowden, Tim, *P.O.W.: Australians under Nippon*, sound recording, ABC Audio, Sydney, 1985.
Braddon, Russell, *The Naked Island*, Werner Laurie, London, 1952.
——, *The Other Hundred Years War: Japan's Bid for Supremacy, 1941–2041*, Collins, Sydney, 1983.
Coates, Albert Ernest & Newman H Rosenthal, *The Albert Coates Story: The Will That Found the Way*, Hyland House, Melbourne, 1977.
Ellis, MH, *Express to Hindustan: An Account of a Motor-Car Journey from London to Delhi*, Bodley Head, London, 1929.
Flanagan, Arch & Martin Flanagan, *The Line*, documentary, 31 January 2010, <www.youtube.com/watch?v=9wZDwJozNDU>.
——, *The Line: A Man's Experience; A Son's Quest to Understand*, One Day Hill, Melbourne, 2005.
Hamilton, Thomas, *Soldier Surgeon in Malaya*, Angus & Robertson, Sydney, 1957.
Harrison, Kenneth, *Road to Hiroshima*, rev. edn of *The Brave Japanese*, Rigby, Adelaide, 1983.
Huxtable, Charles, *From the Somme to Singapore: A Medical Officer in Two World Wars*, Kangaroo Press, Sydney, 1987.
Kent Hughes, Wilfrid S, *Slaves of the Samurai: An Australian Odyssey, Which Gives an Account of the Life and Thoughts of a Slave of the Samurai, during His Three Years and Seven Months as a Prisoner of War in the Hands of the Japanese*, Oxford University Press, Melbourne, 1946.

Lind, Richard A, *My Sabah: Reminiscences of a Former State Secretary*, Natural History Publications, Kota Kinabalu, Malaysia, 2003.
Rivett, Rohan D, *Behind Bamboo: An Inside Story of the Japanese Prison Camps*, Seal Books, Rigby, Adelaide, 1973.
Simons, Jessie Elizabeth, *While History Passed: The Story of the Australian Nurses Who Were Prisoners of the Japanese for Three and a Half Years*, William Heinemann, Melbourne, 1954.

Newspapers and periodicals
Advertiser (Adelaide, SA).
Advocate (Melbourne, Vic.).
Age (Melbourne, Vic.).
Albany Advertiser (WA).
Argus (Melbourne, Vic.).
Argus Woman's Magazine (Melbourne, Vic.).
Army News (Darwin, NT).
Australian (Canberra, ACT).
Australian Women's Weekly (Sydney, NSW).
Barbed Wire and Bamboo (Haymarket, NSW).
Barrier Miner (Broken Hill, NSW).
Bulletin (Sydney, NSW).
Canberra Times (Canberra, ACT).
Cairns Post (Qld).
Catholic Weekly (Sydney, NSW).
Cessnock Eagle and South Maitland Recorder (Cessnock, NSW).
Courier-Mail (Brisbane, Qld).
Daily Mirror (Sydney, NSW).
Daily News (Perth, WA).
Examiner (Launceston, Tas.).
Guardian (Manchester, UK).
Herald (Melbourne, Vic.).
Kalgoorlie Miner (Perth, WA).
Mail (Adelaide, SA).
Makan (Sydney, NSW).
Mercury (Hobart, Tas.).
Molong Express and Western District Advertiser (Molong, NSW).
Mufti (Melbourne, Vic.).
Nation's Forum of the Air (Sydney, NSW).
Newcastle Sun (Newcastle, NSW).
News (Adelaide, SA).
Northern Standard (Darwin, NT).
Northern Star (Lismore, NSW).
P.O.W.: The Monthly Newsletter of the Australian Prisoners of War Relatives Association (Sydney, NSW).
Reveille (Sydney, NSW).
Smith's Weekly (Sydney, NSW).

Bibliography

Southern Argus (Port Elliot, SA).
Straits Times (Singapore).
Sun (Sydney, NSW).
Sun-Herald (Sydney, NSW).
Sunday Herald (Sydney, NSW).
Sunday Mail (Brisbane, Qld).
Sunday Sun and Guardian (Sydney, NSW).
Sydney Morning Herald (Sydney, NSW).
Times (London, UK).
University of Sydney News (Sydney, NSW).
Weekly Times (Melbourne, Vic.).
West Australian (Perth, WA).

Plays and novels

Flanagan, Martin, *Archie's Letter: An Anzac Day Story*, One Day Hill, Melbourne, 2011.
Flanagan, Richard, *The Narrow Road to the Deep North*, Random House, Sydney, 2013.
Malouf, David, *The Great World*, Chatto & Windus, London, 1990.
Parkin, Ray, *Ray Parkin's Wartime Trilogy: Out of the Smoke, Into the Smother, The Sword and the Blossom*, Melbourne University Press, Melbourne, 1999.
Romeril, John, *The Floating World: With Notes on the Yellow Peril and Comment from Allan Ashbolt, Katharine Brisbane and the Official History of Australia in the Second World War*, Currency Press, Sydney, 1975.
Shearer, Jill, *Shimada*, Currency Press, Sydney, 1989.
Simpson, Colin, *Six from Borneo: Documentary Drama of the Death Marches*, transcript, Australian Broadcasting Commission, Sydney, [194–].

Secondary sources

Adam-Smith, Patsy, *Prisoners of War: From Gallipoli to Korea*, Viking, Melbourne, 1992.
AIF Malaya Nursing Scholarship Trust, *AIF Malaya Nursing Scholarship: A Living Memorial*, Australian Red Cross, 2017, <www.redcross.org.au/files/AIF_Brochure.pdf>.
Allen, Judith, *Sex & Secrets: Crimes Involving Australian Women since 1880*, Oxford University Press, Melbourne, 1990.
American Psychiatric Association, Taskforce on Nomenclature and Statistics, *Diagnostic and Statistical Manual of Mental Disorders*, 3rd edn, American Psychiatric Association, Washington, DC, 1980.
Anzac Portal, Department of Veterans' Affairs, 2017, <anzacportal.dva.gov.au>.
'Archibald Henry "Arch" Flanagan', obituary, *Age*, 24 April 2013, <tributes.theage.com.au/obituaries/theage-au/obituary.aspx?pid=164413318>.
Ariotti, Kate, '"At present everything is making us most anxious": families of Australian prisoners in Turkey', in Joan Beaumont, Lachlan Grant & Aaron Pegram (eds), *Beyond Surrender: Australian Prisoners of War in the Twentieth Century*, Melbourne University Press, Melbourne, 2015, pp. 57–74.

——, 'Australian prisoners of the Turks: negotiating culture clash in captivity', in Joachim Bürgschwentner, Matthias Egger & Gunda Barth-Scalmani (eds), *Other Fronts, Other Wars? First World War Studies on the Eve of the Centennial*, Brill, Leiden & Boston, 2014, pp. 146–66.

Aristotle, *Nicomachean Ethics*, trans. Roger Crisp, Cambridge University Press, New York, 2014.

Arneil, SF, *Black Jack: The Life and Times of Brigadier Sir Frederick Galleghan*, Macmillan, Melbourne, 1983.

Ashplant, Timothy G, Graham Dawson & Roper Michael (eds), *Commemorating War: The Politics of Memory*, Transaction, New Jersey, 2006.

Aszkielowicz, Dean, 'Repatriation and the limits of resolve: Japanese war criminals in Australian custody', *Japanese Studies*, vol. 31, no. 2, 2011, pp. 211–28.

Australia, Department of Veterans' Affairs, *Australian Prisoners of War*, Department of Veterans' Affairs, Canberra, 2009.

——, 'Factsheet POW01: benefits available to Australian prisoners of war and their dependants', DVA, 23 February 2017, <www.dva.gov.au/factsheet-pow01-benefits-available-australian-prisoners-war-and-their-dependants>.

Australian Bureau of Statistics, *Women's Safety Australia, 1996*, cat. no. 4128.0, Australian Bureau of Statistics, 1996, <www.abs.gov.au/ausstats/abs@.nsf/cat/4128.0>.

Australian Red Cross Society, *History of the A.I.F. Malayan Nursing Scholarship: Official War Memorial of the 8th Australian Division and A.I.F. Malaya*, Australian Red Cross Society, Melbourne, 1990.

Australians at War Film Archive, UNSW Canberra at the Australian Defence Force Academy, 2017, <australiansatwarfilmarchive.unsw.edu.au>.

Barrett, Craig, '"Matters still outstanding": Australian ex-POWs of the Japanese and claims for reparations', in Martin Crotty & Marina Larsson (eds), *Anzac Legacies: Australians and the Aftermath of War*, Australian Scholarly Publishing, Melbourne, 2010, pp. 187–210.

Bassett, Jan, *Guns and Brooches: Australian Army Nursing from the Boer War to the Gulf War*, Oxford University Press, Melbourne, 1992.

Beaumont, Joan, *Gull Force: Survival and Leadership in Captivity 1941–1945*, Allen & Unwin, Sydney, 1988.

——, 'Hellfire Pass Memorial Museum, Thai–Burma Railway', in Martin Gegner & Bart Ziino (eds), *The Heritage of War*, Routledge, New York, 2012, pp. 19–40.

——, 'The long silence: Australian prisoners of the Japanese', in Peter J Dean (ed.), *Australia, 1944–45: Victory in the Pacific*, Cambridge University Press, Melbourne, 2016, pp. 79–97.

——, 'Officers and men: rank and survival on the Thai–Burma Railway', in Joan Beaumont, Lachlan Grant & Aaron Pegram (eds), *Beyond Surrender: Australian Prisoners of War in the Twentieth Century*, Melbourne University Press, Melbourne, 2015, pp. 174–95.

——, 'Prisoners of war', in Peter Dennis (ed.), *The Oxford Companion to Australian Military History*, Oxford University Press, Melbourne, 1995, pp. 472–81.

——, 'Prisoners of war in Australian national memory', in Bob Moore & Barbara Hately-Broad (eds), *Prisoners of War, Prisoners of Peace: Captivity, Homecoming,*

Bibliography

and Memory in World War Two, Berg, New York, 2005, pp. 185–94.

Beaumont, Joan & Andrea Witcomb, 'The Thai–Burma Railway: asymmetrical and transnational memories', in Christina Twomey & Ernest Koh (eds), *The Pacific War: Aftermaths, Remembrance and Culture*, Routledge, Abingdon, 2015, pp. 67–87.

Bell, David & Joanne Hollows, *Historicizing Lifestyle: Mediating Taste, Consumption and Identity from the 1900s to 1970s*, Ashgate, Aldershot, 2006.

Bessar, Linton, 'POW chief a prisoner of his own lies', *Sydney Morning Herald*, 3 October 2009, <www.smh.com.au/national/pow-chief-a-prisoner-of-his-own-lies-20091002-ggid.html>.

Biess, Frank, *Homecomings: Returning POWs and the Legacies of Defeat in Postwar Germany*, Princeton University Press, Princeton, 2006.

Blackburn, Kevin, 'Commemorating and commodifying the prisoner of war experience in South-East Asia: the creation of Changi Prison Museum', *Journal of the Australian War Memorial*, no. 133, 2000, <www.awm.gov.au/articles/journal/j33/blackburn.asp>.

Boister, Neil & Robert Cryer, *The Tokyo International Military Tribunal: A Reappraisal*, Oxford University Press, Oxford, 2008.

Bomford, Janette, '"A wife, a baby, a home and a new Holden car": family life after captivity', in Martin Crotty & Marina Larsson (eds), *Anzac Legacies: Australians and the Aftermath of War*, Australian Scholarly Publishing, Melbourne, 2010, pp. 107–125.

Bongiorno, Frank, *The Sex Lives of Australians: A History*, Black Inc., Melbourne, 2012.

Bourke, Roger, *Prisoners of the Japanese: Literary Imagination and the Prisoner-of-War Experience*, University of Queensland Press, Brisbane, 2006.

Brawley, Sean, *The White Peril: Foreign Relations and Asian Immigration to Australasia and North America, 1918–1978*, UNSW Press, Sydney, 1995.

Brisbane, Katharine, 'The play in the theatre', in John Romeril, *The Floating World: With Notes on the Yellow Peril and Comment from Allan Ashbolt, Katharine Brisbane and the Official History of Australia in the Second World War*, Currency Press, Sydney, 1975, pp. xxiv–xxviii.

Broinowski, Alison, *The Yellow Lady: Australian Impressions of Asia*, Oxford University Press, Melbourne, 1992.

Brooks, Ronald J, *Under Five Flags*, Pentland Press, Edinburgh, 1995.

Brown, Nicholas, 'Australian intellectuals and the image of Asia, 1920–60', *Australian Cultural History*, no. 9, 1990, pp. 80–92.

'Camps near Hellfire Pass', Anzac Portal, Department of Veterans' Affairs, 2017, <anzacportal.dva.gov.au/history/conflicts/thaiburma-railway-and-hellfire-pass/locations/camps-near-hellfire-pass>.

'Camps of F Force', Anzac Portal, Department of Veterans' Affairs, 2017, <anzacportal.dva.gov.au/history/conflicts/thaiburma-railway-and-hellfire-pass/locations/camps-f-force>.

Carey, Peter, 'Man Booker prize: Peter Carey criticises decision to include US writers', *Guardian*, 14 October 2014, <www.theguardian.com/books/2014/oct/13/-sp-man-booker-prize-peter-carey-criticises-decision-us-writers>.

Carmichael, GA & PF McDonald, 'The rise and fall of divorce in Australia, 1968–1985', in *Proceedings of the Third Australian Population Association Conference 1986*, vol. 1, Flinders University, Adelaide, 1987, n.p.

Caulfield, Michael, *War behind the Wire: Australian Prisoners of War*, Hachette, Sydney, 2008.

Clarke, Hugh V & Colin Burgess, *Barbed Wire and Bamboo: Australian POWs in Europe, North Africa, Singapore, Thailand and Japan*, Allen & Unwin, Sydney, 1992.

Clisby, Mark, *Guilty or Innocent? The Gordon Bennett Case*, Allen & Unwin, Sydney, 1992.

Cochrane, Peter, *Simpson and His Donkey: The Making of a Legend*, Melbourne University Press, Melbourne, 1992.

Cooke, Miriam, 'WO-man, retelling the war myth', in Miriam Cooke & Angela Woollacott (eds), *Gendering War Talk*, Princeton University Press, Princeton, 1993, pp. 177–204.

Cooper, Emmanuel, *Fully Exposed: The Male Nude in Photography*, 2nd edn, Routledge, London, 1995.

Cunningham, Michele, *Defying the Odds: Surviving Sandakan and Kuching*, Lothian, Melbourne, 2006.

——, *Hell on Earth: Sandakan – Australia's Greatest War Tragedy*, Hachette, Sydney, 2013.

Damousi, Joy, *Freud in the Antipodes: A Cultural History of Psychoanalysis in Australia*, UNSW Press, Sydney, 2005.

——, *The Labour of Loss: Mourning, Memory and Wartime Bereavement in Australia*, Cambridge University Press, Melbourne, 1999.

Davison, Graeme, *The Use and Abuse of Australian History*, Allen & Unwin, Sydney, 2000.

de Matos, Christine, 'Diplomacy interrupted? Macmahon Ball, Evatt and Labor's policies in occupied Japan', *Australian Journal of Politics & History*, vol. 52, no. 2, 2006, pp. 188–201.

——, *Encouraging 'Democracy' in a Cold War Climate: The Dual-Platform Policy Approach of Evatt and Labor toward the Allied Occupation of Japan 1945–1949*, Australia–Japan Research Centre, Canberra, 2001.

Dent, OF, B Richardson, S Wilson, KJ Goulston & CW Murdoch, 'Postwar mortality among Australian World War II prisoners of the Japanese', *Medical Journal of Australia*, vol. 150, 3 April 1989, pp. 378–82.

Dingo, Sally, *Unsung Ordinary Men: A Generation Like No Other*, Hachette Australia, Sydney, 2010.

Dower, John W, *War without Mercy: Race and Power in the Pacific War*, Pantheon Books, New York, 1986.

Dunlop, Ernest Edward, *The War Diaries of Weary Dunlop: Java and the Burma–Thailand Railway 1942–1945*, Penguin, Melbourne, 1990.

Ebury, Sue, *Weary: The Life of Sir Edward Dunlop*, Viking, Melbourne, 1994.

Fassin, Didier & Richard Rechtman, *The Empire of Trauma: An Inquiry into the Condition of Victimhood*, Princeton University Press, Princeton, 2009.

Faulkner, Andrew, *Arthur Blackburn, VC: An Australian Hero, His Men, and Their Two World Wars*, Wakefield Press, Adelaide, 2008.

Bibliography

Featherstone, Lisa, '"The one single primary cause": divorce, the family, and heterosexual pleasure in postwar Australia', *Journal of Australian Studies*, vol. 37, no. 3, 2013, pp. 349–63.

Fettling, David, 'An Australian response to Asian decolonisation: Jawaharlal Nehru, John Burton and the New Delhi Conference of Non-Western Nations', *Australian Historical Studies*, vol. 45, no. 2, 2014, pp. 202–219.

Flanagan, Arch, 'Tea and sympathy in the quest for the truth', *Age*, 2 September 2006, <www.theage.com.au/articles/2008/05/27/1211653997962.html>.

Flanagan, Martin & Tom Uren, *The Fight*, One Day Hill, Melbourne, 2006.

Garton, Stephen, 'Changi as television: myth, memory, narrative and history', *Journal of Australian Studies*, vol. 26, no. 73, 2002, pp. 79–88.

——, *The Cost of War: Australians Return*, Oxford University Press, Melbourne, 1996.

Gerster, Robin, *Big-Noting: The Heroic Theme in Australian War Writing*, Melbourne University Press, Melbourne, 1987.

——, 'The old man and the sea', *Age*, 27 October 2012, <www.theage.com.au/entertainment/books/the-old-man-and-the-sea-20121026-28arf.html>.

——, 'Six inch rule: revisiting the Australian occupation of Japan 1946–1952', *History Australia*, vol. 4, no. 2, 2007, pp. 42.1–42.16.

Gilbert, Helen & Jacqueline Lo, *Performance and Cosmopolitics: Cross-Cultural Transactions in Australasia*, Palgrave Macmillan, New York, 2007.

Goldberg, Amos, 'The victim's voice and melodramatic aesthetics in history', *History and Theory*, vol. 48, no. 3, 2009, pp. 220–37.

Goodman, RD, *Our War Nurses: The History of the Royal Australian Army Nursing Corps 1902–1988*, Boolarong Publications, Brisbane, 1988.

Goulston, KJ, OF Dent, PH Chapuis, G Chapman, CI Smith, AD Tait & CC Tennant, 'Gastrointestinal morbidity among World War II prisoners of war: 40 years on', *Medical Journal of Australia*, vol. 143, 1 July 1985, pp. 6–10.

Grant, Lachlan, *Australian Soldiers in the Asia-Pacific in WWII*, NewSouth, Sydney, 2014.

——, 'Monument and ceremony: the Australian Ex-POW Memorial and the Anzac legend', in Karl Hack & Kevin Blackburn (eds), *Forgotten Captives in Japanese-Occupied Asia*, Routledge, London, 2008, pp. 41–56.

——, 'What makes a "national" war memorial? The case of the Australian Ex-Prisoners of War Memorial', *Public History Review*, vol. 12, 2006, pp. 92–102.

Grehan, Helena, 'Testimony and ambivalence in *Sandakan Threnody*', *Australasian Drama Studies*, no. 49, 2006, pp. 89–100.

Griffin, David, 'Galleghan, Sir Frederick Gallagher (1897–1971)', Australian Dictionary of Biography, National Centre of Biography, Australian National University, 2017, <adb.anu.edu.au/biography/galleghan-sir-frederick-gallagher-1027>.

Hack, Karl & Kevin Blackburn (eds), *Forgotten Captives in Japanese-Occupied Asia*, London, Routledge, 2008.

Hajdu, JG, *Samurai in the Surf: The Arrival of the Japanese on the Gold Coast in the 1980s*, Pandanus Books, Canberra, 2005.

Ham, Paul, *Sandakan: The Untold Story of the Sandakan Death Marches*, William Heinemann, Sydney, 2012.

Hamilton, Paula, 'Contested memories of the Pacific War in Australia', in Christina Twomey & Ernest Koh (eds), *The Pacific War: Aftermaths, Remembrance and Culture*, Routledge, Abingdon, 2015, pp. 50–66.

——, 'A long war: public memory and the popular media', in Susannah Radstone & Bill Schwarz (eds), *Memory: Histories, Theories, Debates*, Fordham University Press, New York, 2010, pp. 299–311.

Harding, Eric, *Services Canteens Trust Fund: Steps Leading to the Establishment of the Fund by the Parliament of the Commonwealth of Australia with Effect from the 1st July, 1947*, Services Canteens Trust Fund, Melbourne, 1971.

Hearder, Rosalind, *Keep the Men Alive: Australian POW Doctors under the Japanese*, Allen & Unwin, Sydney, 2009.

Higonnet, Margaret R, Jane Jenson, Sonya Michel & Margaret Collins Weitz, *Behind the Lines: Gender and the Two World Wars*, Yale University Press, New Haven, 1987.

Hill, AJ, 'Wootten, Sir George Frederick (1893–1970)', Australian Dictionary of Biography, National Centre of Biography, Australian National University, 2017, <adb.anu.edu.au/biography/wootten-sir-george-frederick-12073/text21659>.

Hills, Ben, 'God's man in Japan in Japan: the Catholic priest who inspired Australia's post-war reconciliation with Japan', Ben Hills, 2014, <benhills.com/articles/japan-unlimited/gods-man-in-japan-in-japan/>.

Horne, Gerald, *Race War: White Supremacy and the Japanese Attack on the British Empire*, New York University Press, New York, 2004.

Howard, Frederick, *Kent Hughes: A Biography of Colonel the Hon. Sir Wilfrid Kent Hughes*, Macmillan, Melbourne, 1972.

Howard, John, 'Commemorative address at Hellfire Pass, Thailand', PM Transcripts, 25 April 1998, <pmtranscripts.pmc.gov.au/release/transcript-22682>.

Inglis, KS, *Sacred Places: War Memorials in the Australian Landscape*, 3rd edn, Melbourne University Press, Melbourne, 2008.

Ironside, Wallace, 'Cade, John Frederick Joseph (1912–1980)', Australian Dictionary of Biography, National Centre of Biography, Australian National University, 2017, <adb.anu.edu.au/biography/cade-john-frederick-joseph-9657>.

Jacobs, Lyn, 'About face: Asian-Australians at home', *Australian Literary Studies*, vol. 20, no. 3, 2002, pp. 201–214.

Jones, Edgar & Simon Wessely, 'British prisoners-of-war: from resilience to psychological vulnerability; reality or perception', *Twentieth Century British History*, vol. 21, no. 2, 2010, pp. 163–83.

Kaladelfos, Amanda, 'The dark side of the family: paternal child homicide in Australia', *Journal of Australian Studies*, vol. 37, no. 3, 2013, pp. 333–48.

Keating, Gavin Michael, 'Savige, Sir Stanley George (1890–1954)', Australian Dictionary of Biography, National Centre of Biography, Australian National University, 2017, <adb.anu.edu.au/biography/savige-sir-stanley-george-11617>.

Keating, Paul J, 'Speech by the Prime Minister, the Hon P.J. Keating, MP POW ceremony, Australian War Memorial, 14 February 1995', PM Transcripts, <pmtranscripts.dpmc.gov.au/sites/default/files/original/00009476.pdf>.

Kenny, Catherine, *Captives: Australian Army Nurses in Japanese Prison Camps*, University of Queensland Press, Brisbane, 1986.

Bibliography

Kobayashi, Ai, 'Australia and Japan's admission into the Colombo Plan', *Australian Journal of Politics & History*, vol. 60, no. 4, 2014, pp. 518–33.

Lake, Marilyn, 'Female desires: the meaning of World War II', *Australian Historical Studies*, vol. 24, no. 95, 1990, pp. 267–84.

Lake, Marilyn & Joy Damousi, 'Warfare, history and gender', in Joy Damousi & Marilyn Lake (eds), *Gender and War: Australians at War in the Twentieth Century*, Cambridge University Press, Melbourne, 1995, pp. 1–20.

Larsson, Marina, *Shattered ANZACs: Living with the Scars of War*, UNSW Press, Sydney, 2009.

Lawless, Jennifer, *Kismet: The Story of the Gallipoli Prisoners of War*, Australian Scholarly Publishing, Melbourne, 2015.

Leys, Ruth, *Trauma: A Genealogy*, University of Chicago Press, Chicago, 2000.

Linden, Michael, Max Rotter, Kai Baumann & Barbara Lieberei, *Posttraumatic Embitterment Disorder: Definition, Evidence, Diagnosis, Treatment*, Hogrefe, Cambridge, MA, 2007.

Lloyd, Clem & Jacqueline Rees, *The Last Shilling: A History of Repatriation in Australia*, Melbourne University Press, Melbourne, 1994.

Lodge, AB, *Deserter or Hero? The Gordon Bennett Royal Commission*, Sir Robert Menzies Centre for Australian Studies, Institute of Commonwealth Studies, London, 1989.

——, *The Fall of General Gordon Bennett*, Allen & Unwin, Sydney, 1986.

McCormack, Gavan & Hank Nelson (eds), *The Burma–Thailand Railway: Memory and History*, Allen & Unwin, Sydney, 1993.

Macintyre, Stuart, *Australia's Boldest Experiment: War and Reconstruction in the 1940s*, NewSouth, Sydney, 2015.

McKernan, Michael, *This War Never Ends: The Pain of Separation and Return*, University of Queensland Press, Brisbane, 2001.

——, 'War', in W Vamplew (ed.), *Australians: Historical Statistics*, Fairfax, Syme & Weldon Associates, Sydney, 1987, pp. 410–17.

Maga, Timothy P, *Judgment at Tokyo: The Japanese War Crimes Trials*, University Press of Kentucky, Lexington, 2000.

Minear, Richard H, *Victors' Justice: The Tokyo War Crimes Trial*, Princeton University Press, Princeton, 1971.

'Mixed feelings as POW's waited to be released', Australians at War, Department of Veterans' Affairs, 2001, available at Pandora, National Library of Australia, <pandora.nla.gov.au/pan/20401/20020911-0000/www.australiansatwar.gov.au/stories/stories9c3b.html?war=W2&id=121>.

Monteath, Peter, 'Australian POW labour in Germany in World War II', *Labour History*, no. 103, 2012, pp. 83–102.

——, 'Beyond the Colditz myth: Australian experiences of German captivity in World War Two', in Joan Beaumont, Lachlan Grant & Aaron Pegram (eds), *Beyond Surrender: Australian Prisoners of War in the Twentieth Century*, Melbourne University Press, Melbourne, 2015, pp. 116–34.

——, *P.O.W.: Australian Prisoners of War in Hitler's Reich*, Macmillan, Sydney, 2011.

Morris, Narrelle, *Japan-Bashing: Anti-Japanism since the 1980s*, Routledge, New York, 2011.

Muir, Kristy, '"Idiots, imbeciles and moral defectives": military and government treatment of mentally ill service personnel and veterans', *Journal of Australian Studies*, vol. 26, no. 73, 2002, pp. 41–47.

National Archives of Australia, '*Montevideo Maru*: list of prisoners of war and civilian internees on board', National Archives of Australia, 2017, <montevideomaru.naa.gov.au>.

Nelson, Elizabeth, *Homefront Hostilities: The First World War and Domestic Violence*, Australian Scholarly Publishing, Melbourne, 2014.

Nelson, Hank, *P.O.W.: Prisoners of War; Australians under Nippon*, ABC Books, Sydney, 1985.

——, 'The return to Rabaul 1945', *Journal of Pacific History*, vol. 30, no. 2, 1995, pp. 131–53.

Neumann, Klaus, 'Guarding the flood gates: the removal of non-Europeans 1945–9', in Martin Crotty & David Andrew Roberts (eds), *The Great Mistakes of Australian History*, UNSW Press, Sydney, 2006, pp. 186–202.

Nicholls, Glenn, *Deported: A History of Forced Departures from Australia*, UNSW Press, Sydney, 2007.

Northey, RE, 'Haylen, Leslie Clement (Les) (1898–1977)', Australian Dictionary of Biography, National Centre of Biography, Australian National University, 2017, <adb.anu.edu.au/biography/haylen-leslie-clement-les-10466>.

Olick, Jeffrey K, *The Politics of Regret: On Collective Memory and Historical Responsibility*, Routledge, New York, 2007.

Olick, Jeffrey K, Vered Vinitzky-Seroussi & Daniel Levy, *The Collective Memory Reader*, Oxford University Press, New York, 2011.

Ooi Keat Gin, *Post-War Borneo, 1945–1950: Nationalism, Empire, and State-Building*, Routledge, New York, 2013.

——, 'Prelude to invasion: covert operations before the re-occupation of northwest Borneo, 1944–45', *Journal of the Australian War Memorial*, no. 37, 2002, <www.awm.gov.au/journal/j37/borneo.asp>.

Oppenheimer, Melanie, '"Our number one priority": the Australian Red Cross and prisoners of war in the world wars', in Joan Beaumont, Lachlan Grant & Aaron Pegram (eds), *Beyond Surrender: Australian Prisoners of War in the Twentieth Century*, Melbourne University Press, Melbourne, 2015, pp. 57–95.

Panikos, Panayi, *The Enemy in Our Midst: Germans in Britain during the First World War*, Bloomsbury, London, 1991.

Parker, Paul, *The Multi-Function Polis 1987–97: An International Failure or Innovative Local Project?*, Pacific Economic Paper no. 283, Australia–Japan Research Centre, Canberra, 1998.

'Pavitt family, U.K., New Zealand, Australia & North Borneo', Australian Postal History & Social Philately, 2017, <www.auspostalhistory.com/articles/1891.php>.

Piccigallo, Philip R, *The Japanese on Trial: Allied War Crimes Operations in the East, 1945–1951*, University of Texas Press, Austin, 1979.

Pritchard, R John (ed.), *The Tokyo Major War Crimes Trial: The Records of the International Military Tribunal for the Far East; With an Authoritative Commentary and Comprehensive Guide*, 124 vols, E Mellen Press, New York, 1998–2006.

Queensland Ex-Prisoners of War Association, Queensland Ex-POW Reparation

Bibliography

Committee, *Nippon Very Sorry, Many Men Must Die: Submission to the United Nations Commission of Human Rights (ECOSOC Resolution 1503)*, Boolarong, Brisbane, 1990.
Ramsey, Alan, 'How the POW voices were immortalised', *Sydney Morning Herald*, 9 August 2008, <www.smh.com.au/news/alan-ramsey/how-the-pow-voices-were-immortalised/2008/08/08/1218139074481.html>.
Reed, Liz, *Bigger than Gallipoli: War, History and Memory in Australia*, University of Western Australia Press, Perth, 2004.
Reid, Richard, 'In captivity: Australian prisoners of war in the 20th century', in Richard Reid & Peter Stanley (eds), *Stolen Years: Australian Prisoners of War*, Department of Veterans' Affairs & Australian War Memorial, Canberra, 2002, pp. 12–19.
——, *Laden, Fevered, Starved: The POWs of Sandakan, North Borneo, 1945*, Department of Veterans' Affairs, Canberra, 1999.
——, *Sandakan 1942–1945*, Department of Veterans' Affairs, Canberra, 2008.
Reid, Richard & Peter Stanley (eds), *Stolen Years: Australian Prisoners of War*, Department of Veterans' Affairs & Australian War Memorial, Canberra, 2002.
'Remembering Sandakan 1945–1999', Department of Veterans' Affairs, 2017, <anzacportal.dva.gov.au/multimedia/publications/laden-fevered-starved-sandakan/remembering-sandakan-19451999>.
Reynolds, Gary K, *U.S. Prisoners of War and Civilian American Citizens Captured and Interned by Japan in World War II: The Issue of Compensation by Japan*, Congressional Research Service, Washington, DC, 2002.
Reynolds, Robert & Shirleene Robinson, *Gay & Lesbian, Then & Now: Australian Stories from a Social Revolution*, Black Inc., Melbourne, 2016.
Roberts Pedersen, Elizabeth, 'A weak spot in the personality? Conceptualising "war neurosis" in British medical literature of the Second World War', *Australian Journal of Politics & History*, vol. 58, no. 3, 2012, pp. 408–420.
Robinson, Shirleene (ed.), *Homophobia: An Australian History*, Federation Press, Sydney, 2008.
Robson, D, E Welch, NJ Beeching & GV Gill, 'Consequences of captivity: health effects of Far East imprisonment in World War II', *QJM: An International Journal of Medicine*, vol. 102, no. 2, 2009, pp. 87–96.
Rosecrance, Richard N, *Australian Diplomacy and Japan, 1945–1951*, Melbourne University Press, Melbourne, 1962.
Services Canteens Trust Fund, *39th and Final Annual Report, 1986*, Australian Government Publishing Service, Canberra, 1986.
Silver, Lynette Ramsay, *Blood Brothers: Sabah and Australia, 1942–45*, Opus Publications, Kota Kinabalu, Malaysia, 2010.
——, *Sandakan: A Conspiracy of Silence*, Sally Milner Publishing, Sydney, 1998.
Smaal, Yorick, *Sex, Soldiers and the South Pacific, 1939–45: Queer Identities in Australia in the Second World War*, Palgrave Macmillan, London, 2015.
Sobocinska, Agnieszka, '"The language of scars": Australian prisoners of war and the colonial order', *History Australia*, vol. 7, no. 3, 2010, pp. 58.1–58.19.
——, *Visiting the Neighbours: Australians in Asia*, NewSouth, Sydney, 2014.
Spark, Seumas, 'Dishonourable men? The Australian Army, prisoners of war and

Anglo-German POW repatriations in the Second World War', *Australian Historical Studies*, vol. 45, no. 2, 2014, pp. 242–65.
Stanley, Peter, 'Remembering captivity: the prisoners experience as literature', in Richard Reid & Peter Stanley (eds), *Stolen Years: Australian Prisoners of War*, Department of Veterans' Affairs & Australian War Memorial, Canberra, 2002, pp. 91–108.
Starck, Nigel, *Proud Australian Boy: A Biography of Russell Braddon*, Australian Scholarly Publishing, Melbourne, 2011.
Strangio, Paul, *Neither Power Nor Glory: 100 Years of Political Labor in Victoria, 1856–1956*, Melbourne University Press, Melbourne, 2012.
Summerfield, Penny, 'Gender and war in the twentieth century', *International History Review*, vol. 19, no. 1, 1997, pp. 3–15.
Tamura, Keiko, *Michi's Memories: The Story of a Japanese War Bride*, Pandanus Books, Canberra, 2001.
Tavan, Gwenda, *The Long, Slow Death of White Australia*, Scribe, Melbourne, 2005.
Tennant, Christopher, Kerry Goulston & Owen Dent, 'Clinical psychiatric illness in prisoners of war of the Japanese: forty years after release', *Psychological Medicine*, vol. 16, no. 4, 1986, pp. 833–39.
Thorne, Christopher, *Racial Aspects of the Far Eastern War of 1941–1945*, Oxford University Press, London, 1982.
Torney-Parlicki, Prue, *Somewhere in Asia: War, Journalism and Australia's Neighbours 1941–75*, UNSW Press, Sydney, 2000.
Totani, Yuma, *The Tokyo War Crimes Trial: The Pursuit of Justice in the Wake of World War II*, Harvard University Asia Center & Harvard University Press, Cambridge, MA, 2008.
Tracey, Michael, *Australian Prisoners of War*, Department of Defence, Canberra, 1999.
Twomey, Christina, 'Australian nurse POWs: gender, war and captivity', *Australian Historical Studies*, vol. 36, no. 124, 2004, pp. 255–74.
——, '"A body of broken men": POWs in post-war Australia', in Christina Twomey, Stephanie Hodson, Nick Hill & Ann O'Kane (panellists), 'The aftermath of military combat – the history, the personal consequences, the treatment and the recovery', Featured Symposium, moderated by Stephen Brand, TheMHS Conference, Canberra, 25–28 August 2015.
——, 'Trauma and the reinvigoration of Anzac: an argument', *History Australia*, vol. 10, no. 3, 2013, pp. 85–108.
Vamplew, W (ed.), *Australians: Historical Statistics*, Fairfax, Syme & Weldon Associates, Sydney, 1987.
Varney, Denise, 'Political lessons of the "new wave": Romeril's *The Floating World*', *Double Dialogues*, no. 11, 2009, pp. 1–11.
Walker, Allan S, *Medical Services of the R.A.N. and R.A.A.F.: With a Section on Women in the Army Medical Services*, Australia in the War of 1939–45, series 5, Medical, vol. 4, Australian War Memorial, Canberra, 1961.
Walker, David, *Anxious Nation: Australia and the Rise of Asia, 1850–1939*, University of Queensland Press, Brisbane, 1999.
Walker, David & Agnieszka Sobocinska, 'Introduction: Australia's Asia', in David Walker & Agnieszka Sobocinska (eds), *Australia's Asia: From Yellow Peril to Asian*

Bibliography

Century, UWA Publishing, Perth, 2012, pp. 1–23.
'A war widow's long fight', *Sydney Morning Herald*, 10 April 2007, <www.smh.com.au/news/national/a-war-widows-long-fight/2007/04/09/1175971023066.html>.
Waters, Christopher, 'The Macmahon Ball mission to East Asia 1948', *Australian Journal of Politics & History*, vol. 40, no. 3, 1994, pp. 351–63.
——, 'War, decolonization and postwar security', in David Goldsworthy & PG Edwards (eds), *Facing North: A Century of Australian Engagement with Asia*, Melbourne University Press, Melbourne, 2001, pp. 97–133.
Watt, Alan, *The Evolution of Australian Foreign Policy, 1938–1965*, Cambridge University Press, London, 1968.
Wigmore, Lionel, *The Japanese Thrust*, Australian War Memorial, Canberra, 1957.
Willett, Graham, *Living Out Loud: A History of Gay and Lesbian Activism in Australia*, Allen & Unwin, Sydney, 2000.
Winston, CE, 'Walter Edward Fisher', *Medical Journal of Australia*, vol. 2, 6 August 1966, pp. 284–86.
Winter, JM, *Remembering War: The Great War between Memory and History in the Twentieth Century*, Yale University Press, New Haven, 2006.
Woodard, Garry, 'Macmahon Ball's Goodwill Mission to Asia 1948', *Australian Journal of International Affairs*, vol. 49, no. 1, 1995, pp. 129–34.
'The workers', Anzac Portal, Department of Veterans' Affairs, 2017, <anzacportal.dva.gov.au/history/conflicts/thaiburma-railway-and-hellfire-pass/thaiburma-railway-and-hellfire-pass/workers>.
Wotherspoon, Garry, *Gay Sydney: A History*, NewSouth, Sydney, 2016.
Wright, Pattie, *The Men of the Line: Stories of the Thai–Burma Railway Survivors*, Melbourne University Press, Melbourne, 2008.
Yeend, Peter, *Compensation (Japanese Internment) Bill 2001*, Bills Digest no. 6, Information and Research Services, Department of the Parliamentary Library, 2001–02, <parlinfo.aph.gov.au/parlInfo/download/legislation/billsdgs/G1M46/upload_binary/g1m467.pdf;fileType=application/pdf>.
Young, Allan, *The Harmony of Illusions: Inventing Post-Traumatic Stress Disorder*, Princeton University Press, Princeton, 1995.

Index

2nd AIF *see* Australian Defence Forces
7th Division AIF, POWs from 18
8th Division AIF 17, 19, 200–1
8th Division and AIF Malaya Council
    Fisher heads 39
    formation of 32
    reaction to Owen Committee report 72
    supports subsistence allowance claim 58, 63–5
9th Division AIF 190–2, 198

A Town Like Alice xiii
Agreement on Commerce between the Commonwealth of Australia and Japan 182
AIF Malayan Nursing Scholarship 187, 199–209
alcoholism in returned POWs 112–13, 120–1
American Legion 62
amoebiasis, blamed for 'malaise' 49–50
anxiety disorders *see also* mental health issues; post-traumatic stress disorder
    Trust Fund responses to 93
Anzac Day services
    in Thailand ix–x
    Japanese official parties at 183–4
    POWs appear in media coverage 230
    POWs remembered at 234
Anzac legend 25–6
ANZUS defence agreement, affects treaty negotiations 174
Armstrong, Betty 52
Armstrong, Malcolm 196
Army, Department of *see* Defence-related ministries
Arneil, Stanley 'Stan'
    on Asian supervisors 28
    on attitudes to POWs 21
    on 'shame' of capture 22
    One Man's War 219–20, 228
Aspinall, George, photographs by 226
Australasian Meat Industry Employees Union 63

Australia Remembers program 230
Australia–Japan Agreement on Commerce 182
Australian Army *see* Australian Defence Forces
Australian Army Nursing Service 23
Australian Asian Association of Victoria 234–5
Australian Defence Forces *see also* Defence-related ministries
    attitude to POWs 21
    attitude to subsistence allowance claim 55
    repudiate idea of rehabilitation 37, 42–3
Australian Ex-Prisoners of War Memorial 238–9
Australian Imperial Force (AIF) *see* Australian Defence Forces
Australian Labor Party 175–6, 181
Australian prisoners of war *see also* ex-POW associations
    blamed for anti-Japanese feeling 158
    captured by Germany and Italy 4, 17
    changing attitudes to 213–41
    from dysfunctional families 128
    large-scale health studies 104–5
    numbers of 6, 15
    one-off compensation payment 238
    organisations founded by 32
    POW Trust Fund 75–100
    revived media interest in 225–30
    subsistence allowance campaign 56
    therapy required for 9–10
    treatment on return 31
Australian Red Cross *see* Red Cross
Australian Services Reconnaissance Department 188–9
Australian War Memorial
    ceremonial activities 183
    new POW exhibits 2–3
    POW material held by 227
Australian–British Reward Mission 190–2

Index

Bailey, Warrant Officer Eric 138
Ball, William Macmahon 205
Ballarat, Australian Ex-POWs memorial in 238–9
Ballina, camp films screened at 226
Barbed Wire and Bamboo 223
'barbed-wire disease' 35–8
Beaumont, Joan 4, 22
Behind Bamboo 24, 76
Bennett, Lieutenant General Henry Gordon 20
'bitterness' in former POWs 180
Blackburn, Brigadier Arthur Seaforth 'Blackie'
  at NFL Grand Final 33–4
  captured with members of force 18
  chairs POW Trust Fund 79, 93
  death of 231
  heads Services Canteen Trust Fund 79
  on responses to POW Trust Fund letter 84
  on 'sexual neurosis' claims 140
  praise for Dunlop 30
  quote from 33
  returns home to SA 8–10
  seeks reconciliation with Japan 159, 175
  supports subsistence allowance claim 59
  testifies at war crimes tribunal 161
Blackforce 18, 107
Blain, Adair 'Chill' 55–6
Blamey, General Sir Thomas 16, 202
Blood Oath 228–9
Boonpong Sirivejjabhandu 194
Borneo, recognition of local support for POWs 188–99
Bowden, Tim 224–6
Braddon, Russell
  homosexuality 138
  suicide attempt 223
  The Naked Island 31
  The Other Hundred Years War 218
Bridge on the River Kwai, The xi
Brisbane, Katharine 217
British Army 31–2, 36, 164–5
British Borneo Civil Administration Unit 196
British Commonwealth Occupation Force in Japan 166, 168
Bryce, Quentin xi
Bullwinkel, Lieutenant Colonel Vivian
  at dedication of Changi Chapel 227
  imprisoned after surviving massacre 23
  photographed with scholarship nurses 209
  testifies at war crimes tribunal 161
Burton, John 202

Cade, John 52
Cahill, Lloyd 226
Calwell, Arthur
  attempts to repatriate Asian refugees 197
  opposes Japanese immigration 166
  racial abuse by 169
Campbell, Owen 188–9
Canada, monetary compensation for POWs 74
Carey, Peter 228
Carrick, John 226–7
Carter, AG 46
Casey, Richard 181, 231, 234
Catholic Church, missionary work in Japan 171
Changi camp
  chapel from reconstructed at Duntroon 227, 235
  Nursing Scholarship planned in 201
  patrolled for homosexual activity 138
  prisoners in 116
Chia, Alice 205–6
Chia, Maisie 206
Chifley, Ben 62, 202
Chifley Labor Government 59
children, family violence against 147–8
Chinese residents of Malaya 201–3
Civilian Internees' Trust Fund xv–xvi
Clark, Manning 219–20
Coates, Lieutenant Colonel Albert E
  advises Repatriation Commission 38–40
  attends Treaty conference 174
  calls for reconciliation with Japan 172
  death of 231
  dismissive of 'damage' in returned POWs 45–6, 48–9, 222–3
  medical work among POWs 30
  on attitudes to POWs 20
  seeks reconciliation with Japan 159
  testifies at war crimes tribunal 161
Cohen, Norman 50–2, 173
Colombo Plan, Dunlop involved with 234–5
Combined Union Committee, Newport Railway Workshops 174–5
commissioned officers, treatment as POWs 4–5, 11, 58

Commonwealth Employment Services survey of returned POWs 47–8
Commonwealth Yokohama War Cemetery 181
Compensation (Japanese Internment) Act 2001 238
'convention pay' for POW officers 57–8, 61
Convention Relative to the Treatment of POWs *see* Geneva Convention
Council of the 8th Division *see* 8th Division and AIF Malaya Council
Curlewis, Adrian 121, 165
Curtin University, trains memorial scholarship winners 209

Daiichi Torii 242
Dark, Eleanor 176
Davison, Graeme 230
death rates, POWs by country of capture 4
Defence-related ministries
 attitudes to POWs xvii–xviii
 certificates of appreciation for Asians aiding POWs 194
 educational materials on POWs 2
 oppose subsistence payments claim 59, 65–8
 support scholarship scheme 202
Department of... *see* Defence-related ministries; *names of departments*
Derham, Colonel Alfred 40, 46
Dingo, Sally 154
Dulbar, Pardi Bin 190
Duncan, Ian 223
Dunlop, Edward Ernest 'Weary'
 advises Repatriation Commission 38–40
 at dedication of Changi Chapel 227
 attends Owen Committee meeting 66–8
 campaigns to reward Boon Pong 194
 death and funeral 1
 heads POW Trust Fund 80–1
 medical work among POWs 30
 on mental health issues for returning POWs 46
 refuses to attend war crimes tribunal 161
 'reunion tour' xiv–xv, 232–3
 revival of public interest in 1–2, 230–5
 supports subsistence allowance claim 62–4
Dyce, Major Roy K 192

Ellis, Malcolm, reviews *The Naked Island* 31–2
enlisted soldiers
 applications to POW Trust Fund 78
 difficulty finding postwar work 100
 not entitled to 'field allowance' 57
 return from POW camps 6–7, 11
Evans, Richard 192
Evatt, HV 181
Ex Prisoner of War [J] Survey 48–9, 87
ex-POW associations *see also* NSW Ex-Prisoners of War Association
 claim compensation from Japan 237–8
 Dunlop connected with 62, 232
 in South Australia 166
 President fabricates service history 246–7
 trauma discussed by 223
External Affairs Department, 'background material' on Japan 180

Fadden, Arthur 62–3
family life for returned POWs *see also* marital problems
 BCOF troops marrying Japanese women 168–9
 disrupted by mental illness 124, 126–8
 domestic violence issues 144–50
 impotence resulting from imprisonment 7, 132–5, 151–2
 marriage breakups 117
 'unfaithful wives' 150
Fassin, Didier 221
Federated Clerks' Union 175
Field, AE 185
Fisher, Walter Edward 'Ted'
 advises Repatriation Commission 39–41
 appointed to POW Trust Fund 76, 79–81, 93–4
 as Owen Committee member 66, 68–70
 calls for distribution of seized assets 73
 death of 231
 denies POW 'neuroses' 222
 dismissive of 'damage' in returned POWs 48–51
 objects to Japanese PM laying Anzac Day wreath 184
 on 'sob-stuff' 58
 on 'unfaithful wives' 150
 responses to Trust Fund applications 88, 95–6, 140

Index

supports subsistence allowance claim 62, 64–5
supports war crimes trials 165
Fit for Work photograph 226
Flanagan, Arch 243–4
Flanagan, Keith 232–4
Flanagan, Martin 232–3, 243–4
Flanagan, Patrick 244
Flanagan, Richard 2, 233, 243
Floating World, The 215–18, 222
Forde, Frank 59
Formosa, senior officers interned in 4
Fort Siloso, Singapore xiii
Fraser, Malcolm, at Dunlop's funeral 1
Friends and Neighbors 181
Funk, Johnny 195–9
Funk, Melvyn Francis 197

Galleghan, Brigadier Sir Frederick 'Black Jack'
   death of 231
   on attitudes to POWs 20–1
   on death rates among Japanese POWs 23–4
   racial identity of 28–9
Gallipoli, subsistence claim for troops at refused 58
Garland, Alf 185
Garrett, Jack 138
Garton, Stephen 34
Geneva Convention
   Japan fails to ratify 16
   on forwarding pay to POW officers 57–8
   stipulates rations for POWs 61
   women protected by 24
Geraty, John 157
Germany, POWs captured by
   Australian POWs 4, 17
   exchanges of 36
   malnourished 56
   treatment violates Geneva Convention 70
Gerster, Robin 22
Gilmore, Mary 176
Glynn, Father Tony 171
Great World, The 229
Gull Force 17–18

Harper, Norman 158
Hawke, Bob 1, 235–6
Haylen, Leslie
   on seized Japanese funds 73
   on Treaty of Peace with Japan 176

response to POW Trust Fund letter 83–4
supports subsistence allowance claim 71–2
health issues *see also* mental health issues
   for returned POWs 34
   large-scale health studies 104–5
   'malaise' among former prisoners of Japan 46–7
   obesity in returned POWs 112
   psychosomatic conditions 136–7
Hellfire Pass Memorial Museum ix–xi, xiv
Henderson, John and Mary 168–9, 177–8
Hinsuke, Yashiro, visits Australia 171
Hirohito, Emperor 180
Holland, George 185
Holt, Harold 60, 177
homosexuality
   in response to confinement 138
   perceived as mental illness 112, 137, 139
Hood, Bill 223
Howard, John, at Dunlop's funeral 1
Hutchinson, Garrie 228
Huxtable, Charles
   on anti-Japanese feeling 180
   on Japanese athletes at Melbourne Olympics 166–7
   on Russian treatment of POWs 164
   on war crimes trials 162–3
   quote from 157

Immigration Restriction Act 1901 see White Australia Policy
Imperial Japanese Army *see also* Japan
   Australian POWs captured by 17
   death rate among POWs of 4, 18–19
   greater compensation for POWs of 57–8
   'malaise' among former prisoners of 46–7
   poor mail service for POWs of 150
   POWs of seen as special case 70
   recovers war dead from PNG 181
   war criminals from released 182
   women POWs captured by 23
impotence resulting from imprisonment 7, 132–5, 151–2
Indonesia, conflict with Malaysia 198–9
'inferiority complex' resulting from imprisonment 111–12, 119
Information, Department of, advertises scholarship scheme 202
International Military Tribunal for the Far East 161

International Olympic Committee, readmits Japan 168
Italy, Australian POWs captured by 4, 17

Jackson, Major Henry 'Harry' 190, 193–4
Jackson, Oscar 'Ossie' 226
Japan *see also* Imperial Japanese Army
   arts and crafts of exhibited 171
   Australian residents from interned 165
   economic power of 215–17
   moral grounds for resisting 228–9
   post-war reconciliation with 157–86, 245
   racial denigration of 27, 167–70
   treatment of immigrants from 165–7
   Treaty of Peace with 72–3, 172–4
JEATH War Museum xii, xiv
Jeffery, Michael 238
Jeffrey, Betty 25
Johnston, George, on shame felt by POWs 29

Kanchanaburi War Cemetery
   Anzac Day service at x–xi
   author visits xi–xii, xv
   Hawke visits 235–6
Keating, Paul 1, 230, 236–7
Kempetai, torture and atrocities by 124–5
Kent Hughes, Wilfred
   advocates ratifying treaty 175–6
   changes views on reconciliation 159–63
   death of 231
   diaries of exhibited 227
   on 'Christian duty to the vanquished' 170
   on internment camps for Boers 164–5
   on Japanese athletes at Melbourne Olympics 167–8
   on Japanese participation in Anzac Day ceremonies 184
   on suspended scholarship scheme 207–8
   visits war graves in Asia 180
   writes to Trust Fund on behalf of applicants 93–4
Kipling, Rudyard, 'Recessional' 172
Kirkpatrick, John Simpson 233
Kishi, Nobusuke 182, 184–6
Konfrontasi period 198
Korea, prisoners in 116
Kulang, Orang Tuan 188–9

Lark Force, POWs from 18
Legacy organisation, Savige founds 66

Legal Aid Society 151
Lewis, JR 166
'libidinal impairment' 7, 132–4, 151–2
Lim Han Hoe 203
Line, The 244

MacFarlane, Bill 190
Mahoney, Reg, on 'living like white men' 28
Malaya 17, 199–209
Malayan Union 204
Malaysia, conflict with Indonesia 198–9
Malouf, David 15, 213, 229
Man Booker prize for Flanagan novel 243
Marist Japanese Mission League 171
marital problems 132–56 *see also* family life for returned POWs
   BCOF troops marry Japanese women 168–9, 177
   de facto relationship not regarded as marriage 150–1
   family violence 144–7
   marriage breakdowns 140–4
   sexual problems 132–41
Marsden, Father Lionel 170–1
masculinity
   effect of imprisonment on 21–30
   family violence and 147–8
   'inferiority complex' resulting from imprisonment 111–12
   reconciliation campaign appeals to 180
Massey, Claude 203–4, 206
'material prejudice' question 132–3
Matthews, Captain Lionel 189–90
McEachern, Brigadier Cranston 175
McEwen, Jack 178
McKernan, Michael 24
medical officers among POWs
   continue work while imprisoned 30
   on mental health issues 38–41, 46–53
   privileged status of 233–4
Melbourne appeal for funds for needy ex-POWs and families 63
Melbourne Olympics, Japan attends 166
mental health issues 33–54 *see also* suicides and suicide attempts
   addiction to prescription drugs 119
   ADF dismissive of 42–53
   anxiety disorders 93
   difficulties with authority and routine 118–19
   from Trust Fund records 105–6

Index

homosexuality perceived as 112, 137–9
impotence resulting from imprisonment 7, 132–5, 151–2
marriage breakdown due to 140–4
'nervous breakdown' 36
'neurosis' 36, 44, 124
post-traumatic stress disorder 220–4
'trauma' 221
'wanderlust' as after-effect of imprisonment 118
worsening over time 52
Menzies, Robert
  accepts Owen Committee report 71
  appeals for reconciliation with Japan 178–9
  appoints Kent Hughes as treaty advocate 175
  campaigns for inquiry 55, 62–3
  opens arts and crafts exhibition 171
  visits Japan 182
Menzies Coalition government
  appoints Hughes to organise Olympics 168
  inquiry into subsistence payments claim 65
  policy for POW Trust Fund 75–7, 93
  prioritises closer relations with Japan 178–9
  seeks to prevent Japanese rearmament 158
  Services Canteen Trust Fund used for information by 80–1
Mills, Jonathan, *Sandakan Threnody* 2
Mitchell River Mission 109–10
Montevideo Maru 19
Mountbatten, Louis xiii
Moxham, Susan 134
Mudge, Bert 161–2
Mufti magazine (RSL) 30
Multifunction Polis planned 218
Myer Mural Hall exhibition 227

Naked Island, The 138
Narrow Road to the Deep North, The 2, 233
National Football League Grand Final, POWs honoured at 33–4
National Police Reserve (Japan) 174
National Roads and Motorists Association 106
Nelson, Hank 224–6
'nerves' *see* mental health issues
'nervous breakdown', symptoms of 36

'neurosis' 36, 44, 124
Newman, Major PH 37
Newman-Morris, John 41
Nippon Very Sorry, Many Men Must Die 238
Nishi, Haruhiko 183
Nishisato, Fuyuko 244–5
No 1 Cycle Camp, prisoner assaulted in 107
Norrie, Sir Charles Willoughby 33
North Borneo *see* Borneo; Sabah
North Borneo Volunteer Force 196
NSW Ex-Prisoners of War Association
  accuses Pollard of 'insult' 61
  Cohen heads 50–2
  demands reparations 173
  provides information to POW Trust Fund 94
nurses
  AIF Malayan Nursing Scholarship 199–209
  as POWs 23–5 *see also* women POWs

obesity in returned POWs 112
O'Byrne, Justin 73
officers, preferential treatment of 4–5, 11, 58
Official History of Australia in the War of 1939-1945 184–5
Olick, Jeffrey 224
One Day of the Year, The 214
One Man's War 219–20, 228
Ooi Soh Im 205–6
Other Hundred Years War, The 218
'other ranks' *see* enlisted soldiers
Owen Committee of inquiry 66–71

Parkin, Ray 213, 234
Pavitt, Ernest 196
PEN Award for *One Man's War* 219
Plimsoll, James 181
'politics of regret' 224
Pollard, Reg 60–1
Pond, Lieutenant Colonel Samuel 202
post-traumatic stress disorder 220–4
P.O.W.: Australians Under Nippon 225–6
POW Research Network (Japan) 243–4
prisoners of war *see also* Australian prisoners of war
  captured by Turkey 4
  death rates by country of capture 4
  exchanges of 16
  from British Army 31–2, 36
  from Canada 74

299

Russian treatment of 164
women POWs 23
Prisoners of War Trust Fund 75–100
applications to xvi–xvii, 84–6
Blackburn heads 10
Dunlop heads 232
letter to former POWs 81–3
methods of determining claims 86–94, 97–100
sources of information 94–7
Probyn, Major Leo 176
psychiatric conditions *see also* mental health issues
emphasis on sexuality 137, 139–40
PTSD 220–4

racial issues *see also* White Australia Policy
among POWs 27
changing attitudes to 216–20
Japanese seen as 'barbarous' 167
scholarship offered to Malaysian Chinese 204–5
Radic, Leonard 222
Ramsay, James 223
ranks other than officers *see* enlisted soldiers
'Recessional' (Kipling) 172
Rechtman, Richard 221
Red Cross
cares for convalescent cases 44–5
criticises scholarship scheme 208
Japanese tourist donates blood to 172
Newman-Morris heads 41
on mental health issues 37–8
POW support campaigns 16
relations with POW Trust Fund 94–7
seized Japanese funds transferred to 72–3
supports attempt to legitimise marriage 151
supports scholarship scheme 202
'reduced status' grant applicants 91
rehabilitation studies 36–7, 41–5
Repatriation Commission *see* Repatriation Department
Repatriation Department *see also* Defence-related ministries; Veterans' Affairs Department
hospitals run by 123
policy on returned POWs xvii–xviii, 38–43, 76
relations with POW Trust Fund 86–7, 95–6

renamed Department of Veterans' Affairs 236
'restitution of conjugal rights' applications 142, 148
Returned and Services League (RSL)
attitudes to relations with Japan 185–6
concern over treatment of returned POWs 30–1
on Japanese athletes at Melbourne Olympics 166
petitions for better mental health care 44
POWs entitled to join 32
reaction to Owen Committee report 72
reconciliation with Germany and Italy 167
relations with Council of the 8th Division 65
response to POW Trust Fund letter 83
sends Coates to Treaty conference 174
submission to Owen Committee 66–7
supports subsistence allowance claim 56, 59–61
Riches, Les 196–7
Rivett, Rohan 24, 39, 76
Rocklea housing camp 126
Romeril, John, *The Floating World* 215–18, 222
Royal Military College Duntroon, Changi Chapel re-erected at 227, 235
Ruxton, Bruce 185, 218

Sabah, establishment of 198
Sage, Annie 23
Sandakan camp 3, 189–91
Sandakan Threnody 2
Savige, Lieutenant General Stanley 54, 66–9
'Selarang' (journalist) 30
Services Canteens Trust Fund 80
Seymour, Alan, *The One Day of the Year* 214
shame, as effect of imprisonment 21–30
Shapper, G 177
Shearer, Jill, *Shimada* 218
shell-shock, symptoms of 34–6
Shimada 218
Simpson, Colin 190, 193–4
Singapore xii–xiii, 18 *see also* Changi camp
Six from Borneo documentary 190
Sixth World Conference Against Atomic and Hydrogen Bombs 163–4
Slaves of the Samurai 159–60
Slaves of the Sons of Heaven 226

Index

Slessor, Kenneth 37
Smallwood, Margaret 203–4
Some Aspects of Medical Investigation and Treatment 49
Soni, Lieutenant 107
Spender, Percy, signs Treaty of Peace 174
Spowers, Colonel Allan 80–1, 91
St Vincent de Paul society 127
Stahl, Fred 173–4
Stanley, Massey 164, 166–7
Statham, Vivien *see* Bullwinkel, Lieutenant Colonel Vivian
status, loss of, as reason for grant 91
Stephen, Ninian 1, 235
Stephens, Donald 199
Sticpewich, Warrant Officer William 190
Stoller, Alan
    advises Repatriation Commission 43
    on mental health issues for returning POWs 46
    survey of 'sex activity' 52
subsistence allowance claim 54–74
suicides and suicide attempts
    Bill Moxham 134
    linked to mental health issues 103–4, 122–3
    numbers of unknown 103
    Russell Braddon 223
Surrender Chambers at Fort Siloso xiii
Survey of Selected Groups of Those Who Served 47–8
'survivor effect' 5
Swartz, Reginald 209
Sweeting, AJ 184–5

Taisei Maru 181
Tenko TV series xiii
Thai–Burma Railway
    author visits ix
    deaths among POWs working on 19
    Dunlop revisits 233
    Hawke visits 235–6
    in Yushukan War Memorial Museum 242
    Memorial Centre at xiv
    mental health issues due to work on 107–8
    sold to Thai government 73
Thailand, Anzac Day services in ix–xi
The Bridge on the River Kwai xi
The Era of the the Witness 221

The Floating World 215–18, 222
The Great World 229
The Line 244
The Naked Island 138
The Narrow Road to the Deep North 233
The One Day of the Year 214
The Other Hundred Years War 218
The War Diaries of Weary Dunlop xiv, 235
TheMHS Learning Network 245
Timson, Frank 197
Trade Department, pursues Japanese trade relations 178–9
Trading with the Enemy Act 1939 72–3
'trauma' 221 *see also* mental health issues
Treaty of Peace with Japan 72–3, 172–3
Tuol Sleng Genocide Museum, Cambodia 3
Turkey, Australian POWs captured by 4
Turnbull, Winton 55–6, 68
Two Minutes' Silence 71

'unfaithful wives', problems blamed on 150
Union of Australian Women, opposes ratifying treaty 176–7
United Nations
    Educational, Scientific and Cultural Organization 203
    Human Rights Commission 238
    Relief and Rehabilitation Administration 71–2
United States 61, 73
Uren, Tom
    campaigns for POW recognition 236–7
    Dunlop friendly with 231–2, 234
    supports Japanese disarmament 163
Uyehara, Hilary M 171–2

Veterans' Affairs Department 2, 236, 239–40
Vietnam War, effect of on attitudes 214–15, 227–8
Vischer, Adolf 35–6
Vyner Brooke, sunk with POWs aboard 23

Walker, E Ronald 158
War Claims Commission (US) 62
War Diaries of Weary Dunlop, The xiv, 235
war gratuity payments 59
War Memorial Gallery, POW exhibition at 226–7
war service homes 127
Ward, Russel 220, 228
Warner, Dennis 197

Watanabe, Mina 243
welfare recipients, information network 94–100
White, J Glyn 46
White, Thomas 75–7
White Australia Policy *see also* racial issues
   abandonment of 214–15
   growing opposition to 170
   overridden for Melvyn Funk 197
   treatment of Japanese under 165
White Coolies 25
'white coolies', POWs as 27–8
Whitecross, Roy 226–7
Whitlam, Gough 199
Whitlam Labor Government 205, 236

Wieviorka, Annette, *The Era of the the Witness* 221
Wigmore, Lionel 184–5
Windsor, Major Henry 'Harry' 24
women POWs 23–5, 133
Wootten, George 38–40, 46
World Council of Churches 170
World War I, attitude to POWs after 60–1
Worry Centre (RSL) 44–5
Wounds, Scars and Healing conference 243–4

Yasukuni Shrine 241–3
Yeo, William 72, 185, 236
Yushukan War Memorial Museum 241

www.ingramcontent.com/pod-product-compliance
Lightning Source LLC
Chambersburg PA
CBHW030606230426
43661CB00053B/1866